DISCARD

SHARKS

SHARKS

CONSULTING EDITOR
John D. Stevens

ILLUSTRATIONS BY
Tony Pyrzakowski

Facts On File Publications
New York, New York ● Oxford, England

Produced by
Intercontinental Publishing Corporation Limited
4th Floor, 69 Wyndham Street, Central Hong Kong
Telex 83499 PPA HX; Fax 5-8101683
A member of the Weldon-Hardie Group of Companies
Sydney. Auckland. Hong Kong. London. Chicago.

Published in the United States of America by
Facts on File, Inc.
460 Park Avenue South,
New York, New York 10016
First published 1987
Reprinted 1988, 1989
ISBN 0 948075 68 6

Editorial director: Elaine Russell
Project coordinator: Sheena Coupe
Editors: Carson Creagh, Robert Coupe
Captions: Carson Creagh
Index: Dianne Regtop
Maps: Greg Campbell
Designer: Sue Burk
Production: Sue Tickner, Kate Smyth

© 1987 Intercontinental Publishing Corporation Limited

Library of Congress Cataloging-in-Publication Data

Sharks.

Bibliography: p.
Includes index.
1. Sharks.   2. Shark attacks.   I. Stevens, John D.
QL638.S454 1987   591'.31   87-601
ISBN 0-8160-1800-6

Typeset by Amazing Faces, Sydney, Australia
Production by Mandarin Offset, Hong Kong
Printed by Kyodo-Shing Loong Printing Industries Pte Ltd
Printed in Singapore
10 9 8 7 6 5 4

A KEVIN WELDON PRODUCTION

Cover:
Tiger sharks are confirmed maneaters, but they are nonetheless among the most efficient and
elegant predators of tropical waters.
Photo by Ben Cropp

Endpapers:
A truly gentle giant, the whale shark is the largest fish in the world, but hunts only
small fish, tiny plankton and krill.
Photo by Marty Snyderman

Page 1:
Despite its fearsome appearance, the sand tiger or grey nurse shark has never been positively
identified in attacks on humans.

Page 2:
Species of hammerhead sharks are found in temperate and tropical seas around the world.

Page 3:
Small sharks are common predators of tropical reefs.

Page 5:
A shark with its yolk-sac still attached illustrates one of the efficient reproductive methods
developed by these surprisingly sophisticated fishes.

Page 7:
The graceful pelagic blue shark lives and hunts in the open ocean and is only rarely
encountered close to land.

Page 8
Requiem or whaler sharks are found in a variety of habitats, from coral reefs to deep ocean waters,
mangrove swamps and freshwater lakes and rivers.

Page 9:
The great white shark's reputation for ferocity is justified by its speed, savagery and intelligence.

Page 11:
A diver revives a 'drowning' shark, captured as part of a scientific research program,
by forcing water through its gills.

Jeff Rotman

CONSULTING EDITOR

Dr John D. Stevens
Senior Research Scientist, Division of Fisheries, CSIRO Marine Laboratories, Hobart, Tasmania, Australia

CONTRIBUTORS

Dr Leonard J. V. Compagno
Senior Research Scientist, J. L. B. Smith Institute of Ichthyology, Grahamstown, South Africa

Carson Creagh BSc
Editor and natural history writer, Sydney, New South Wales, Australia

Dr Guido Dingerkus
Director, Natural History Consultants, Goshen, New York, USA

Hugh Edwards
Marine photographer and author, Perth, Western Australia

Richard Ellis M.A.
Marine artist and author, New York, USA

Dr Edward S. Hodgson
Professor of Biology, Tufts University, Medford, Massachusetts, USA

Roland Hughes BSc
Former editor, *Australian Natural History,* Sydney, New South Wales, Australia

Dr C. Scott Johnson
Research Scientist, Biological Services Branch, Naval Ocean Systems Center, San Diego, California, USA

Dr John G. Maisey
Associate Curator, Department of Vertebrate Paleontology, American Museum of Natural History, New York, USA

Dr Arthur A. Myrberg Jr
Professor of Marine Science, Rosenstiel School of Marine and Atmospheric Sciences, University of Miami, Miami, Florida, USA

A.M. Olsen MSc
Former Chief Fisheries Officer, Department of Agriculture and Fisheries, Adelaide, South Australia

Larry J. Paul BSc (Hons)
Fisheries Research Division, Ministry of Agriculture and Fisheries, Wellington, New Zealand

Marty Snyderman
Marine photographer, cinematographer and author, San Diego, California, USA

Dr John D. Stevens
Senior Research Scientist, Division of Fisheries, CSIRO Marine Laboratories, Hobart, Tasmania, Australia

Dr Leighton R. Taylor Jr
Deputy Executive Director, California Academy of Sciences, San Francisco, California, USA

Valerie Taylor
Marine photographer and author, Sydney, New South Wales, Australia

Dr Timothy C. Tricas
Research Associate, Washington University School of Medicine and Woods Hole Marine Biological Laboratory, St Louis, Missouri, USA

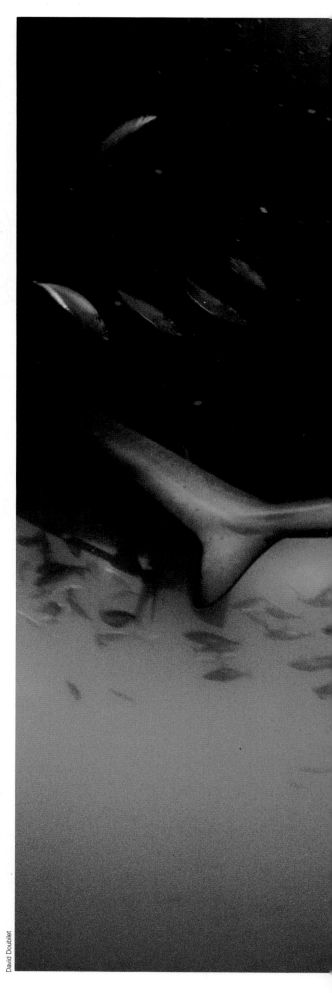

David Doubilet

CONTENTS

David Doubilet

INTRODUCTION

Sharks have occasionally exacted a terrible price from humans who have trespassed on their territory. No better understood than the medium they inhabit, these animals have inspired a complex mythology that reflects the mixture of fear and fascination with which people have always regarded them. The superstition behind this mythology pervades such modern-day extravaganzas as Peter Benchley's *Jaws* and the popular media's often morbid fascination with shark attacks.

Attitudes deeply ingrained in the human psyche still persist, despite the detailed and painstaking research of recent years which has thrown new light on the biology and behaviour of sharks and dispelled a great deal of the mystique surrounding them.

Written by some of the world's leading experts on the subject, and global in its scope, this book presents the interested general reader with a balanced and comprehensive survey of sharks, their habits and habitats. Its subject matter is wide, ranging from the evolution, biology and behaviour of sharks, to an examination of their commercial use and place in the ecological system. There are chapters on the kinds of sharks and their distribution, and others surveying the cause and incidence of shark attacks in the waters of Australia, New Zealand, the Pacific, the United States and South Africa. Those who work with sharks or whose studies have thrown new light on these creatures write about their experiences and conclusions. Myth and reality confront each other as the latest research findings are presented along with an examination of the shark's peculiar role in myth-making, both historic and contemporary. This enlightening and informative text is supported by revealing and often spectacular photographs, paintings and diagrams culled from the finest collections or created especially for this publication.

John Stevens

John D. Stevens
CONSULTING EDITOR

▲ The power and grace of the shark are
products of more than 300 million years
of unparalleled evolutionary success.

THE SHARK

EVOLUTION OF THE SHARK

JOHN G. MAISEY

The fossil record of sharks is three times as long as that of the dinosaurs. It extends back through the pages of earth history more than a hundred times as far as that of humans.

This pedigree represents more than 450 million years of independent evolution. There were sharks in the oceans of the prehistoric world long before the first backboned animals crawled onto land, before the first insects took to the air, even before many plants had effectively colonised the continents. If we could be transported to that distant time, sharks would be one of the few familiar sights in a world of unfamiliar organisms.

Familiar, but somehow different. Not the sinister profile of the great white, the streamlined hydrofoil of the hammerhead or the wicked serrated teeth of the tiger shark. No modern sharks would be recognisable. The most ancient fossil assigned by paleontologists to a still living group of sharks is approximately 180 million years old – certainly a respectable ancestry – but the majority of modern groups can be traced back a 'mere' 100 million years.

▼ A hybodont shark from the Pennsylvanian rocks of Kansas. This is one of the earliest complete examples of this group and shows that very little evolutionary change took place in the group between 350 and 100 million years ago.

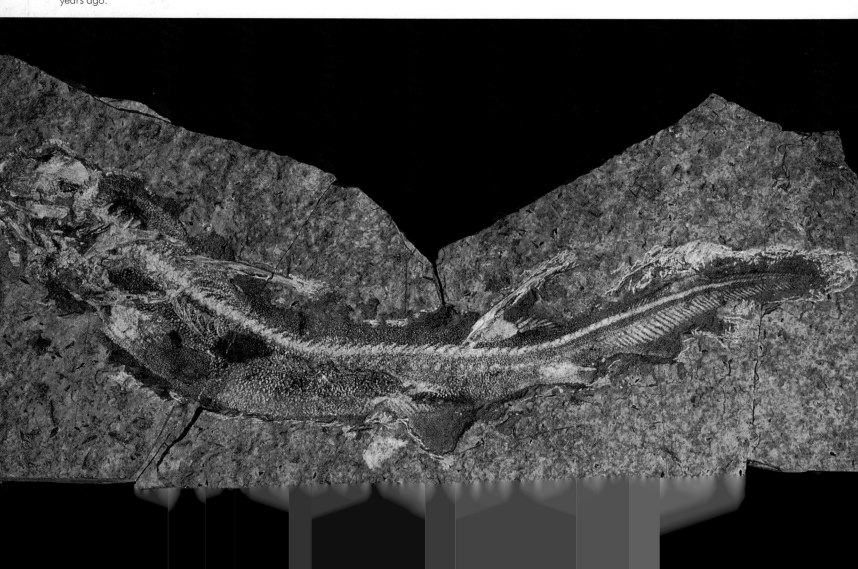

FOSSIL EVIDENCE

For the most part, the shark fossil record is fragmentary. Usually all we find is their teeth, sometimes in great abundance.

In exceptional cases, pieces of the internal skeleton and even complete fossil sharks have been discovered. Such finds are subjected to the most detailed investigation in order to extract the maximum scientific information. To understand why the fossil record should be so biased it is worthwhile considering some aspects of shark anatomy.

Unlike a bony fish, whose head is usually sheathed by large bones and whose body is clad in big bony scales, the skin of a shark is covered from nose to tail – except around the eyes, corners of the mouth, cloaca and gills – by a fine shagreen of minute denticles. As the shark ages these denticles are periodically shed and replaced or augmented by new ones; they do not grow larger. In many ancient sharks, however, the denticles grew incrementally before they were shed. Although fossil shark denticles are abundant they are usually overlooked except by micropaleontologists. On the other hand, virtually every paleontologist, amateur as well as professional, has found fossil shark teeth.

Estimates suggest that over the span of just a few years a shark may grow, utilise and then discard tens of thousands of teeth. Since this prodigious output has been a characteristic of sharks for much of their history, it is small wonder that shark teeth are probably the world's most common vertebrate fossils. Besides being produced over the ages in unimaginable quantities, shark teeth are solid and resilient objects, easily prone to fossilisation. The inorganic material in shark teeth is the mineral apatite (calcium phosphate), the same as in bone. Vast quantities of phosphate are therefore metabolised by sharks during their lifetime.

Instead of internal bones, the shark has a cartilaginous skeleton, with a superficial bonelike layer broken up into thousands of isolated apatite prisms, each no larger than one of the denticles that cover the skin. When a shark dies, the decomposing skeleton rapidly disintegrates and the apatite prisms scatter. Fossil sharks have been preserved only where the bottom sediments have permitted rapid burial and there has been little disturbance by currents or scavengers.

PALEOZOIC SHARKS

Among the most ancient and primitive sharks is *Cladoselache,* about 400 million years old, found within Paleozoic strata of Ohio, Kentucky and Tennessee. These rocks were once the soft muds that formed the floor of a shallow ocean extending over much of North America. *Cladoselache* was of unexceptional size – it was only about a metre long – with stiff triangular fins supported by elongate bars of cartilage and long, slender jaws. Its teeth had

several pointed cusps that are often worn down and blunted, evidently by prolonged use; *Cladoselache* probably did not replace its teeth as frequently as modern sharks. Its tail (caudal fin) was similar in shape to those of fast-swimming mako and white sharks. Some *Cladoselache* specimens contain whole fishes swallowed tail first. This suggests that *Cladoselache* had great speed and agility, a characteristic that no doubt helped it to avoid being eaten by the giant armoured fishes (arthrodires) that were over six metres long and shared the oceans with it.

We are only just beginning to understand the diversity achieved by other Paleozoic sharks. New discoveries in the United States, Europe and Australia reveal that some were armoured by bladelike spines projecting from the dorsal fins. In others only the males possessed these structures, which sometimes curved grotesquely over the head. Yet others had great spirals of serrated teeth, like slowly growing circular-saw blades, wedged under their chin. Around 350 million years ago some sharks began evolving into bizarre creatures from which the living chimaeroids (rabbitfishes) are descended.

▲ Exquisite preservation of muscles, gills and skeleton is seen in this silicone elastic cast of a 400 million year old *Cladoselache* from Tennessee. Although smaller than most dogfishes, *Cladoselache* represents one of the earliest sharks in which the anatomy can be studied.

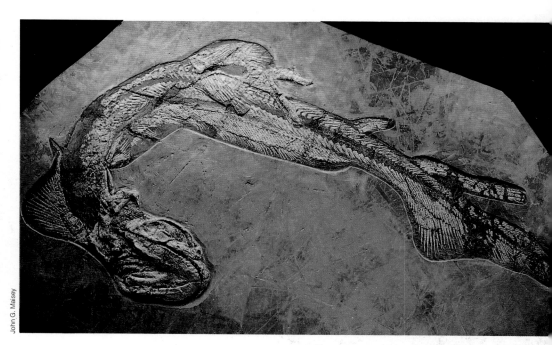

▲ This gigantic xenacanth shark, almost two metres long, swam in the lakes and rivers of western Europe some 250 million years ago. It is so finely preserved that its sex (male) can be determined from its pelvic fin structure.

THE PERIOD OF EVOLUTION

Following this great period of shark radiation there seems to have been prolonged evolutionary stasis. From about 300 to 150 million years ago most fossil sharks can be assigned to just two groups. One of these (called xenacanths) was almost exclusively confined to freshwater environments. In spite of this, between its origin (approximately 450 million years ago) and its extinction (about 220 million years ago) it achieved worldwide distribution. For such an ecologically specialised group xenacanths achieved a remarkable longevity. The other group

▶ One of the oldest known 'modern' sharks is *Palaeospinax*, from the Lower Jurassic (approximately 180 million years ago) of Europe. It has well-formed vertebrae and its teeth, scales and skeleton reveal many other advanced features.

John G. Maisey

(called hybodonts) appeared some 320 million years ago and was predominant in oceans and freshwater habitats throughout the age of dinosaurs. It was gradually ousted by modern forms toward the end of that era and finally become extinct at the same time as the last dinosaurs. Dinosaur and hybodont fossils occur together in Upper Cretaceous strata of Wyoming.

THE 'MODERN' PERIOD
What is the earliest geological record of modern maneaters? Fossil mako and mackerel shark teeth occur in the Lower Cretaceous (approximately 100 million years ago), and teeth of primitive carcharhinids are recorded soon after. The oldest white shark teeth date from 60 to 65 million years ago.

Early in white shark evolution there are at least two lineages: one with coarsely serrated teeth that probably gave rise to the modern great whites, and another with finely serrated teeth and a tendency to attain gigantic size. This group reached maximum development worldwide during the Miocene (approximately 10–25 million years ago) and includes the gargantuan *Carcharodon megalodon*, whose teeth exceed eighteen centimetres in height and whose body length may have exceeded twelve metres. Contrary to popular belief, *C. megalodon* did not get to 25 or 30 metres; these old estimates were based on miscalculations and inaccurate comparisons with living sharks. Nor does *C. megalodon* seem to be directly ancestral to living great whites. Nonetheless it is impressive!

What factors contributed to the rise of the large predator sharks like the great white? It may be significant that their first appearance coincides with the extinction of dinosaurs and the widespread diversification of mammals. We know that some early mammalian groups evolved into aquatic forms around that time. Certainly wherever we find fossil teeth of the big sharks we also get an abundance of marine mammal bones, including those of seals, porpoises and whales; and these bones frequently show signs of having been chewed on by sharks. One scenario, then, would link later shark evolution with the rise of marine mammals, some 60 million years ago – long before humans were there to get eaten.

▼ This photograph allows a comparison of fossil teeth from *Carcharodon megalodon* with a tooth from a present-day great white.

Ron & Valerie Taylor

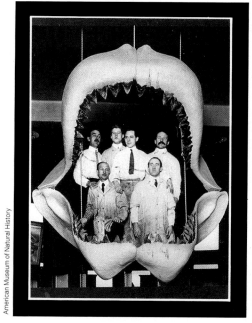

▲ The grand-daddy of them all, Professor Bashford Dean's reconstruction of *Carcharodon megalodon* in New York's Museum of Natural History. Modern calculations suggest it is oversized by two or even three times.

▲ Another *bête ancienne*, this time hanging from the ceiling of the Natural History Museum in Brussels, with a string of vertebrae for good measure.

RECONSTRUCTING AN ANCIENT MONSTER
Carcharodon megalodon

In 1982 John Maisey was invited to oversee the construction of a new restoration of the jaws of *C. megalodon* for the Smithsonian Institution in Washington DC. It had been known for years that the original reconstruction by Professor Bashford Dean (in the American Museum of Natural History, New York) was grossly oversized and technically inaccurate. Since Dean's model several other, more or less fanciful, attempts have been made to reproduce the jaws of the ancient monster. The opportunity for a more authentic restoration stemmed from the discovery by Pete Harmatuk, an avid amateur collector, of a partial set of Miocene teeth in a North Carolina phosphate quarry. Now that some more morphometric data about an individual fossil white shark had come to light, it was possible to make accurate comparisons with modern great whites and to come up with a more reasonable restoration.

The Smithsonian's version went on public display in October 1985. In the new restoration the jaws, to the great disappointment of some people, are only two-thirds the size of those in Professor Dean's version.

▼ Shark jaws, fanciful and otherwise. The version at left, bearing an uncanny resemblance to a set of dentures, hangs in a Massachusetts college. The teeth have been simply graded according to size and are inserted back to front. The concrete choppers in the centre delight a visitor to Florida Marineland. The jaws below are the 1985 restoration now hanging in the Smithsonian Institution.

KINDS OF SHARKS

LEONARD J.V. COMPAGNO

Living sharks are divided into eight major groups or *orders*, each easily recognisable by certain external characteristics. Each order contains one or more smaller groups, or *families*. In all there are 30 families of sharks and they contain the 350 or more different kinds or *species* of sharks. The living sharks are reviewed below by order and family in a roughly phylogenetic (evolutionary) order.

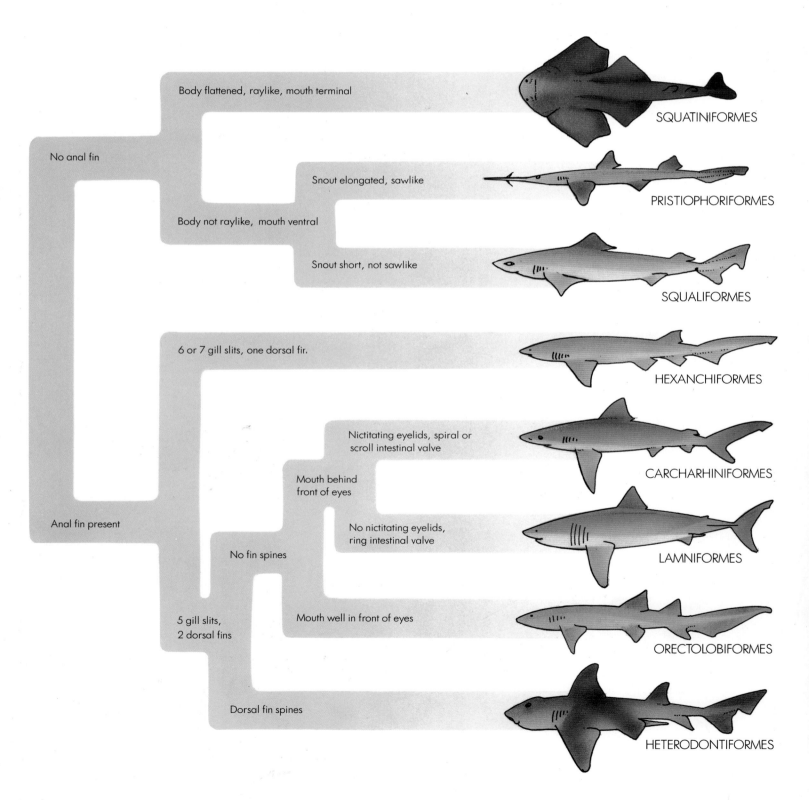

No anal fin

Body flattened, raylike, mouth terminal — SQUATINIFORMES

Body not raylike, mouth ventral

Snout elongated, sawlike — PRISTIOPHORIFORMES

Snout short, not sawlike — SQUALIFORMES

Anal fin present

6 or 7 gill slits, one dorsal fin — HEXANCHIFORMES

No fin spines

Mouth behind front of eyes

Nictitating eyelids, spiral or scroll intestinal valve — CARCHARHINIFORMES

No nictitating eyelids, ring intestinal valve — LAMNIFORMES

5 gill slits, 2 dorsal fins

Mouth well in front of eyes — ORECTOLOBIFORMES

Dorsal fin spines — HETERODONTIFORMES

1 ORDER HEXANCHIFORMES: SIXGILL, SEVENGILL AND FRILLED SHARKS

Sharks with a single spineless dorsal fin, six or seven pairs of gill openings and an anal fin. This small group contains two families and five species, is worldwide in distribution and occurs mostly in deep water. Members of this are ovovivaporous livebearers (the young hatch from eggs within the body).

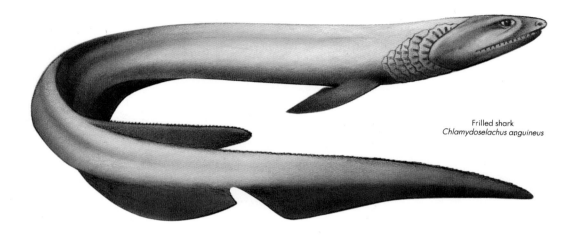

Frilled shark
Chlamydoselachus anguineus

Family Chlamydoselachidae
Frilled Sharks

SPECIES *Chlamydoselachus anguineus* frilled shark.
APPEARANCE This slender, almost eel-like shark is unmistakable. It has a fierce-looking snake-like head with a terminal mouth, small tricuspid teeth in both jaws, six pairs of gill openings with large frilly margins and low fins.
SIZE Maximum length 196 centimetres.
HABITAT Usually on or near the bottom on outer continental and island shelves and upper slopes at depths between 120 and 1280 metres, but occasionally inshore or at the surface.
DISTRIBUTION Scattered marine localities worldwide.
REPRODUCTION Litters of eight to twelve young and a gestation period of up to two years.
DIET Little is known; the remains of a small shark were found in one South African example.

Broadnose or spotted sevengill shark
Notorynchus cepedianus

Family Hexanchidae
Six and Sevengill Sharks

NUMBER OF SPECIES Four.
APPEARANCE Heavy-bodied sharks with high fins and subterminal mouths behind long snouts. The upper teeth have high narrow cusps suitable for impaling prey; the lower, cutting teeth are like broad-tooth combs. Two of the species have six pairs of gill openings; the other two have seven pairs.
SIZE The dwarf of the group, the sharpnose sevengill, does not exceed 1.4 metres; the largest, the giant bluntnose sixgill, grows to almost five metres.
HABITAT The two sixgills and the sharpnose sevengill occur mostly in deeper water on outer shelves and upper slopes from 90 to 1875 metres; the spotted sevengill favours continental shelves and breeds in shallow bays.
DISTRIBUTION Wide-ranging in coastal and offshore waters of all cold temperate to tropical seas. None are oceanic.
REPRODUCTION Large litters of between nine and 108 young.
DIET Relatively large prey: bony fishes, other sharks, rays, chimaeras, squid, crabs, shrimps and carrion. The bluntnose sixgill and broadnose seven gill are indiscriminate feeders on all kinds of carrion as well as live prey.

2 ORDER SQUALIFORMES: DOGFISH SHARKS

Sharks with two dorsal fins (often with fin spines), no anal fin, cylindrical bodies, short mouths and long snouts. Many have powerful cutting teeth in both jaws. In some species these are in the lower jaw only and the upper teeth serve to hold the food.

This large and varied group contains three families and about 82 species. It is found in all oceans, sometimes at depths of 6000 metres. All species are ovoviviparous livebearers.

Bramble shark
Echinorhinus brucus

Family Echinorhinidae
Bramble Sharks

SPECIES *Echinorhinus brucus* bramble shark
Echinorhinus cookei prickly shark.
APPEARANCE Large sharks with stout, cylindrical bodies, small spiracles, broadly arched mouths with smooth lips. They have no dorsal fin spines; the first dorsal fin is over the pelvic fins. The bramble shark has large, heavy platelike denticles; the prickly shark has small conical denticles.
SIZE The bramble shark reaches a length of 3.1 metres, and the prickly shark grows to about four metres.
HABITAT Both species are primarily deepwater slope dwellers. They range down to 900 metres but occur on the shelves in water as shallow as eleven metres.
DISTRIBUTION The bramble shark ranges widely in temperate and tropical seas. At present the prickly shark is known only as a Pacific Ocean dweller.
REPRODUCTION Litters of between fifteen and 24 young.
DIET Both species eat a variety of bottom prey including bony fishes, other smaller sharks, octopuses, squid, crabs and eggcases of sharks and chimaeras.

Family Squalidae
Dogfish Sharks

Piked or spiny dogfish
Squalus acanthias

NUMBER OF SPECIES Approximately 73.
APPEARANCE This diverse group ranges from vary small to gigantic. They have stout to slender cylindrical, or somewhat compressed bodies, small to large spiracles, mouths that vary from broadly arched to transverse, and the first dorsal fin in front of the pelvic fins. Most species have dorsal fin spines, but several species lack these.
SIZE Some dogfish sharks are mature between fifteen and twenty centimetres and are among the smallest of living sharks; many reach between 30 and 90 centimetres; the giants of the family, the Greenland and Pacific sleeper sharks, may grow to between six and seven metres.
HABITAT Most dogfish sharks are found on or near the bottom on the temperate to tropical continental and insular slopes. Some occur on the continental shelves; a small number of species are oceanic.
DISTRIBUTION Their range is probably greater than that of any other shark family. Different species are found in all seas from the Arctic to the sub-Antarctic.
REPRODUCTION Litters range in size from one or two to more than twenty.
DIET Dogfish sharks feed on a variety of prey including bony fishes, other sharks, batoids, cephalopods, crustacea and other invertebrates. Larger members of the family also eat marine mammals.

Family Oxynotidae
Roughsharks

NUMBER OF SPECIES Five.
APPEARANCE Small, bizarre-looking sharks with high compressed bodies, rough skin, small to large spiracles, transverse mouths with lip papillae, strong dorsal fin spines and the first dorsal well in front of the pelvic fins.
SIZE Most grow to less than one metre long. One species sometimes reaches 1.5 metres.
HABITAT Upper continental and insular slopes and outer shelves at depths of between 40 and 720 metres.
DISTRIBUTION The family has a wide, though not uniform, distribution in temperate and tropical seas.
REPRODUCTION Litters contain seven or eight young.
DIET Bottom invertebrates and small fishes.

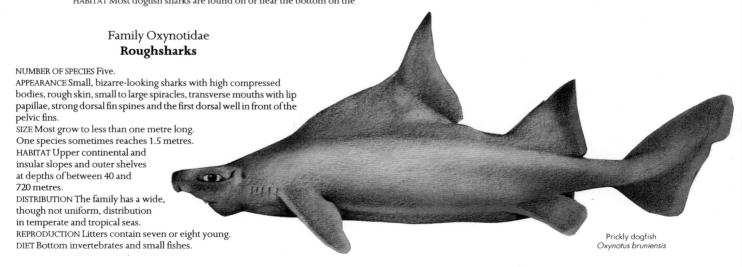

Prickly dogfish
Oxynotus bruniensis

3 ORDER PRISTIOPHORIFORMES: SAWSHARKS

Sawsharks are a minor group of harmless bottom sharks that resemble small sawfishes. The saw snouts are probably used to disable prey. The order comprises a single family with about five species. All are ovoviviparous livebearers.

Family Pristiophoridae
Sawsharks

Shortnose sawshark
Pristiophorus nudipinnis

NUMBER OF SPECIES About five.
APPEARANCE Sawsharks have long, flat bladelike snouts, edged with slender, needle-sharp lateral teeth and a pair of long barbels in front of the nostrils. They have two dorsal fins and no anal fin, short transverse mouths and small cuspidate holding teeth in both jaws.
SIZE Between one and 1.6 metres long.
HABITAT Sawsharks occur at moderate depths on the shelves and upper slopes, on mud, sand and gravel bottoms. The Bahamas sawshark ranges down to a depth of 915 metres.

DISTRIBUTION Different species occur in the western Pacific, the western North Atlantic, the southeastern Atlantic and the western Indian oceans.
REPRODUCTION Litters contain between five and twelve young.
DIET Small fishes, crustaceans and squid.

4 ORDER SQUATINIFORMES: ANGELSHARKS

This highly distinctive group of sharks comprises a single family of about thirteen species. All are ovoviviparous livebearers.

Family Squatinidae
Angelsharks

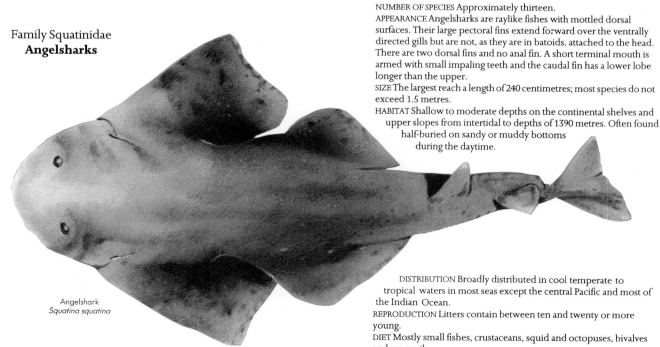

Angelshark
Squatina squatina

NUMBER OF SPECIES Approximately thirteen.
APPEARANCE Angelsharks are raylike fishes with mottled dorsal surfaces. Their large pectoral fins extend forward over the ventrally directed gills but are not, as they are in batoids, attached to the head. There are two dorsal fins and no anal fin. A short terminal mouth is armed with small impaling teeth and the caudal fin has a lower lobe longer than the upper.
SIZE The largest reach a length of 240 centimetres; most species do not exceed 1.5 metres.
HABITAT Shallow to moderate depths on the continental shelves and upper slopes from intertidal to depths of 1390 metres. Often found half-buried on sandy or muddy bottoms during the daytime.

DISTRIBUTION Broadly distributed in cool temperate to tropical waters in most seas except the central Pacific and most of the Indian Ocean.
REPRODUCTION Litters contain between ten and twenty or more young.
DIET Mostly small fishes, crustaceans, squid and octopuses, bivalves and sea-snails.

5 ORDER HETERODONTIFORMES: BULLHEAD SHARKS

These are the only living sharks that combine fin spines on their two dorsal fins and an anal fin. They comprise a single family that contains eight species.

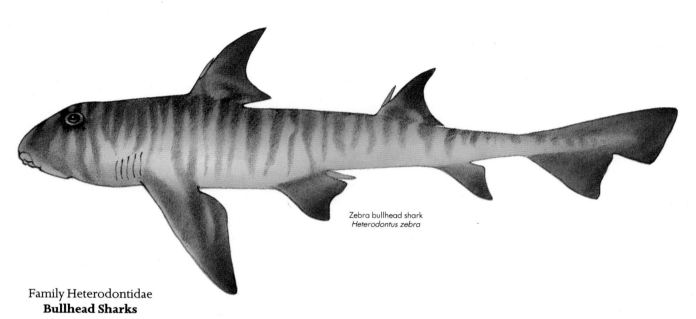

Zebra bullhead shark
Heterodontus zebra

Family Heterodontidae
Bullhead Sharks

NUMBER OF SPECIES Eight.
APPEARANCE Bullhead sharks have big, thick heads with a broad crest over each eye. They have very short, piglike snouts and short, nearly transverse mouths. Grooves connect the mouth and the nostrils. Their jaws characteristically have enlarged, flattened crushing teeth in the rear and small cusped holding teeth in front.
SIZE Adults grow to between 55 and 165 centimetres long.
HABITAT Shallow to moderately deep continental and insular waters at depths from intertidal to at least 275 metres.
DISTRIBUTION Warm temperate to tropical waters in the western Indian and the western and eastern Pacific oceans.
REPRODUCTION Bullhead sharks are oviparous. They lay eggs – enclosed in conical eggcases with screwlike flanges and sometimes terminal tendrils – and deposit them in nest sites among rocks in late winter or spring. These hatch out after seven to twelve months. The young may take ten or more years to mature.
DIET Mostly invertebrates: they crush sea-urchins, starfishes, crabs, shrimps, barnacles, marine worms, sea-snails and other hard prey with their rear teeth. They also catch small fishes.

Port Jackson shark
Heterodontus portusjacksoni

6 ORDER ORECTOLOBIFORMES: CARPETSHARKS

This small but diverse group of seven families and 33 species of warm-water sharks have piglike snouts and short mouths that in most species are connected to the nostrils by grooves. There is an anal fin but, unlike the bullhead sharks, no fin spines on the two dorsal fins. They have uniquely formed barbels at the inside edges of the nostrils.

All are warm temperate or tropical sharks of shallow to moderate depths. Their distribution centres on the tropics of the western Pacific, especially Australia, and the Indian Ocean, though some species range more widely.

Collared carpetshark
Parascyllium collare

Family Parascylliidae
Collared Carpetsharks

NUMBER OF SPECIES Seven.

APPEARANCE These attractively coloured sharks have narrow heads and slender bodies and tails. They have colour patterns of dark and light spots and saddle markings. The anal fin is partly in front of the second dorsal fin and well ahead of the short caudal fin.
SIZE Maximum length ranges from 34 to about 97 centimetres.
HABITAT Moderate depths on continental and insular shelves, from close inshore to 183 metres.

DISTRIBUTION The western Pacific Ocean. Four species occur off southern Australia and three off the Philippines, Taiwan, China and Japan.
REPRODUCTION At least some of the species are oviparous.
DIET Virtually nothing is known. Food probably includes small invertebrates and fishes.

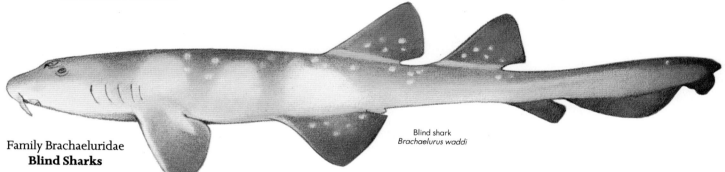

Blind shark
Brachaelurus waddi

Family Brachaeluridae
Blind Sharks

SPECIES *Brachaelurus waddi* blind shark
Heteroscyllium colcloughi bluegrey carpetshark (a Queensland rarity about which little is known).
APPEARANCE Blind sharks have broad heads and moderately stout bodies and tails. The anal fin is behind the second dorsal fin and just in front of the short caudal fin. They have small light spots but no colour pattern or saddle markings.

SIZE Maximum length 122 centimetres.
HABITAT Inshore reef-dwellers from the intertidal to depths of 110 metres.
DISTRIBUTION Restricted to temperate and tropical waters of Australia: off New South Wales, Queensland, the Northern Territory and Western Australia.
REPRODUCTION Ovoviviparous, with seven or eight young per litter.
DIET Small fishes, crabs, shrimps, cuttlefish and sea anemones.

Family Orectolobidae
Wobbegongs

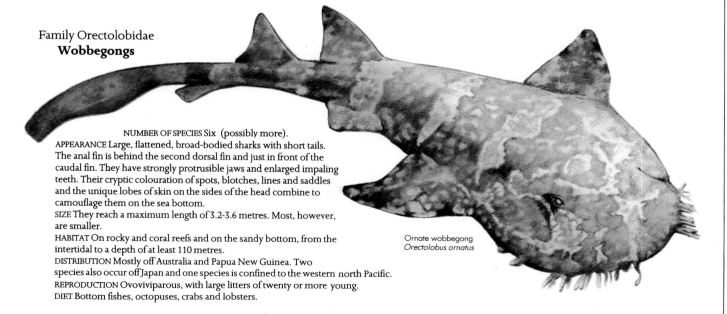

NUMBER OF SPECIES Six (possibly more).
APPEARANCE Large, flattened, broad-bodied sharks with short tails. The anal fin is behind the second dorsal fin and just in front of the caudal fin. They have strongly protrusible jaws and enlarged impaling teeth. Their cryptic colouration of spots, blotches, lines and saddles and the unique lobes of skin on the sides of the head combine to camouflage them on the sea bottom.
SIZE They reach a maximum length of 3.2-3.6 metres. Most, however, are smaller.
HABITAT On rocky and coral reefs and on the sandy bottom, from the intertidal to a depth of at least 110 metres.
DISTRIBUTION Mostly off Australia and Papua New Guinea. Two species also occur off Japan and one species is confined to the western north Pacific.
REPRODUCTION Ovoviviparous, with large litters of twenty or more young.
DIET Bottom fishes, octopuses, crabs and lobsters.

Ornate wobbegong
Orectolobus ornatus

6 ORDER ORECTOLOBIFORMES: CARPETSHARKS (continued)

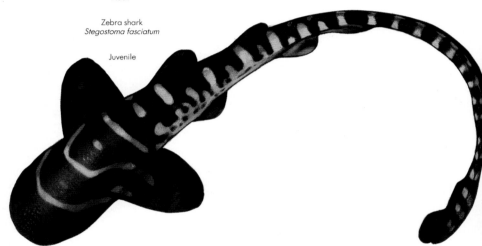

Adult

Zebra shark
Stegostoma fasciatum

Juvenile

Family Stegostomatidae
Zebra Sharks

SPECIES *Stegostoma fasciatum* zebra shark.
APPEARANCE The zebra shark is unmistakable with its broad caudal fin as long as its body. Zebra sharks have broad, bluntly rounded heads, no grooves around the outer edges of their nostrils, moderately stout bodies and tails with strong lateral grooves. The anal fin is well behind the second dorsal fin and just in front of the caudal fin. Young zebra sharks have a colour pattern of yellow stripes on a dark brown background; in the adult shark there is pattern of small brown spots and blotches on a yellow background.
SIZE Most grow to a length of less than three metres; some grow to 3.5 metres.
HABITAT Mainly coral reefs and sandy areas adjacent to reefs, at moderate depths on or near the bottom.
DISTRIBUTION Ranges widely in the Indian Ocean and western Pacific.
REPRODUCTION Oviparous, depositing large, round eggcases on the sea bottom.
DIET Mainly bivalves and sea-snails, but also crabs, shrimps and small bony fishes.

Slender bambooshark
Chiloscyllium indicum

Family Hemiscylliidae
Longtailed Carpetsharks

NUMBER OF SPECIES At least twelve.
APPEARANCE Plain to strikingly patterned sharks with narrow heads, moderately stout bodies and greatly elongated, slender tails. The anal fin is formed as a low rounded keel well behind the second dorsal fin and just in front of the short caudal fin.
SIZE Maximum length is about a metre.
HABITAT Coral and rocky reefs and on sandy and muddy bottoms, mostly in the intertidal but ranging down to 100 metres.

DISTRIBUTION Range widely in the Indian Ocean and the western Pacific, from Madagascar and the Persian Gulf to Japan, the Philippines and Australia.
REPRODUCTION At least some of the species are oviparous and deposit eggs on the bottom in oval eggcases.
DIET Little is known; probably includes small fishes and bottom invertebrates.

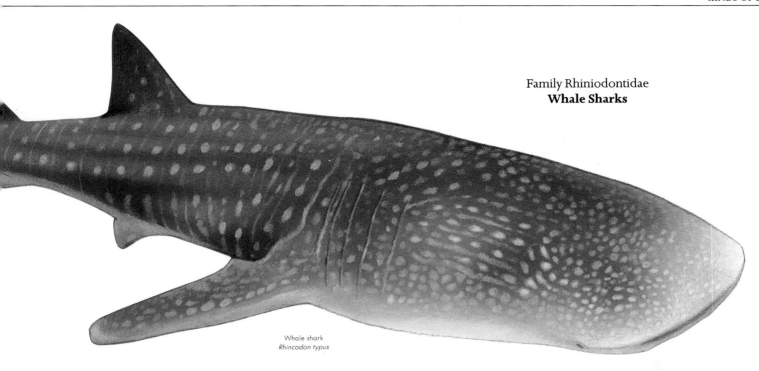

Family Rhiniodontidae
Whale Sharks

Whale shark
Rhincodon typus

SPECIES *Rhincodon typus* whale shark.
APPEARANCE This very distinctive shark has a broad flat head, truncated snout, terminal mouth and tiny teeth. It has huge gill openings, lateral ridges on the trunk and tail and a huge crescent caudal fin with a long lower lobe. Light spots and vertical horizontal lines against a dark background create a unique checkerboard colour pattern.
SIZE Huge specimens, possibly eighteen metres long, have been sighted. The largest accurately measured was 12.1 metres long. It is the world's largest fish.
HABITAT Usually near the surface, close inshore and far from land in the great ocean basins.

DISTRIBUTION All warm temperate and tropical seas.
REPRODUCTION May be oviparous or ovoviviparous. A large egg with a near-term hatchling inside found on the bottom of the Gulf of Mexico may have been normally deposited or prematurely aborted.
DIET A filter-feeder that can ingest a wide variety of food organisms, from one-celled algae and minute crustaceans to mackerel and small tuna.

NUMBER OF SPECIES Three.
APPEARANCE These sharks vary from small to large. They have broad heads, no grooves around the outer edges of their nostrils and moderately stout bodies and tails. The anal fin is slightly behind the second dorsal fin and just in front of the short caudal fin. There is no colour pattern; at most there are scattered dark spots and obscure saddles in young sharks.
SIZE The short-tail nurse shark reaches a length of only 75 centimetres; the other species exceed three metres.
HABITAT Off sandy beaches, mud and sand flats, and from the intertidal on coral and rocky reefs to depths of at least 70 metres.
DISTRIBUTION In all warm seas, including the eastern Pacific, the eastern and western Atlantic and the Indian Ocean.
REPRODUCTION At least one species, the nurse shark, is ovoviviparous and produces litters of twenty to 30 young. The tawny nurse shark has been variously reported as ovoviviparous and oviparous.
DIET Small fishes, crabs, lobsters, shrimps, octopuses, squid, bivalves, sea-snails, sea-urchins and corals.

Family Ginglymostomatidae
Nurse Sharks

Tawny nurse shark
Nebrius ferrugineus

7 ORDER LAMNIFORMES: MACKEREL SHARKS

The mackerel sharks, with seven families and fifteen or sixteen species, are found in all seas except for high Arctic and Antarctic latitudes. Most of them have elongated snouts, long mouths that reach behind the eyes, an anal fin and two spineless dorsal fins.

They range from the intertidal to depths of more than 1200 metres, and from the surfline to the great ocean basins. They are apparently unique in their form of ovoviviparous reproduction – uterine cannibalism – in which embryo sharks feed on their younger siblings and fertilised eggs for a protracted period before birth.

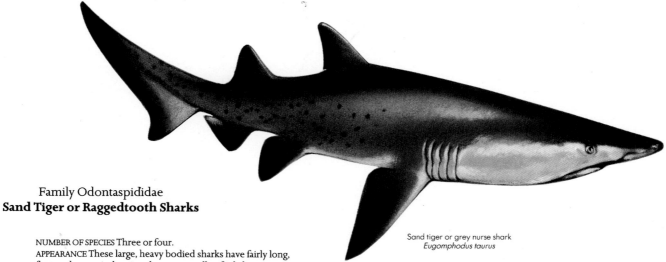

Sand tiger or grey nurse shark
Eugomphodus taurus

Family Odontaspididae
Sand Tiger or Raggedtooth Sharks

NUMBER OF SPECIES Three or four.
APPEARANCE These large, heavy bodied sharks have fairly long, flattened or conical, pointed snouts, small to fairly large eyes, protrusible jaws with large, slender-cusped teeth. The gill openings are short and there are precaudal pits but no lateral caudal keels. The short, asymmetrical caudal fin has a short ventral lobe.
SIZE All species are large and reach a maximum length of between three and 3.6 metres.
HABITAT These sharks are associated with continental or insular landmasses; none are oceanic. They reach depths of 191 to 1200 metres. They occur both at the bottom and near the surface.

DISTRIBUTION Found in all warm temperate and tropical seas, though distribution of individual species may be patchy.
REPRODUCTION Only known in the grey nurse shark; it has two young per litter.
DIET Bony fishes, small sharks and rays, cephalopods and large crustaceans.

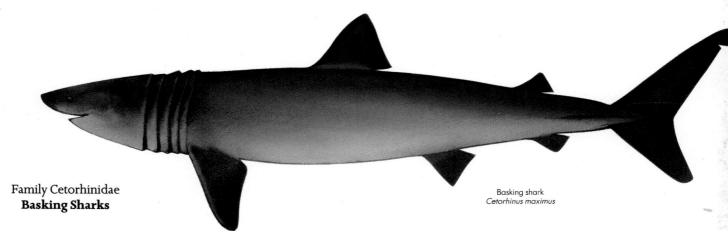

Basking shark
Cetorhinus maximus

Family Cetorhinidae
Basking Sharks

SPECIES *Cetorhinus maximus* basking shark.
APPEARANCE A gigantic, heavy-bodied, spindle-shaped shark with minute eyes, a moderately long hooked or conical snout, a large mouth with only slightly protrusible jaws and minute hooked teeth. It has enormous gill openings that virtually encircle the head, precaudal pits and strong caudal keels. A short, nearly symmetrical, crescent-shaped caudal fin has a long ventral lobe.
SIZE Second only to the whale shark in size. Individuals between 12.2 and 15.2 metres long have been reported, but most do not exceed 9.8 metres.

HABITAT Most abundant in cold temperate coastal continental waters. In shelf waters basking sharks occur well offshore but range right up to the surf-line and into enclosed bays.
DISTRIBUTION The north and south Atlantic and the north and south Pacific.
REPRODUCTION Uncertain, but presumably ovoviviparous.
DIET A filter-feeder that traps minute planktonic crustaceans, principally copepods, on rows of unique gill-raker denticles.

Goblin shark
Mitsukurina owstoni

Family Mitsukurinidae
Goblin Sharks

SPECIES *Mitsukurina owstoni* goblin shark.
APPEARANCE Perhaps remarkable for being the ugliest of living sharks, the gobin shark has a long, flat, daggerlike snout, tiny eyes, a soft flabby body, long protrusible jaws with large, slender, needlelike teeth, and a long low caudal fin without a ventral lobe or precaudal pits.
SIZE Reaches a length of about 3.6 metres.
HABITAT This sluggish bottom-dwelling shark occurs mainly on the continental shelves and outer slopes in depths down to at least 726 metres. Occasionally it is found close inshore.

DISTRIBUTION Its distribution is spotty but spans most oceans, including the western and eastern Atlantic and the western Pacific.
REPRODUCTION Very little known.
DIET Probably includes small soft-bodied prey including fishes, shrimps and squids.

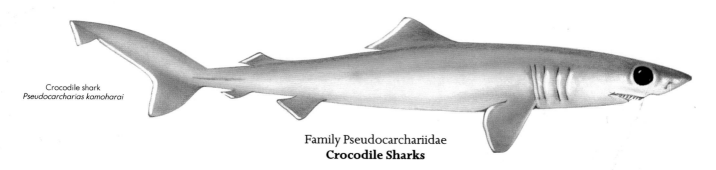

Crocodile shark
Pseudocarcharias kamoharai

Family Pseudocarchariidae
Crocodile Sharks

SPECIES *Pseudocarcharias kamoharai* crocodile shark.
APPEARANCE It is named for its prominent, long, narrow-cusped teeth. The crocodile shark is a small, spindle-shaped oceanic shark with huge eyes, a long, conical, pointed spout, protrusible jaws and fairly long gill openings. It has precaudal pits and low lateral caudal keels and a short asymmetrical caudal fin with a moderately long ventral lobe.

SIZE Maximum length about 1.1 metres.
HABITAT Mainly in the open ocean and off continental waters.
DISTRIBUTION A spotty distribution in the eastern Atlantic, western Indian Ocean, western north Pacific, the central Pacific and the eastern Pacific.
REPRODUCTION Four young per litter.
DIET Midwater bony fishes, squid and crustaceans.

Megamouth shark
Megachasma pelagios

Family Megachasmidae
Megamouth Sharks

SPECIES *Megachasma pelagios* megamouth shark.
APPEARANCE A large heavy-bodied, flabby, cylindrical oceanic shark with small eyes, short, bluntly rounded snout, huge mouth and protrusible jaws with very small, and numerous, hook-shaped teeth. It has short gill openings, precaudal pits but no caudal keels, and a long asymmetrical caudal fin with a moderately long ventral lobe.
SIZE About 4.5 metres long.

HABITAT Only two specimens have so far been caught. These were at depths of between seven and 163 metres in the open ocean or over the upper continental slope.
DISTRIBUTION The central and eastern Pacific.
REPRODUCTION Nothing currently known.
DIET A filter-feeder on small euphausiid shrimps, copepods and pelagic jellyfish.

7 ORDER LAMNIFORMES: MACKEREL SHARKS (continued)

Family Alopiidae
Thresher Sharks

NUMBER OF SPECIES Three.
APPEARANCE Large, stout-bodied, cylindrical sharks with moderately large to huge eyes, short conical snouts, small mouths with slightly protrusible jaws and small bladelike teeth. They have short gill openings, precaudal pits but no caudal keels. A gigantic scythe-shaped caudal fin, about as long as the rest of the shark, has a short ventral lobe.
SIZE Maximum length between 3.3 and 6.1 metres.
HABITAT In oceanic and coastal waters, and near the bottom down to at least 500 metres.
DISTRIBUTION All temperate and tropical seas.
REPRODUCTION Litters of two to four young.
DIET Small prey: pelagic and bottom schooling fishes and squid, octopuses and crustaceans.

Thresher shark
Alopias vulpinus

Family Lamnidae
Mackerel Sharks

Great white shark
Carcharodon carcharias

NUMBER OF SPECIES Five.
APPEARANCE Large, heavy-bodied, spindle-shaped sharks with small to moderately large eyes, long conical snouts, large mouths and only slightly protrusible jaws with large cuspidate or bladelike teeth. The large gill openings do not encircle the head. They have precaudal pits and strong caudal keels. A short, nearly symmetrical, crescent-shaped caudal fin has a long ventral lobe.
SIZE The shortest of the group reach between three and 3.7 metres; the largest, the great white, reaches about 6 metres in length.
HABITAT Oceanic and coastal waters, from the surface, intertidal, surfline and enclosed bays down to depths of 1280 metres.

DISTRIBUTION Found in all cold temperate to tropical seas.
REPRODUCTION Litters of between two and sixteen young.
DIET Small to large bony fishes, squid, other sharks and, in the case of the great whites, sea turtles, seabirds, seals, sea lions, porpoises and carrion from dead whales and other mammals.

Shortfin mako
Isurus oxyrinchus

8 ORDER CARCHARHINIFORMES: GROUNDSHARKS

This group dominates the world's shark fauna, with approximately 197 known species. They swarm in the tropics, are very common in temperate continental waters, share habitats with squaloids and other groups in deep benthic waters. Some species, such as the blue, silky and oceanic whitetip sharks, form the bulk of the oceanic sharks. The group is varied in a gradient from the most primitive small, inactive, small-toothed catsharks, through the intermediate houndsharks and weasel sharks to the large, powerful requiem sharks and hammerheads, which dominate warm seas. Most of the dangerous species occur in this group.

The typical groundshark has an elongated snout, a long mouth that reaches behind the eyes, an anal fin and two spineless dorsal fins. The eyes have movable, nictitating lower eyelids worked by unique muscles. Teeth vary from small and cuspidate or flattened to large and bladelike. Ground sharks have no enlarged rear crushing teeth.

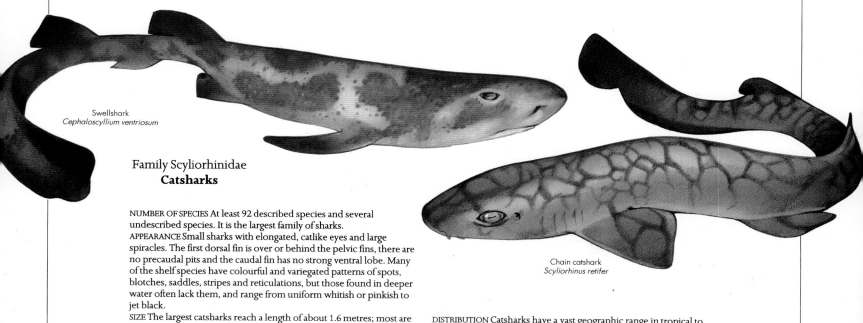

Swellshark
Cephaloscyllium ventriosum

Chain catshark
Scyliorhinus retifer

Family Scyliorhinidae
Catsharks

NUMBER OF SPECIES At least 92 described species and several undescribed species. It is the largest family of sharks.
APPEARANCE Small sharks with elongated, catlike eyes and large spiracles. The first dorsal fin is over or behind the pelvic fins, there are no precaudal pits and the caudal fin has no strong ventral lobe. Many of the shelf species have colourful and variegated patterns of spots, blotches, saddles, stripes and reticulations, but those found in deeper water often lack them, and range from uniform whitish or pinkish to jet black.
SIZE The largest catsharks reach a length of about 1.6 metres; most are smaller – less than 80 centimetres long – and some dwarf species do not exceed 28-30 centimetres.
HABITAT The majority of catshark species are deepwater slope sharks. None are oceanic and most occur on or near the bottom, though some deepwater slope species range well above the substrate. Catsharks occur in coastal marine waters, from the intertidal to the outer shelf, and down the slopes to depths of over 2000 metres. None occur in fresh water.

DISTRIBUTION Catsharks have a vast geographic range in tropical to cold temperate and boreal waters, in all oceans except the Antarctic.
REPRODUCTION Most are oviparous and lay elongated, flattened egg cases with tendrils at their corners. A few are ovoviviparous and produce litters of from two to ten young.
DIET Catsharks feed primarily on invertebrates, especially crustaceans and cephalopods, small bony fishes and small sharks and rays; many take bottom prey but a number of species feed on midwater bony fishes such as lanternfishes and lightfishes.

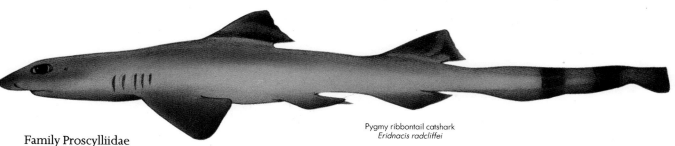

Pygmy ribbontail catshark
Eridnacis radcliffei

Family Proscylliidae
Finback Catsharks

NUMBER OF SPECIES About six.
APPEARANCE This family of small, plain or brightly patterned sharks is very similar to the true catsharks (Scyliorhinidae), but its members have their first dorsal fins positioned in front of the pelvic fins. They also have elongated, catlike eyes, comblike rear teeth, no precaudal pits and no strong ventral caudal lobe.
SIZE The giant of the group, the slender smoothhound, reaches about one metre; the pygmy ribbontail catshark matures at between fifteen and eighteen centimetres.

HABITAT Outer shelves and upper slopes at depths of 50 to 716 metres.
DISTRIBUTION A scattered distribution in the western north Atlantic and Indo-west Pacific.
REPRODUCTION All species are ovoviviparous livebearers except the graceful catshark, which is oviparous.
DIET Small bony fishes, crustaceans, cephalopods and bivalves.

8 ORDER CARCHARHINIFORMES: GROUNDSHARKS (continued)

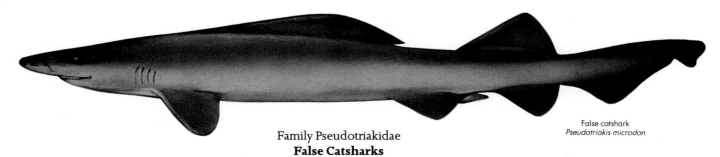

False catshark
Pseudotriakis microdon

Family Pseudotriakidae
False Catsharks

SPECIES *Pseudotriakis microdon* false catshark.
APPEARANCE A large and unmistakable shark with a long, low keel-like first dorsal fin on the back in front of the pelvic fins. It has elongated, catlike eyes, very large spiracles, a large mouth, very numerous small teeth, no precaudal pits and a caudal fin without a strong ventral lobe.
SIZE Adults are up to 295 centimetres long.
HABITAT A singular inhabitant of continental and insular slopes at depths of between 200 and 1500 metres. Sometimes occurs inshore.
DISTRIBUTION Ranges widely in the north Atlantic; also occurs in the western Indian Ocean and in the western and central Pacific.
REPRODUCTION Ovoviviparous with a litter of two to four foetuses that may grow to one metre or more before birth.
DIET Probably feeds on a variety of deepwater bottom fishes and invertebrates.

Barbeled houndshark
Leptocharias smithii

Family Leptochariidae
Barbeled Houndshark

SPECIES *Leptocharias smithii* barbeled houndshark.
APPEARANCE Closely resembles the true houndsharks and the finback catsharks, but differs from both in its longer labial furrows and in combining nearly circular eyes, minute spiracles, and nostrils with barbels. Its tail lacks precaudal pits and its caudal fin lacks a strong ventral lobe.
SIZE Maximum length 82 centimetres.
HABITAT Common at depths from ten to 75 metres, especially off river mouths. It favours muddy bottoms.
DISTRIBUTION The West African tropics, from Mauritania to Angola; may range north off Morocco and into the Mediterranean.
REPRODUCTION Viviparous (placental livebearers), with a unique globular yolk-sac placenta; litters of seven young.
DIET Crustaceans, octopuses, sponges and a variety of small bony fishes.

Snaggletooth shark
Hemipristis elongatus

Family Hemigaleidae
Weasel Sharks

NUMBER OF SPECIES Six.
APPEARANCE Small to moderately large sharks that are very similar to the requiem sharks. They have nearly circular eyes, small spiracles and nostrils without barbels. The first dorsal fin is in front of the pelvic fins and there are precaudal pits. The caudal fin has a strong ventral lobe.
SIZE Most do not exceed 1.4 metres in length. One species, the snaggletooth shark, reaches 2.4 metres.
HABITAT Inshore sharks, occurring in shelf waters at modest depths, from the intertidal to about 100 metres.
DISTRIBUTION Except for one species in the eastern Atlantic, weasel sharks are characteristic of the Indo-west Pacific, from South Africa and the Red Sea to Japan and Australia.
REPRODUCTION All are viviparous with between one and fourteen young per litter.
DIET Bony fishes, small sharks and rays, crustaceans, cephalopods and other invertebrates.

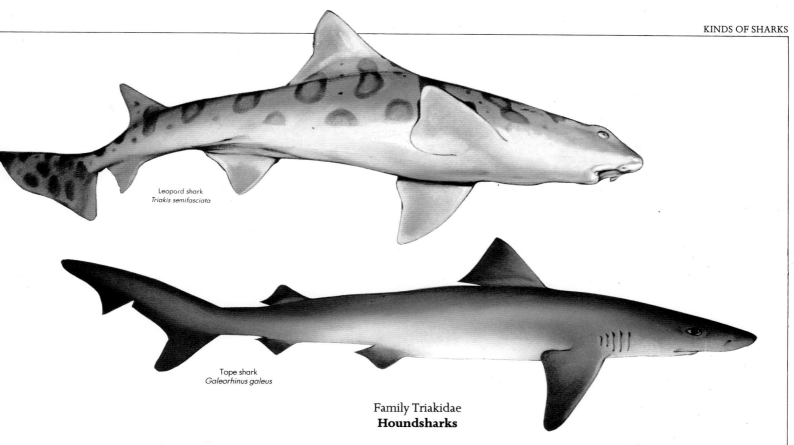

Leopard shark
Triakis semifasciata

Tope shark
Galeorhinus galeus

Family Triakidae
Houndsharks

NUMBER OF SPECIES About 34 described species.
APPEARANCE Small to moderately large sharks with elongated to nearly circular eyes, large to minute spiracles, and nostrils with anterior flaps usually not formed as barbels. The first dorsal fin is in front of the pelvic fins, there are no precaudal pits and the caudal fin may or may not have a strong ventral lobe.
SIZE A few species reach a length of two metres, but most do not exceed 1.2 metres; some reach maturity at less than 30 centimetres.
HABITAT Most occur on the continental and insular shelves. A few species are deepwater slope dwellers, and range to below 2000 metres; none are oceanic. Houndsharks occur mostly on mud, sand and rock bottoms, commonly in enclosed bays, but at least one species occurs on coral reefs.
DISTRIBUTION Found in all tropical and temperate seas.
REPRODUCTION All are livebearers. Slightly more than half the species are viviparous; the rest are ovoviviparous. Litters range from one to fifty-two.
DIET Most feed on bottom invertebrates, particularly crustaceans; some feed heavily on bony fishes and a few specialise on cephalopods. None regularly eat carrion.

Family Sphyrnidae
Hammerhead Sharks

NUMBER OF SPECIES Nine.
APPEARANCE Hammerheads are unmistakable; when viewed from above or below their uniquely expanded and flattened heads have the shape of a hammer or a mallet. They have circular, widely spaced eyes and lack spiracles and barbels on the nostrils. The first dorsal fin is in front of the pelvic fins. They have precaudal pits and the caudal fin has a strong ventral lobe.

SIZE Five of the species are small and do not exceed 1.5 metres in length. The other four reach lengths of between three and more than five metres.
HABITAT Confined to coastal and offshore continental and insular waters, from the intertidal and surface down to at least 275 metres. None are benthic, deepwater or oceanic in habitat.
DISTRIBUTION All warm temperate and tropical seas.
REPRODUCTION All are viviparous livebearers, with litters of between four and 37 young.
DIET Bony fishes, other sharks, batoids, squid, octopuses, and cuttlefish, crabs, shrimps and other crustaceans and sea-snails.

Great hammerhead
Sphyrna mokarran

8 ORDER CARCHARHINIFORMES: GROUNDSHARKS (continued)

Blue shark
Prionace glauca

Family Carcharhinidae
Requiem sharks

NUMBER OF SPECIES 48.

APPEARANCE Small to large sharks with circular or nearly circular eyes,
usually without spiracles or barbels. The first dorsal fin is in front of the
pelvic fins, there are precaudal pits and the caudal fin has a strong
ventral lobe.

SIZE Many species are large and grow to more than two or three metres
long. Some of the small species do not exceed 70 centimetres. The
tiger shark reaches a length of 5.5, possibly 7.4 metres.

HABITAT A very wide habitat range: from estuaries and the intertidal to
the open ocean; from muddy bays and hypersaline estuaries to coral
and rocky reefs; and in freshwater rivers and lakes. None are specialist
deepwater bottom dwellers, but at least two species range down to
400-600 metres and three species are truly oceanic.

DISTRIBUTION Extremely wide. Found in all tropical and temperate
seas. This group dominates the tropical shark fauna in the diversity of
species and often in numbers of individuals.

REPRODUCTION All species are viviparous except the tiger shark, which
is ovoviviparous. Litters vary from one to 135, though most are
between two and twenty.

DIET Requiem sharks are among the most important large marine
predators and take a broad spectrum of prey: bony fishes, sharks and
rays, cephalopods, sea-snails, crustaceans, carrion, even sea-turtles,
sea-snakes, seabirds and marine mammals. Smaller species take less
variety.

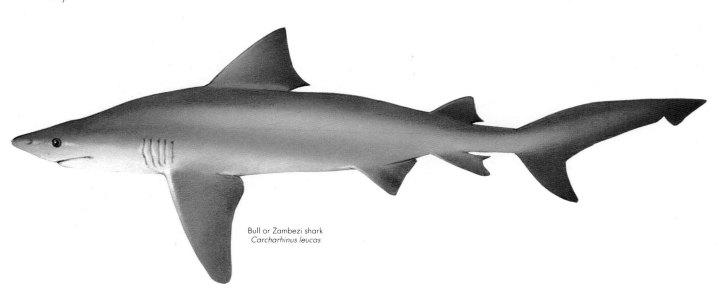

Bull or Zambezi shark
Carcharhinus leucas

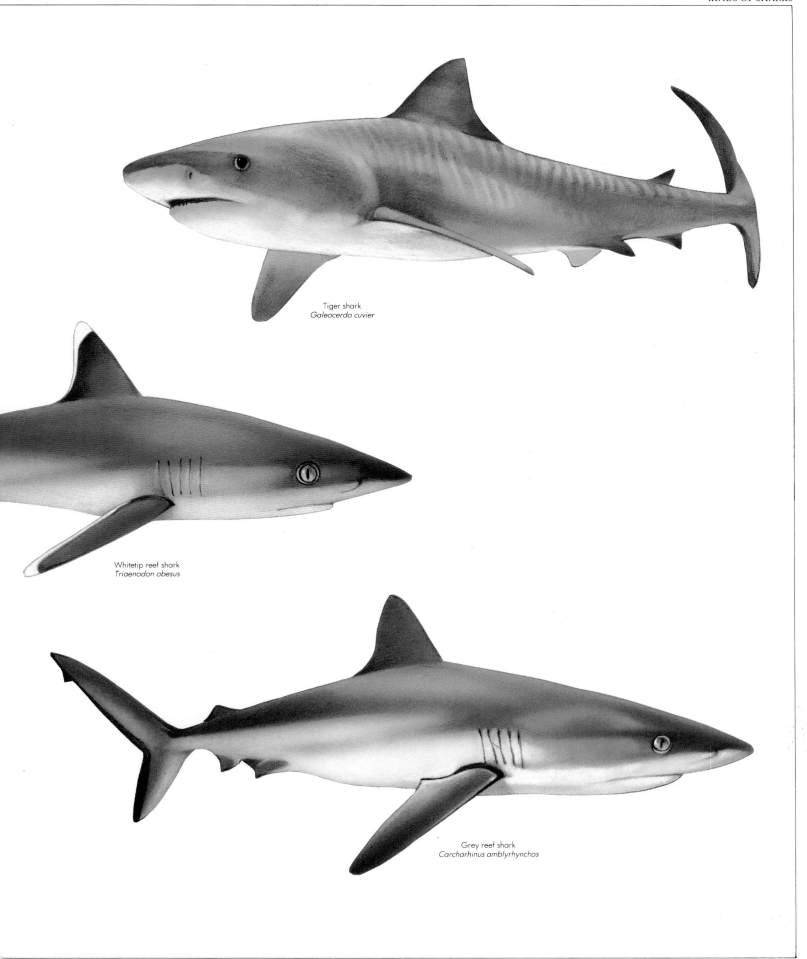

Tiger shark
Galeocerdo cuvier

Whitetip reef shark
Triaenodon obesus

Grey reef shark
Carcharhinus amblyrhynchos

▲ The sand tiger or grey nurse's South African common name of 'raggedtooth' comes from its habit of swimming with its mouth open, exposing its jagged, doglike teeth.

Kevin Deacon/Auscape

WHAT'S IN A NAME?

CARSON CREAGH

Requiem or whaler . . . grey nurse or sand tiger? The confusing variety of common names we use for sharks (and, indeed, for all animals) can mean that two people may be talking about the same animal and not know it. *Eugomphodus taurus* – the sand tiger, according to the International Commission on Zoological Nomenclature – is known as the grey nurse in Australia. In North America and New Zealand, it is referred to as the sand tiger; in South Africa it is the spotted raggedtooth shark.

The variety of names given to this species seems to stem from its appearance and from media coverage of shark attacks: it *is* a fierce-looking shark, with long, protruding teeth and the yellow eyes we would like to associate with the terror of the oceans. In fact, as shark expert Dr Leonard Compagno has recorded, it is relatively inoffensive and unaggressive unless provoked. Its unwarranted reputation as a maneater seems to be due to no more than its name: 'grey nurse' looks much more stirring in a newspaper headline than 'whaler', which is the Australian common name for members of the family Carcharhinidae, to which most of the sharks known to be responsible for attacks on humans belong.

How much more stirring, though, is 'requiem', with its funeral associations, than 'whaler'? Perhaps if Australians had adopted 'requiem' instead of 'whaler' to describe sharks that are truly dangerous, the inoffensive grey nurse would not have been killed in such numbers by divers. No doubt they felt they were ridding the waters of danger but, as Compagno says, theirs was a 'crude and barbaric sport, analogous to shooting domestic cattle with a pistol'. The decline in numbers that resulted from such 'sport' has, fortunately, been halted and the grey nurse is now a protected species in Australia.

It seems that dangerous sharks attract the greatest number of common names. *Carcharodon carcharias*, the great white shark, is also known as the white pointer, the white shark, the great blue shark or, dramatically, as white death. The shortfin mako, *Isurus oxyrinchus*, is sometimes called the blue pointer; a name that causes confusion with the blue shark, *Prionace glauca*, and the great white – or blue – shark.

The value of scientific names is therefore to remove much of this confusion: a single, internationally recognised name that not only defines a particular species but helps to place it in a standardised taxonomic position. Taxonomy (from the Greek words *tasso*, to arrange, and *nomia*, distribution) refers to the classification of organisms within related groups of various sizes. Sharks belong to the phylum Chordata, the subphylum Vertebrata, the class Chondricthyes, one of eight orders, 29 families, around 99 genera and approximately 350 species.

The cautious 'around' 99 genera and 'approximately' 350 species are indications of the dynamic nature of taxonomy: new species, and new discoveries about familiar species, keep the classification of all organisms in a state of flux. In 1984, Dr Leonard Compagno noted that four species of shark – the

▲ The great white shark's alternative common name – white death – was conferred in recognition of its awesome power and ferocious attacks on whales.

Australian school shark, the commercially important soupfin shark, the north Atlantic tope and the South American 'vitamin' shark – are all, in fact, members of a single species, *Galeorhinus galeus*. The value of his discovery lies in increasing our knowledge of shark distribution and populations; knowledge that will help scientists monitor populations and fishing pressures and develop a greater understanding of the processes of evolution.

School sharks grow to a length of around one and a half metres. Another species, almost ten times as long, has also been the subject of changes and not a little confusion in its scientific name. The whale shark, at nearly fourteen metres the world's largest fish, has seen considerable variation in the spelling of its scientific name: from *Rhiniodon typus* to *Rhinodon*, *Rhincodon* and *Rhineodon*. The International Commission on Zoological Nomenclature decides which scientific name is most valid, usually on the basis of priority (which name was used first), and has given *Rhincodon typus* official status. The variety in this case is all the more confusing because each of the names means roughly the same thing: literally 'nose-tooth', in reference to the terminal mouth of this species.

▲ The whale shark may be unique as the world's largest fish, but its zoological history has seen a number of variations in its scientific name.

SHARK DISTRIBUTION

GUIDO DINGERKUS

The distribution of sharks around the world can be largely explained in terms of water temperature and water depth. In some cases there is a positive correlation between temperature and depth; in other cases there is not. When classified according to water temperatures, sharks can be divided into three groups: tropical, temperate and cold water sharks.

ACTIVE TROPICAL SHARKS

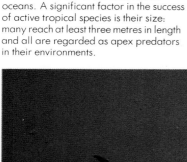

▼ Tropical sharks such as the great hammerhead (*Sphyrna mokarran*) favour warmer waters and are found in all oceans. A significant factor in the success of active tropical species is their size: many reach at least three metres in length and all are regarded as apex predators in their environments.

Tropical sharks live in areas where the water is usually warmer than 21°C (70°F). Sharks living in these regions include most of the carcharhinids (typical or requiem sharks), the sphyrnids (hammerhead sharks), many of the triakids (smooth houndsharks), the orectolobids (wobbegong or carpet sharks), the rhiniodontids (nurse and whale sharks), the hemiscylliids (banded catsharks), and some of the squatinids (angelsharks). These sharks can further be separated into the active types, which swim almost continuously, and the bottom-dwelling or benthic types, which move relatively little.

In the active group are included the requiem sharks, hammerhead sharks, triakids and the whale shark. Individuals in this group travel considerable distances every day and undertake seasonal migrations. In these seasonal migrations they follow changes in water temperatures. In winter active tropical sharks will be closer to the equator, whereas in summer they will be found much further north or south, depending on hemisphere. Being such active swimmers, and following the seasonal water currents, many of the larger members of these species are found in all the world's tropical waters. Examples are the tiger shark (*Galeocerdo cuvier*), bull shark (*Carcharhinus leucas*), sandbar shark (*C. plumbeus*), dusky shark (*C. obscurus*), oceanic whitetip shark (*C. longimanus*), blacktip shark (*C. limbatus*), silky shark (*C. falciformis*), scalloped hammerhead shark (*Sphyrna lewini*), great hammerhead shark (*S. mokarran*), smooth hammerhead shark (*S. zygaena*), and the whale

Ron & Valerie Taylor/ANT

DISTRIBUTION OF THE WINGED HAMMERHEAD SHARK, *Eusphyra blochii*

The winged hammerhead is restricted to the Indo-Pacific region. It typifies the limited range of many smaller species of sharks.

DISTRIBUTION OF THE BULL SHARK, *Carcharhinus leucas*

The bull shark is the only known species to penetrate deeply and for prolonged periods into fresh water.

shark (*Rhincodon typus*). Most of these species grow to larger than three metres, a factor that helps to explain their worldwide distribution in tropical seas.

One of these species, the bull shark (*Carcharhinus leucas*) is also sometimes called the freshwater shark because of its habit of entering freshwater rivers and lakes in most of its range around the world. It has been recorded in such waters as the Amazon River, the Rio San Juan and Lake Nicaragua, the Mississippi River, the Congo River, the Zambezi River, the Bombay River, the Brisbane River, Lake Jamoer and the Panama Canal. In the Amazon River it has been recorded more than 3000 kilometres upstream from the ocean.

The bull shark is the only species of shark that invades fresh waters to such an extent, and will spend long periods of time in fresh water. However, studies by Dr Thomas B. Thorson, mainly on the Lake Nicaragua–Rio San Juan area, have shown that the bull shark does not spend its entire life in fresh water, but enters it for periods of up to several weeks. Just why it enters fresh water for these periods is not known, but it has been theorised that it is to exploit food resources there or to breed – perhaps even to rid itself of marine parasites that cannot survive in fresh water. No species of shark lives exclusively in fresh water. It might be mentioned here that various fishes sold in petshops as fresh water 'sharks' are not sharks at all; they are species of large cyprinids (minnows).

Smaller species of tropical marine sharks (usually less than three metres in length) tend to have smaller ranges. Many species are restricted to the Indo–Pacific region. These include the winghead hammerhead shark (*Eusphyra blochii*), whitetip reef shark (*Triaenodon obesus*), sicklefin lemon shark (*Negaprion acutidens*), spottail shark (*Carcharhinus spallanzani*), blackspot shark (*C. sealei*), blacktip reef shark (*C. melanopterus*), grey reef shark (*C. amblyrhynchos*) and snaggletooth shark (*Hemipristis elongatus*).

David Doubilet

◄ It has often been said that we know more about outer space than the oceans that cover seven-tenth's of the earth's surface. The bizarre filter-feeding megamouth shark (*Megachasma pelagios*), discovered in 1982, is known only from two specimens but may be wide ranging, though rare, in the midwater zone of the open ocean.

An interesting pattern is found in the western Atlantic and eastern Pacific oceans, where many of these smaller species have populations in the tropical coastal waters on either side of Central America. These species include the bonnethead shark (*Sphyrna tiburo*), scooped hammerhead shark (*S. media*), lemon shark (*Negaprion brevirostris*) and smalltail shark (*Carcharhinus porosus*). Such a distribution is probably due to a geological upheaval in Central America that occurred about three million years ago. Before then the western Atlantic and eastern Pacific oceans were one uninterrupted body of water and these species formed one continuous population throughout the area. Given enough time, and assuming that the Central American barrier remains, the two populations will probably diverge

DISTRIBUTION OF THE TIGER SHARK, *Galeocerdo cuvier*

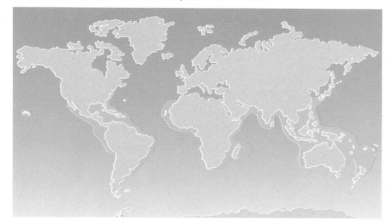

Like many of the larger sharks, the tiger shark is an active swimmer, travelling considerable distances each day and migrating according to seasonal changes.

DISTRIBUTION OF THE WHALE SHARK, *Rhincodon typus*

The whale shark – the largest of all – also has one of the widest distributions. It is one of a small group of large sharks that is both continental and oceanic.

and become distinct species. These will then become sister species pairs, with one sister species on the Atlantic side and the other on the Pacific side of Central America. Indeed this already seems to have occurred with some species that diverge more rapidly.

Examples of already existing sister species pairs on opposite sides of Central America are: the scalloped bonnethead shark (*Sphyrna corona*) and the smalleye hammerhead shark (*S. tudes*); the Pacific sharpnose shark (*Rhizoprionodon longurio*) and the Brazilian sharpnose shark (*R. lalandii*); the sharptooth smooth houndshark (*Mustelus dorsalis*) and the smalleye smooth houndshark (*M. higmani*); and the whitenose shark (*Nasolamia velox*) and the blacknose shark (*Carcharhinus acronotus*). (In each of the above pairs the Pacific species is given first.)

The smallest species of tropical sharks, reaching only about a metre in length, have very small ranges and, hence, limited distributions. These forms occur only around a particular archipelago or in one region of an ocean. Their limited range may be due to their small size and their inability to swim long distances. Examples of such species in the Indo–Pacific region are: the spadenose shark (*Scoliodon laticaudus*), Australian sharpnose shark (*Rhizoprionodon taylori*), grey sharpnose shark (*R. oligolinx*), broadfin shark (*Lamiopsis temmincki*), speartooth shark (*Glyphis glyphis*), Ganges shark (*G. gangeticus*), blacktail reef shark (*Carcharhinus wheeleri*), Pondicherry shark (*C. hemiodon*), creek whaler shark (*C. fitzroyensis*), whitecheek shark (*C. dussumieri*), nervous shark (*C. cautus*), Borneo shark (*C. borneensis*), straighttooth weasel shark (*Paragaleus tengi*), sicklefin weasel shark (*Hemigaleus microstoma*), hooktooth shark (*H. macrostoma*), banded houndshark (*Triakis scyllium*), sharptooth houndshark (*T. megalopterus*), spotted houndshark (*T. maculatus*), sharpfin houndshark (*T. acutipinna*), Arabian houndshark (*Mustelus mosis*), starspotted houndshark (*M. manazo*) and the spotless houndshark (*M. griseus*). In the Atlantic examples of these species include the Caribbean sharpnose shark (*Rhizoprionodon porosus*), daggernose shark (*Isogomphodon oxyrhynchus*), Caribbean reef shark (*Carcharhinus perezi*), Atlantic weasel shark (*Paragaleus pectoralis*), blackspotted houndshark (*Mustelus punctulatus*), narrowfin houndshark (*M. norrisi*), starry houndshark (*M. asterias*), and barbeled houndshark (*Leptocharias smithii*).

▼ The nurse shark (*Ginglymostoma cirratum*) is common off western Africa, the east coast of both North and South America and from California to Peru in the Pacific. All three populations are distinct, differing in a range of body measurements and colour, and appear to have become separated from each other around three million years ago.

Dick Clarke/Seaphot

▲ One of the most attractive sharks, the 3-metre-long zebra shark (*Stegostoma fasciatum*) is common in shallow continental and island waters and on coral reefs throughout the eastern Pacific and Indian Ocean, from the Red Sea to Madagascar, southern Japan and Australia. Its diet consists mainly of molluscs, crabs, shrimp and small fish.

BOTTOM-DWELLING TROPICAL SHARKS

The bottom-dwelling tropical sharks have, on the whole, relatively small ranges. They spend most of their time just sitting on the ocean floor, moving only in order to hunt their food. Indeed, many of them do not actively hunt. They simply sit, camouflaged, on the bottom, waiting for an appropriate meal to come up to them. When the prey comes close enough they dart out, seize it and then settle back to await more prey. As a result, they do not swim great distances. Data seem to show that in their whole lifetime many of these sharks do not travel more than several kilometres from where they were born. Many of them are fairly small, growing to less than two metres long. Like the small active swimming sharks discussed above, most of these species will be restricted to a particular archipelago or a region of a sea. Examples of tropical bottom-dwellers are the banded catsharks, species of the genera *Hemiscyllium* and *Chiloscyllium;* the carpetsharks or wobbegongs, species of the genera *Orectolobus, Sutorectus* and *Eucrossorhinus;* and species of angelsharks, genus *Squatina.*

Three species of fairly large bottom-dwelling sharks – the nurse shark (*Ginglymostoma cirratum*), zebra shark (*Stegostoma fasciatum*) and tawny nurse shark (*Nebrius ferrugineus*) – do not fit this pattern. Being much larger sharks, growing on average to between three and four metres, and good swimmers when they need to be, they appear to travel much more than the smaller bottom-dwelling sharks. The zebra shark and the tawny nurse shark are both found all throughout the Indo–Pacific region. They range from South Africa up to and throughout the Red and Arabian seas, along the coasts of India and China to as far north as the southernmost part of Japan, throughout the Indonesian archipelago to Australia and even as far as Pacific islands such as Fiji. The nurse shark has a very interesting distribution. In the eastern Atlantic Ocean it extends along the west coast of tropical Africa from around Senegal to Angola; in the western Atlantic Ocean it is found in tropical waters from the southern United States to Brazil, including the Caribbean and the Gulf of Mexico; and in the tropical eastern Pacific it is found from California to Peru.

These three populations are quite distinct and can be told apart on the basis of morphometric measurements and differences in coloration. The western Atlantic and eastern Pacific populations are more similar to one another than either is to the eastern Atlantic population. This suggests that, as

with some of the active swimming sharks, the western Atlantic and eastern Pacific populations were separated between one and three million years ago when Central America arose. Since then they have changed, but not enough to warrant calling them separate species.

The eastern Atlantic population differs quite markedly from both of these and it does not appear that the nurse sharks cross the Atlantic Ocean. Nor have they ever been caught at the Azores islands or Ascension Island. As they are restricted to relatively shallow waters, the best explanation for their distribution may be in terms of continental drift. It is possible that before the Atlantic Ocean spread to its present width, the nurse shark lived in the quite shallow waters between Africa and South America. Then, as the continents drifted apart and the Atlantic Ocean attained its great depths, the populations may have been separated. These two populations would, then, have been separated for about ten million years and in that time the differences between them would have developed. Further studies should show whether this hypothesis is accurate.

◄ The Pacific angelshark (*Squatina californica*) is one of the most widely distributed members of the family Squatinidae, and is common to abundant from southern Alaska to Chile, though they are not found in the warm coastal waters of Central America. Like other angelsharks, it is an ambush predator of the sea floor.

TEMPERATE WATER SHARKS

Temperate water sharks live mostly at water temperatures between 10 and 21°C. They include some of the carcharhinids (requiem sharks), heterodontids (horn sharks), triakids (smooth houndsharks), scyliorhinids (catsharks), lamnids (mackerel sharks), alopiids (thresher sharks), odontaspidids (sand tiger sharks), many of the squalids (dogfish sharks), some of the squatinids (angel sharks) and the pristiophorids (saw sharks).

As with the tropical sharks, temperate water sharks can be divided into active swimmers and bottom dwellers. The active swimmers follow water currents as the temperatures change. In winter they tend to be closer to the equator, and in summer they will be further away from it; depending on the hemisphere, they will be further

DISTRIBUTION OF ANGELSHARKS, genus *Squatina*

Like most bottom-dwelling sharks, the various species of angelsharks are limited in their distribution.

north, or further south, than tropical sharks. As with tropical sharks the larger species (more than three metres) are found virtually worldwide. However, because of their preference for cooler waters, they have what is called an anti-tropical distribution. This means that, while there are northern hemisphere and southern hemisphere populations, they are generally absent in tropical, or equatorial, seas.

Species having wide distribution include most of the lamnids: the basking shark (*Cetorhinus maximus*), mako shark (*Isurus oxyrinchus*), great white shark (*Carcharodon carcharias*) and the carcharhinid blue shark (*Prionace glauca*), as well as the alopiid thresher sharks (species of the genus *Alopias*), and odontaspidid sand tiger sharks (species of the genus *Eugomphodus* and *Odontaspis*). The blue shark is probably one of the widest travelling species. Individuals tagged off

◄ Although they are often encountered resting on the bottom close to shore, sand tigers (*Eugomphodus taurus*) are active predators from the surfline to depths of at least 190 metres. Sand tigers are found in tropical and temperate waters of the Atlantic, Indian and western Pacific oceans, and many populations appear to be strongly migratory.

Long Island, New York, have been recaptured off Spain, and individuals tagged off England have been recaptured off Brazil and New York. With individual animals travelling such distances, it is no wonder that the species is found worldwide!

Although these species are most common north or south of tropical or equatorial regions they are also sometimes present in the deeper, cooler waters of tropical regions. In some tropical areas where the temperature of the surface water may be 27°C, at depths of between 30 and 60 metres the water temperature may be as low as 15°C. The blue shark, for example, is quite common near the surface in temperate areas and at depths of 60 metres in the tropics. Other temperate water sharks also venture into tropical waters, but to a lesser extent than the blue shark.

Two species of lamnids, the porbeagle (*Lamna nasus*) and the salmon shark (*L. ditropis*), are very similar and have exclusive ranges. The

▲ *Prionace glauca*, the blue shark, is a wide-ranging open ocean and coastal species that is found from the surface to depths of 150 metres. Although it is primarily an offshore species, it may venture close to shore at night and in temperate waters has been netted at the edges of littoral kelp forests, where it hunts fish, squid and pelagic crabs.

43

▲ Collared catsharks – members of the family Parascylliidae – are restricted to the island and continental shelves of Australia, the China Sea and Japan, and each species is known from a very small range. The Tasmanian spotted catshark (*Parascyllium multimaculatum*), as its name suggests, is restricted to the inshore waters of Tasmania.

dogfish shark (*S. mitsukurii*) and soupfin shark (*Galeorhinus galeus*), as well as houndsharks (genus *Triakis*) and smoothhound sharks (genus *Mustelus*).

BOTTOM-DWELLING TEMPERATE WATER SHARKS

Bottom-dwelling sharks in temperate waters are small, growing to less than two metres in length. As they move very little, their distributions are quite limited. Usually they are only found around one archipelago or in only a restricted portion of one sea. Examples include angelsharks (species of the genus *Squatina*), sawsharks (species of the genera *Pristiophorus* and *Pliotrema*); horn sharks (species of the genus *Heterodontus*) and catsharks (species of the genera *Scyliorhinus*, *Atelomycterus*, *Poroderma*, *Halaelurus* and *Cephaloscyllium*).

COLD WATER SHARKS

Cold water sharks inhabit water colder than 10°C. Many of them live very far north or south, in or close to arctic or antarctic waters. Others live in the deep, cold waters of temperate and even tropical regions. One species, the Portuguese shark (*Centroscymnus coelolepis*), has been caught at a depth of 1500 metres. Another species, the Greenland, or sleeper, shark (*Somniosus microcephalus*) has actually been reported from under polar icefloes. Sharks found in cold water include cowsharks (family Hexanchidae), the frilled shark (Chlamydoselachidae), some of the catsharks (Scyliorhinidae), the false catshark (Pseudotriakidae), the goblin shark (Mitsukurinidae), and some of the dogfish sharks (families Squalidae and Oxynotidae). As in the other groups, these sharks can be divided into active swimming and bottom-dwelling groups.

Among the active swimming cold water sharks, large forms (more than two metres in length) were once thought to be found only very far north or very far south. As more deep water

salmon shark is found only in the cold and temperate waters of the northern Pacific Ocean. The porbeagle has an amphitemperate distribution in the North and South Atlantic, the Indian Ocean and the southern fringes of the Pacific basin.

Like the smaller tropical species, the smaller active temperate sharks (usually less than two metres in length) have more limited ranges than the larger species. However, like the larger forms they have northern and southern hemisphere populations and are more or less absent in tropical waters. If they are occasionally found in tropical areas, it is in deeper, cooler waters. Examples of these sharks are: the spiny dogfish shark (*Squalus acanthias*), Cuban dogfish shark (*S. cubensis*), Japanese dogfish shark (*S. japonicus*), shortspine

DISTRIBUTION OF THE GREAT WHITE SHARK, *Carcharodon carcharias*

The great white, the killer shark of so many legends, has a distinctly coastal distribution.

DISTRIBUTION OF THE BONNETHEAD SHARK, *Sphyrna tiburo*

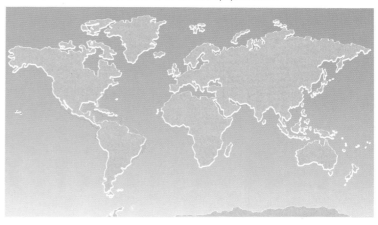

A geological upheaval may account for the appearance of distinct populations of this species on either side of Central America.

▲ Horn sharks (family Heterodontidae) are necessarily restricted in their ranges, since their favoured diet of molluscs, sea urchins and crustaceans can only be found relatively close to shore in temperate and tropical waters. The Port Jackson shark (*Heterodontus portusjacksoni*) is strongly migratory and returns each year to favoured breeding sites.

research is done, we are finding that these species seem to be almost worldwide in distribution. In the far north and far south they seem to come into shallow water, especially during winter months. However, in other areas they are found at depths of 300 metres and more. These are depths at which the water temperature is almost the same as that of arctic or antarctic waters. Among the larger active cold water sharks are the six and seven-gilled sharks (species of the genera *Hexanchus* and *Notorynchus*), frilled shark (*Chlamydoselachus anguineus*), false catshark (*Pseudotriakis microdon*), goblin shark (*Mitsukurina owstoni*) and the sleeper sharks (species of the genus *Somniosus*). Although tagging or tracking studies

of these species have not yet been done, I predict that when they are, we will find that individuals travel very great distances, because food is relatively scarce in such cold waters.

The smaller species of active cold water sharks (less than one metre in length) all live at depths of 300 metres or more. Even in the far north and south, they are not known to come close to the surface. Originally they were thought to be rather rare and to have only limited distributions. However, recent research at greater depths has shown them to be more common and to be much more widely distributed than was once thought. In fact most recent studies seem to show that most of these species have global distributions in the deep

DISTRIBUTION OF THE SHARPTOOTH HOUND SHARK, *Triakis megaloptera*, ● and spotted hound shark, *Triakis maculata* ●

The very limited distribution of these sharks is typical of many active temperate and tropical sharks.

DISTRIBUTION OF COOKIECUTTER SHARKS, genus *Isistius*

The cookiecutters exemplify 'spotty' distribution. Although widespread, their distribution is limited to specific areas.

▲ One of the many reasons for sharks' evolutionary success stems from the fact that unrelated species occupy similar niches in different environments. Thus, the blue shark (*Prionace glauca*) occupies the same free-ranging, predatory niche in temperate seas as the oceanic whitetip (*Carcharhinus longimanus*) does in tropical waters.

small distributions. They seem to be very sedentary and to move only short distances during their entire lives. Indeed, many species seem to have ranges that cover only a few thousand square kilometres. The deepwater catsharks (genus *Apristurus*) are worldwide in distribution, but there are at least 25 species (according to some estimates there might actually be twice that number) and each seems to have its own small 'pocket' on the ocean floor. The only other group of bottom-dwelling cold water sharks, the prickly sharks (species of the genus *Oxynotus*, family Oxynotidae), has only four which, however, have somewhat larger distributions.

Because in certain areas sharks live at different depths, according to the water temperature, a stratification often occurs. It occurs most frequently in tropical areas where variations in water temperature are most marked. In the same general area tropical, temperate and cold water shark species will be found at different depths. Some species, however, live only in areas where particular temperatures and depths coincide. For these species both the temperature and the water depth must be right. For example, most requiem sharks (family Carcharhinidae) and hammerhead sharks (family Sphyrnidae) prefer tropical, shallow waters. In the middle of a tropical ocean – say the Pacific – where the water depth is 1500 metres, one will not find hammerhead sharks or most species of requiem sharks, even near the surface. On the other hand, the oceanic whitetip shark (*Carcharhinus longimanus*), a pelagic species of requiem shark, prefers tropical waters that are, on average, at least 60 metres deep. This species does not come close into shore in shallow tropical water, but remains in the upper, tropical layers in the middle of the Pacific Ocean where the depth is 1500 metres.

In temperate waters, the oceanic whitetip shark is replaced by the blue shark, a temperate pelagic species. Most species of temperate and

seas. Further studies will probably show that, like the larger species, these smaller cold water sharks travel extensively in order to find enough prey to sustain themselves. All the smaller cold water sharks are dogfish sharks of the family Squalidae (species of the genera *Squaliolus*, *Isistius*, *Etmopterus*, *Deania*, *Dalatias*, *Centroscymnus* and *Centrophorus*).

BOTTOM-DWELLING COLD WATER SHARKS

The bottom-dwelling cold water sharks, too, are found only in very deep cold waters and never come close to the surface, even in the far north or south. They are all less than one metre in length but, unlike the active swimming species, have very

DISTRIBUTION OF THE OCEANIC WHITETIP SHARK, *Carcharhinus longimanus*

The oceanic whitetip shark has a very wide distribution that is typical of many of the larger species of sharks.

DISTRIBUTION OF THE BASKING SHARK, *Cetorhinus maximus*

The basking shark has an anti-tropical distribution. It is typical of a number of species that are more common away from tropical and equatorial seas.

Ken Lucas/Seaphot

tropical sharks are shallower water species that inhabit water less than 30 metres deep. Pelagic sharks form only a small group: as well as the blue shark and oceanic whitetip shark, pelagic species include the whale shark (*Rhincodon typus*), mako shark (*Isurus oxyrinchus*); basking shark (*Cetorhinus maximus*), porbeagle shark (*Lamna nasus*) and salmon shark (*L. ditropis*). As well, all species of the family Lamnidae, including the great white shark (*Carcharodon carcharias*) and all the species of thresher shark (*Alopias* spp.) are pelagic.

When active swimming species from temperate and cold waters move into deeper waters they stratify themselves in the water layers.

When in this stratified condition they are called midwater sharks, as they are at neither the water's surface nor near the bottom. The active swimming species of cold water sharks, except for the few species that come into cold shallow water in the far north or south, always behave as midwater species, finding the depth where the water temperature suits them.

A survey of the distribution patterns outlined in this chapter will show that sharks are found in all of the world's marine waters – from the deepest parts of the oceans to the shallowest tropical waters, from the coldest arctic and antarctic waters to temperate and tropical rivers and lakes.

▲ Wide-ranging in temperate and cold waters, the broadnose sevengill shark (*Notorhynchus cepedianus*) is a powerful and indiscriminate predator whose diet of other sharks, bony fishes, stingrays and carrion has enabled it to thrive in a range of habitats from the surfline to at least 46 metres deep.

DISTRIBUTION OF THE SALMON SHARK, *Lamna ditropis*

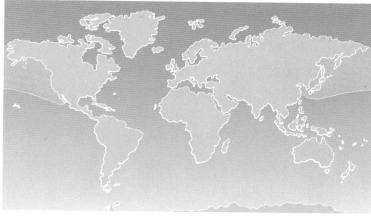

The salmon shark provides a good example of an exclusive distribution. It is found only in the northern Pacific Ocean.

DISTRIBUTION OF THE GREENLAND SHARK, *Somniosus microcephalus*

This cold water shark has been recorded underneath polar ice floes. Although it may reach seven metres, it is sluggish when captured.

SHARKS: LARGE, SMALL AND DANGEROUS

CARSON CREAGH

Contrary to the popular *Jaws* image, most sharks are small and harmless to humans. Fifty per cent of living species reach a maximum length of between fifteen centimetres and one metre, and 82 per cent do not reach two metres. The average maximum length for living sharks is about 1.5 metres. Only about 4 per cent of sharks are gigantic – four to twelve or more metres long. These include the largest living fishes, the whale and basking sharks, which broadly overlap the larger cetaceans in size. In contrast some sharks are dwarfs and mature at a length of fifteen to twenty centimetres.

Almost all dangerous sharks are large, over two metres long. Dangerous, as applied to sharks, is a relative term, used for rating different species. It does not signify that sharks are any more than minimally dangerous to people when compared with such hazards as motor cars, heart attacks, communicable diseases, the sea or war. A person is more likely to be struck by lightning or bitten by a poisonous snake than attacked by a shark. Experts suggest that the worldwide shark attack rate is less than 100 per year, with 25 to 30 fatalities. This is very low when we take into account the number of people who swim in or otherwise use the sea.

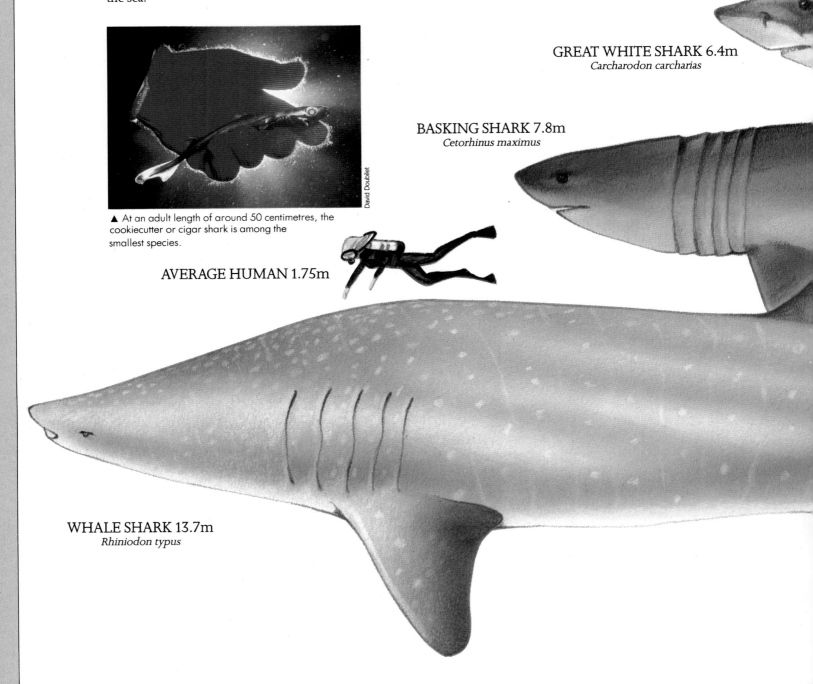

David Doubilet

▲ At an adult length of around 50 centimetres, the cookiecutter or cigar shark is among the smallest species.

GREAT WHITE SHARK 6.4m
Carcharodon carcharias

BASKING SHARK 7.8m
Cetorhinus maximus

AVERAGE HUMAN 1.75m

WHALE SHARK 13.7m
Rhiniodon typus

PYGMY RIBBONTAIL CATSHARK 0.24m *Eridacnis radcliffei*
PIKED DOGFISH 1.6m *Squalus acanthias*
PORT JACKSON SHARK 1.65m
Heterodontus portusjacksoni
ORNATE WOBBEGONG 2.88m
Orectolobus ornatus
BULL SHARK 3.4m
Carcharhinus leucas

The lengths represented in the diagram are the maximum recorded sizes of each species as reported in Leonard J. V. Compagno's 1984 FAO Species Catalogue, *Sharks of the World*.

SHARK BIOLOGY

JOHN D. STEVENS

Sharks arose some 350 million years ago and have remained virtually unchanged for the past 70 million years, yet still comprise a dominant group. Admittedly, they live in an environment that is fairly resistant to fluctuations and have been subject to minimal interference from humans, but considering the geological time scale they have spanned, sharks appear to be exceptionally successful. Their success is due to the original 'building blocks' they inherited from their primitive ancestors, but sharks demonstrate some fascinating adaptations to a variety of ecological niches and to the constraints of a demanding environment – adaptations that have enabled them to become the most important predators in the sea.

Sharks almost certainly evolved from the placoderms, a group of primitive jawed fishes. Placoderms experimented with different jaw and fin designs; the variety of these in this group is surprising. By contrast, even early sharks were fairly conservative in design and had already settled on a predatory existence similar to many of the modern forms.

▼ A shark's body form is closely related to its way of life. The 'typical' shark, represented by the whaler genus, has a streamlined body and highly efficient system of movement to complement its active predatory lifestyle. Mackerel sharks are conico-cylindrical and stouter than the whaler sharks. Their bodies are close to the perfect hydrodynamic shape. In contrast, the catshark is adapted to its sluggish bottom-dwelling existence. Its tapering body and weak tail enable it to swim with an eel-like motion.

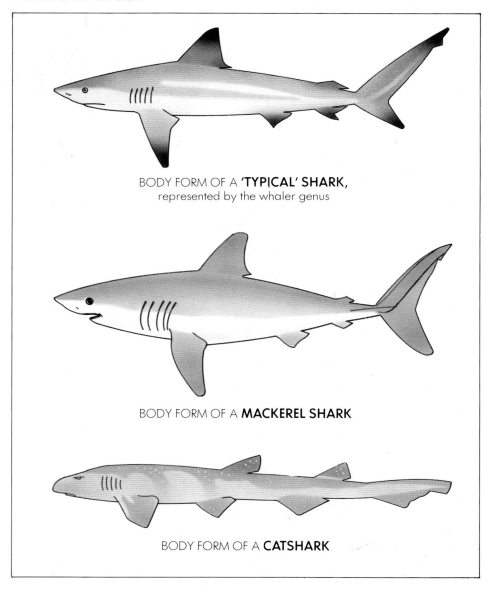

BODY FORM OF A **'TYPICAL' SHARK,**
represented by the whaler genus

BODY FORM OF A **MACKEREL SHARK**

BODY FORM OF A **CATSHARK**

BODY FORM AND LOCOMOTION

If asked to draw a typical shark, most of us would sketch something like the top diagram (*left*), which is best represented by the whaler genus (*Carcharhinus*). An active, predatory lifestyle in a demanding medium 800 times denser than air requires an efficient locomotory system and, while a swimmer can be forgiven for not appreciating the finer points of an approaching shark, its superb grace is indisputable.

The body form of sharks can be related to their way of life. Our typical shark has a streamlined, slender body, a longish snout and pectoral fins, a tail fin with the upper lobe longer than the lower lobe and a thickish caudal peduncle or tail stem. The forward part of the shark's body is flattened to reduce drag during rapid turning and to allow lateral movement during normal swimming. The elevated middle sections induce more drag, acting as a fulcrum when the shark turns.

These sharks swim with a slightly sinuous eel-like motion, their muscles sending transverse waves down the body. Since the amplitude of these waves reaches a peak near the tail, this section is also flattened to reduce drag while providing lift to the tail.

In general, sharks control their position in the water by balancing opposing forces generated during forward motion. The longer upper tail lobe drives the shark down through the water, and this is counteracted by lift generated from the pectoral fins and the flattened ventral surfaces of the head region.

Buoyancy control with minimal expenditure of energy is important in maintaining an animal's position in the water. While bony fishes developed

Ron & Valerie Taylor

gas bladders, sharks solved this problem by acquiring large, oily livers and reducing the density of body tissues. One of the most important developments was the replacement of bone as the body's framework with cartilage, which is both lighter and more elastic.

The less dense the body of a shark, the less lift is required to maintain its position in the water. The difference in the density of various species is related to their way of life: typical sharks, which tend to be active pelagic and midwater swimmers, are less dense than bottom-living forms. The blue shark (*Prionace glauca*) and piked dogfish (*Squalus acanthias*) weigh in water only 2.5 per cent and 2.7 per cent of what they weigh in air, compared with 5.5 per cent for the bottom-living angelshark (*Squatina squatina*).

It would seem logical for fast-swimming species to reduce their density even further so that they could reduce the area of the fins needed to provide lift, thus minimising drag. However, there would be no real advantage in being neutrally buoyant, because the fins need to be a certain size for adequate manoeuvrability. Reduction in density can be accomplished instead by developing a large, oily liver containing oil of low specific gravity. In the blue shark, for example, the liver can account for up to 20 per cent of the body weight. The other major tissues that contribute to an overall reduction in density are the white muscles,

skeletal tissues and skin. Blue sharks also have a low-density 'jelly' in the snout.

The skin of sharks consists of dermal denticles (actually modified teeth), which give the skin its sandpaper texture. Each denticle consists of a basal plate or root, a pedicel and a crown that caps the pedicel and may expand outwards from it. At first sight it is curious that sharks have a rough skin, as this might appear to increase drag due to friction. However, it has been suggested that the alignment of the denticles channels the water, resulting in a laminar flow that acts to reduce friction. The arrangement of the denticles may also make sharks 'hydrodynamically quiet', which would be an advantage in stalking prey. The denticles of faster pelagic sharks are smaller and lighter than those of the more sluggish benthic or bottom-living species.

A shark's fins provide lift, braking and turning power, acceleration and tracking and prevent pitch, roll and yaw. It has been postulated that the typical body form of sharks is an adaptation for cruising, a requirement of their predatory way of life. In the typical shark, the placement of the pectoral and dorsal fins probably results in poor acceleration, but the spacing between them is critical in interacting with the water flow to increase efficiency and thrust.

Sharks have two main types of muscle, red and white. In the typical shark, the red muscle lies in a thin layer just under the skin and outside the white

▲ The whaler or requiem sharks (members of the genus *Carcharhinus*) epitomise the 'typical' sharks: streamlined, powerful animals. There are around 29 species of *Carcharhinus*, ranging from less than a metre to more than four metres in length and found in virtually every habitat from fresh water to estuaries, tropical reefs and the open ocean.

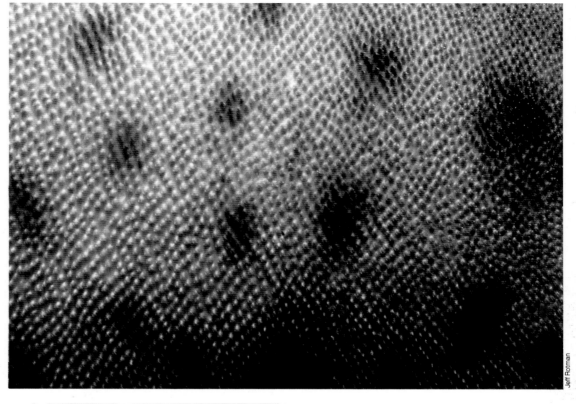

► A shark's skin is covered with a sort of flexible armour — thousands of small, scale-like denticles composed of a flattened basal plate and a backwards-facing spine. In bullhead sharks the denticles have lost the spines and resemble hexagonal columns; in the prickly dogfish (*Oxynotis bruniensis*), the skin is so rough that it can cause painful abrasions.

▼ It was once believed that sharks are less efficient than bony fishes because they lack a gas-filled swim bladder. However, sharks can move up and down in the water column more easily than bony fishes since they obtain close to neutral buoyancy through oily livers that are not affected by variations in pressure due to depth.

muscle. It has a good blood supply and uses aerobic oxidation of fat as its energy source. Red muscle functions in sustained slow swimming and in a typical shark, such as the blue shark, comprises around eleven per cent total muscle. White muscle has a poor blood supply, functions by the anaerobic breakdown of glycogen and is only used during fast sprint swimming: because white muscle operates anaerobically, sharks cannot sustain sprint speeds and quickly become exhausted.

Cruising speeds of typical sharks have been calculated in various ways. A 2-metre bull shark (*Carcharhinus leucas*) was observed swimming at around 2.5 kilometres per hour (70 centimetres per second) over a measured distance. Telemetry studies on blue sharks indicated speeds of 1.3 kilometres per hour during the day and 2.8 kilometres per hour at night, when the sharks were more active. Maximum speed generally decreases with length and the smaller piked dogfish cruise at around one kilometre per hour (30 centimetres per second). Sprint speeds are less well known, but in one questionable series of experiments a 60-centimetre-long blue shark reputedly maintained its position in a current equivalent to 38 kilometres per hour and in short bursts attained 69 kilometres per hour. A blacktip reef shark (*Carcharhinus melanopterus*) hooked on rod and line achieved bursts of 29 kilometres per hour and a similar speed was estimated for an individual of the same species chased by a boat in shallow water. In general, typical sharks (pelagic, midwater and near-bottom feeders) are better designed for sprinting than sustained cruising.

SHARK TAILS: DIVERSITY OF FORM AND FUNCTION

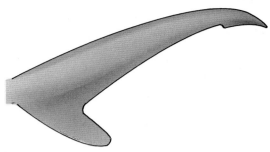

TIGER SHARK

The tiger shark's tail is strongly *epicercal* (the upper lobe is longer and heavier than the lower lobe). This species moves by swinging its body from side to side, and the large upper lobe delivers the maximum amount of power for slow cruising or sudden bursts of speed in pursuit of prey. The tiger shark's varied diet means that it must be able to twist and turn rapidly when hunting turtles, fish, stingrays and other sharks.

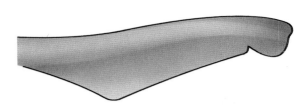

NURSE SHARK

Common in shallow waters on the tropical coasts of America and Africa, the nurse shark (*Ginglymostoma cirratum*) is a nocturnal species that spends daylight hours resting on the bottom or in caves and crevices: its prey consists mainly of invertebrates such as crabs, lobsters, sea urchins and octopuses. The nurse shark swims with an eel-like motion, using broad sweeps of its elongated tail to propel it slowly in search of food.

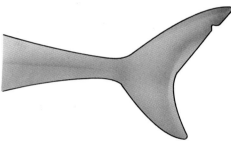

PORBEAGLE

The porbeagle (*Lamna nasus*) is a heavily built pelagic shark related to the mako and great white and is a voracious feeder on school fishes such as mackerel and herring. Porbeagles use their tails for propulsion rather than swinging their bodies from side to side; the large lower lobe of the tail fin provides greater speed after fast-moving prey, and lateral 'keels' at the base of the tail may reduce drag for efficient hunting.

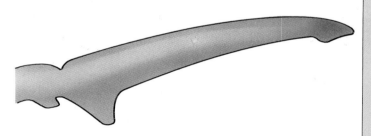

THRESHER SHARK

Thresher sharks are found in tropical and temperate oceans around the world and are active hunters of fish and squid, which they are believed to herd, then stun, with the powerful and incredibly elongated upper lobe of their tails. All three species are active and strong-swimming sharks; the development of a tail that is almost as long as the rest of the body has not been at the expense of speed or predatory efficiency.

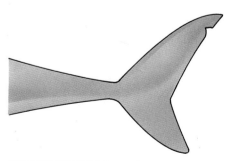

GREAT WHITE SHARK

The great white shark is primarily a coastal and offshore species, but has been encountered far from land. The great white has evolved a body and tail that are remarkably similar in shape to the tuna. It relies on its tail, in which the upper and lower lobes are nearly of equal size, for both low-speed cruising and high-speed dashes after fast-moving and agile prey.

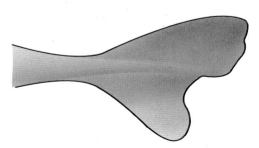

COOKIECUTTER SHARK

The cookiecutter shark (*Isistius brasiliensis*) hunts squid and crustaceans, but will also attach itself to marlin, tuna, dolphins – even the little-known megamouth shark – with its strong suction lips, then use its scoop-shaped lower jaw to cut out a conical plug of flesh. Its tail has broad upper and lower lobes of almost the same size. Because it is luminescent, the tail may lure prey towards the shark.

▲ Despite common belief, remoras are active and strong swimming fish that do not rely on sharks to provide them with food; indeed, they seem to 'hitch a ride' only when it suits them and are often found attached to turtles, which are vegetarians and do not provide scraps of food for their companions.

FRIENDS AND ENEMIES

CARSON CREAGH

S harks do not exist in an ecological vacuum: as predators, they play a vital part in the complex web of interactions that make up the oceanic food chain and, like all organisms, associate with other species in symbiotic relationships.

Symbiosis is popularly defined as mutual dependence, but in its widest sense can be regarded simply as 'living together'. Where one organism benefits from the relationship and the other is not affected, the relationship is called *commensalism;* where both parties benefit it is called *mutualism;* and if one organism benefits at the expense of the other the relationship is called *parasitism.*

The relationship between sharks and pilot fish is a classic case of commensalism. It was once believed that pilot fish guided – literally piloted – their shortsighted and dimwitted 'masters' to food, and in return were protected from other predators and spared by their grateful companions.

Unfortunately, pilot fish neither direct sharks to food, nor are their lives spared if they are slow, ill or weak. The fish themselves certainly benefit from the relationship by stealing scraps of food, and it has recently been suggested that they derive other advantages from the relationship. Smaller pilot fish gain some hydrodynamic benefits, riding the shark's 'bow wave' in much the same way as dolphins will with a ship. More intriguing is the idea that pilot fish, being schooling fishes, are attracted to moving objects that offer contrasts in brightness – a diver, a school of other pilot fish, a manta ray . . . or a shark. They are more robots than guides, attracted to sharks merely through instinctive schooling responses rather than any knowledge of feeding advantages.

Diskfish, commonly known as remoras or sucker fish (family Echeneidae) were once thought to 'take advantage' of sharks in the same way as their relatives the pilot fish – simply attaching themselves by their louvred suction cups (actually highly modified dorsal fins) and 'hitching a ride' in order to steal food scraps.

▲ The remora or sucker fish (*Echeneis naucrates*) grows to 60 centimetres in length and smaller specimens are sometimes found living inside the gill cavities of sharks, manta rays or marlin without causing any apparent harm to their hosts. The remora's ridged suction disk is actually formed from its highly modified first dorsal fin.

The truth is more complex, and demonstrates some of the adaptations bony fishes have made to take advantage of their supposedly more primitive relatives. The eight species of diskfish have evolved to live with more or less specific hosts: the remora (*Remora remora*), sharksucker (*Echeneis naucrates*) and white suckerfish (*Remorina albescens*) are usually found with sharks or rays, and the whalesucker (*Remorina australis*) with baleen whales and larger toothed whales. The sharksucker does not spend most of its time attached to a shark. Instead, like the pilotfish, it rides the shark's bow wave, only using its suction disk when its host changes direction or slows down.

However, the stomach contents of both sharksuckers and remoras reveal that their relationship with sharks must be regarded as mutualism. Almost all of their food consists of parasitic copepods, and the remora and white suckerfish have adapted so well to their role as cleaners that they have short, stumpy bodies and reduced fins, and are most often found inside the mouths or gill chambers of sharks and rays.

Other organisms also provide a service to sharks, apparently ridding them of external parasites, or ectoparasites, that are too small for diskfish to remove. Most tropical reefs have a resident population of cleaner fishes (usually wrasses or blennies) and shrimps that earn a living by removing parasites from a range of elasmobranchs and bony fishes. These animals move purposefully over a shark's skin, picking off copepods and often entering the mouths or gill chambers of their 'clients'. Both lemon sharks and nurse sharks will rest on the bottom to be cleaned and nurse sharks have been observed to halt the movements of their gills for up to two minutes while they are serviced by cleaners.

Just as 'big fleas have little fleas', so sharks – like all other organisms – have parasites that survive at the expense of their unwilling host. As well as flatworms and roundworms, there are specialised marine leeches that live only around the cloaca and claspers of sharks. But the most common ectoparasites are undoubtedly the copepods, highly evolved crustaceans that range from less than a millimetre to around 30 centimetres in length. Copepods usually feed on the skin tissues of their hosts, especially on the trailing surfaces of fins, but one species, *Ommatokoita elongata*, attaches itself to the cornea of Greenland shark eyes. Even more strangely, this species is bioluminescent and may act as a lure to attract prey to these lethargic bottom-dwelling sharks.

The trend in shark evolution towards urea retention as a means of establishing a chemical balance between the interior of the body and the surrounding seawater has made life difficult for most parasites, but tapeworms appear to have rallied to the challenge and comprise the most abundant – more than 400 species – internal parasites, or endoparasites, of elasmobranchs. Although few grow to more than 20 centimetres long, thousands of smaller tapeworms have been recovered from the intestine of a single shark.

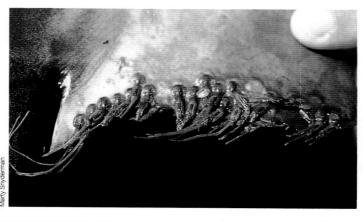

▲ Among the most common body and skin parasites of sharks are copepods, crustaceans often referred to as sea lice. Most of the 4500 species of copepods are free-living, but a thousand or so are parasites ranging in size from less than one millimetre to 30 millimetres long and usually found attached to the fins or gills of their hosts.

◄ A banded coral shrimp (*Stenopus hispidus*) removes tiny parasites from the skin of a wobbegong as it rests on the sea floor. These shrimp set up 'cleaning stations' near coral outcrops and clean parasites from the skin and mouths of fish and sharks – which will even cease breathing to allow the shrimp to rid their gills of parasites.

▲ The main thrust of shark evolution has been towards a highly efficient predatory lifestyle, epitomised by the great white shark – a 'true superpredator' that hunts in the open ocean and can survive for long periods without food. When it finds prey, the great white tears away chunks of flesh with its powerful jaws and daggerlike teeth.

David Doublet

Al Giddings/Ocean Images

▶ *Carcharodon carcharias*, the great white shark, is almost perfectly hydrodynamic. Its stiff, tuna-like body allows it to cruise for long periods at a relatively low speed until it encounters one of the many animals it includes in its diet: from salmon and tuna to other sharks, gannets, dolphins, porpoises and seals.

SPECIALISATION

Body form and locomotion are related to way of life, and having looked at a typical shark we can now examine the ways in which species have become specialised. Over and above size differences, around 40 per cent of species differ significantly from the typical shark body plan.

One family, the Lamnidae or mackerel sharks, which contains the great white shark (*Carcharodon carcharias*), shortfin mako (*Isurus oxyrinchus*) and porbeagle (*Lamna nasus*), has become highly specialised for a pelagic existence. The mako is probably the fastest and most active shark and is renowned as a sportfish, often repeatedly leaping clear of the water when hooked – and for a mako to jump clear of the water it must have a starting velocity of at least 35 kilometres per hour.

The body form of the mackerel sharks is conico-cylindrical, with the maximum width occurring well forward on the body. They are stouter than the typical shark and most closely conform to a 'perfect' hydrodynamic shape. They have a bluntly pointed snout, thin caudal peduncle and a lunate tailfin (lobes about equal in length). The tail has a high aspect ratio (ratio of height to length), which produces maximum thrust with minimum drag and provides almost all of the propulsion; these sharks swim with a particularly rigid action.

One of the major adaptations of the mackerel sharks is an elevated body temperature and the ability to maintain temperatures 5–11°C above ambient water temperature. The effect of this is to make the muscles operate more efficiently: in a unique experiment conducted off New York, a 4.6-metre white shark was tracked for three and a

half days while its depth, muscle temperature and the water temperature were recorded by acoustic telemetry. The shark swam at an average speed of 3.2 kilometres per hour and stayed mainly in the thermocline (the boundary between warm and cold water), where it kept its muscle temperature at 3–5°C above ambient temperature.

Mackerel sharks have larger amounts of red muscle which, in contrast with other species, is sited deep in the body close to the vertebral column. The red muscle is connected to the circulatory system by a complicated capillary network that acts as a heat exchanger to reduce heat loss.

Mackerel sharks are well adapted for maintaining high cruising speeds and parallel many of the adaptations shown by tuna, which have a similar lifestyle among the bony fish. Mackerel sharks' bodies tend to be slightly denser than those of the typical sharks: the porbeagle, for example, has a density of about 3.2 per cent in water and has a relatively smaller pectoral and caudal fin area. But because their cruising speed is higher, mackerel sharks are able to develop sufficient lift with a heavier body and smaller fins.

Another group of sharks adapted to a fairly sluggish existence, feeding on or near the bottom in shallow water, includes the carpetsharks (Orectolobiformes) and catsharks (Scyliorhinidae). They are characterised by a large head, tapering body and weak, thin tail. They swim with a pronounced eel-like motion, with the motive force being provided by the whole rear end of the body, not just the tail. The front of the body swings in a wide arc with the pivot point being near the first dorsal fin, which is situated well back on the body.

Because they spend much of their time on or near the bottom, buoyancy is not so important; neither is it necessary to have large amounts of red

▲ Bottom-dwelling sharks such as this ornate wobbegong (*Orectolobus ornatus*) lie in wait for suitable prey — octopuses, crabs, lobsters and bony fish — which they grasp with their sharp, fanglike teeth. Most wobbegongs have tassels, called dermal lobes, that help to break up their outline against a sandy or rocky bottom.

◄ Many of the smaller reef sharks, especially the blacktip reef shark (*Carcharhinus melanopterus*), rest in caves or beneath coral outcrops during the day. They may even 'sleep' in these protected spots. They are often cleaned by shrimp or cleaner fish at such times and their respiration and heart rates slow down considerably.

nurse shark (*Ginglymostoma cirratum*).

Some species of shark, notably the dogfish sharks (*Squaliformes*), the frilled shark (*Chlamydoselachus anguineus*) and the goblin shark (*Mitsukurina owstoni*), have invaded the deep sea. Many of these species have large livers (around 25 per cent of body weight) that contain up to 90 per cent oil, much of which is of very low specific gravity. One of these low specific gravity compounds, squalene, is still extracted commercially from shark livers and used as a base in the cosmetics industry.

Many of the deep-sea sharks either have a very low body density or are neutrally buoyant; food is scarce in the deep sea and these species probably need to be more active than their shallow-water benthic counterparts. Because the density of liver oil varies little with water depth, these sharks can rise quickly toward the surface after prey more easily than can bony fish, which have gas bladders for buoyancy.

The two largest sharks, the whale shark (*Rhincodon typus*) and basking shark (*Cetorhinus maximus*), feed on plankton by cruising at three to five kilometres per hour (75 to 100 centimetres per second), filtering water through their gill slits. The basking shark has a large liver containing squalene and is close to neutral buoyancy; it can thus travel slowly, using its small pectoral fins to provide lift. The whale shark has not been closely studied, but it, too, is probably also close to neutral buoyancy.

The basking shark and, to a lesser extent, the whale shark are similar in body form to the mackerel sharks and though slow are powerful swimmers, as fishermen who hunt them for their liver oil can attest.

▲ The giant basking shark (*Cetorhinus maximus*) is a filter feeder like the whale and megamouth sharks and obtains plankton simply by swimming along with its mouth open. Its gill slits are so large that they almost encircle the head. Basking sharks are hunted commercially for their large, oil-rich livers and their flesh is used for fishmeal.

muscle for continuous cruising. This is illustrated by the smallspotted catshark (*Scyliorhinus canicula*), which has a density of 4.7 per cent and around 8 per cent red muscle. Since drag is not a major consideration, these sharks tend to have larger fins that give them greater manoeuvrability on the bottom. Many species do, however, need to be able to accelerate rapidly to catch their prey, which they do with the help of larger, more posteriorly placed median fins, such as those of the

PARTS OF A SHARK

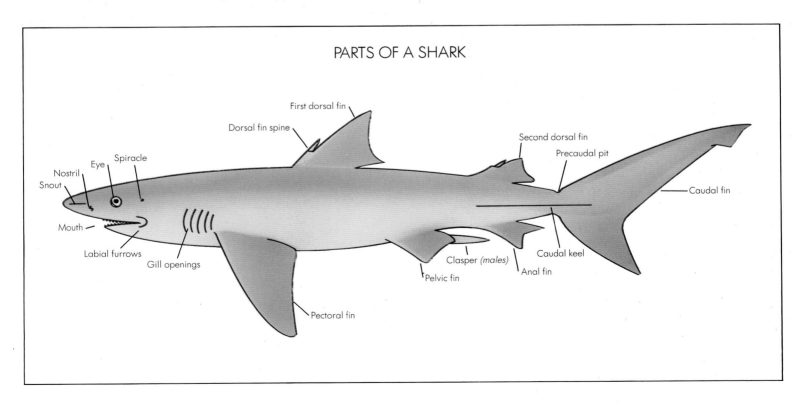

First dorsal fin

Dorsal fin spine

Second dorsal fin

Precaudal pit

Nostril

Eye

Spiracle

Snout

Caudal fin

Mouth

Labial furrows

Gill openings

Clasper (*males*)

Caudal keel

Anal fin

Pelvic fin

Pectoral fin

AI Giddings/Ocean Images

◀ ▼ Even more bizarre than the thresher sharks, hammerheads (family Sphyrnidae) have evolved winglike structures that are thought to aid their manoeuvrability. The location of the eyes at the end of the 'wings' gives them superior binocular vision and the wings contain greatly developed olfactory (smell) and electroreceptive organs.

In contrast, the third planktivorous shark, the recently discovered megamouth (*Megachasma pelagios*), appears to be a weak swimmer with its soft, flabby body and fins. It is a deep-swimming shark; its density is reduced by extremely poor calcification, soft, loose skin and flabby, loose connective tissue and muscles. This reduction of body tissues and weak swimming ability are probably responses to a nutrient-poor environment.

Some extremes of body form are shown by the hammerheads (*Sphyrna* spp.), threshers (*Alopias* spp.), angelsharks (*Squatina* spp.) and the frilled shark. One function of the bizarre head of hammerheads is to act as a 'wing', providing extra lift at the front of the shark that enables it to bank quickly and make rapid vertical movements. The dorso-ventrally flattened head induces minimal drag during turning.

The scalloped (*Sphyrna lewini*) and smooth hammerhead (*S. zygaena*) feed extensively on squid, which are jet-propelled and extremely manoeuvrable. The 'hammer' enables these sharks to catch their fast and agile prey, but it has been taken beyond mere hydrodynamic considerations in the winghead shark (*Eusphyra blochii*), whose head width is 40 to 50 per cent of its body length.

The thresher sharks, which have an upper tail lobe up to 50 per cent of their body length, are especially interesting. Apart from their tails, their streamlined bodies are much like those of the mackerel sharks; they also have the same elevated body temperature and the associated internal red muscle and heat-exchange system – features unique to threshers and mackerel sharks. They are powerful swimmers – as demonstrated by their ability to jump clear of the water. The thresher's tail seems totally out of place in a powerful swimmer, yet does not seem to be a hindrance.

The angelsharks have become dorso-ventrally flattened like the rays, and are an extreme case

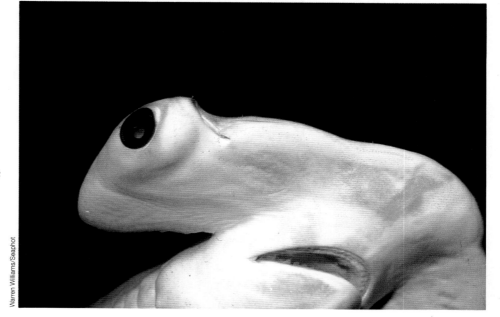

Warren Williams/Seaphot

among the sharks of specialisation for a bottom-living existence. Buoyancy is not important; they are, along with some of the rays, among the most dense of elasmobranchs. The angelshark has a density of 5.5 per cent; its liver contributes little buoyancy and its muscle and skeleton are relatively dense. The swimming mechanism of the angelshark has not been investigated, but it presumably moves by creating vertical waves along the flattened pectoral fins, as rays do.

The frilled shark is an example of extreme elongation. Its deep-sea habits are poorly known, but its long, eel-like body may be an adaptation to life on a rocky sea bottom, where this species may hunt for prey hidden in crevices. The frilled shark's jaws can be protruded so it can feed on large prey, rather as a snake does; the long body provides less resistance in the water should the shark be dragged along by its prey.

Edward S. Hodgson

▶ Sophisticated adaptations for different lifestyles; a lemon shark (*Negaprion brevirostris*), a common predator in tropical America, swims over a partially concealed stingray (*Dasyatis* sp.). The lemon shark is large, fast swimming and active, hunting fish, shellfish, seabirds and small rays, while the stingray eats molluscs and crustaceans.

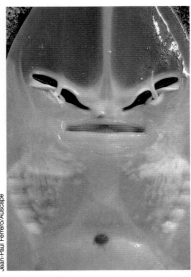

▲ One of the many myths concerning sharks and their relatives is that they must 'swim or die', since they lack swim bladders and rely on movement to force water through their gills. The myth is exploded by the success of bottom-dwelling sharks and rays, like this guitarfish, which spends most of its time partially buried in sand on the sea floor and has its nostrils and gills on its ventral surface.

SHARKS AND THEIR RELATIVES

LEONARD J.V. COMPAGNO

Sharks belong to a major group – the class Chondrichthyes. The other members of this group are their close relatives – the rays, or batoids – and more distant relatives – the chimaeras and elephantfishes (Holocephali). All have mouths and nostrils on the underside of the head, ampullae of Lorenzini in the head, teeth in conspicuous rows or in fused tooth plates, scales in the form of dermal denticles, paired and unpaired fins that are supported only by cartilaginous radials and ceratotrichia (horny, cartilaginous rods). They all have simplified cartilaginous skeletons without bone. The males have claspers and the females are fertilised internally and produce large eggs.

The approximately 470 species of batoids or rays are flattened shark derivatives that are most closely related to the sawsharks (Pristiophoridae). They include the sawfishes, guitarfishes, skates, torpedo rays, stingrays, butterfly rays, eagle rays, cownosed rays and mantas. They differ from sharks in having their pectoral fins expanded forward and fused to the sides of their heads over the gill openings, so that their gill openings are on the undersides of their heads. They have short, flat bodies and long tails. Some species have long, shark-like caudal and dorsal fins; other species lack them altogether. The pectoral fins, which are greatly enlarged in more specialised rays, supplement or replace the caudal fin as a means of propulsion.

The chimaeras, or ratfishes, are compressed cartilaginous fishes with only four gill openings that are covered with a soft gill cover or operculum without bony plates. These small, harmless, often silvery fishes differ from sharks in a number of ways: their upper jaws are fused to the braincase; the jaws are not supported by the hyoid arch; they have largely naked skins without denticles; and their rodent-like teeth consist simply of three pairs of ever-growing tooth plates. They have simplified guts and their stomachs merge with their valvular intestines. As well as pelvic claspers a male chimaera has an unpaired frontal clasper on the forehead and paired prepelvic claspers in front of the pelvic fins. All of the claspers have specialised dermal denticles to help the male hold the female during copulation.

Lynn Cropp/Auscape

Jean-Paul Ferrero/Auscape

▲ The manta or devilfish is the most spectacular member of the order Batoidea, which includes the rays, skates, guitarfishes and electric rays. Unlike most batoids, however, it is pelagic (an open-ocean dweller) and a filter feeder on plankton and small fish. Mantas grow to nearly seven metres wide and can weigh almost 1400 kilograms.

◄ The common Australian stingray or stingaree (*Urolophus mucosus*), first collected by Joseph Banks in 1770, is often found in water less than ten centimetres deep in bays and estuaries. Its caudal spine can inflict painful wounds and fishermen or others walking in shallow water are advised to shuffle their feet to avoid being 'stung'.

RESPIRATION AND CIRCULATION

Swimming at cruising speeds, like other aerobic activities, depends on the efficiency with which the respiratory and vascular systems supply oxygen. Oxygen is extracted from the water by the gills, from where it is transferred to the blood. The circulatory system then delivers oxygenated blood to the tissues and organs.

Shark gills consist of a series of cartilaginous arches from which extend two alternating rows of

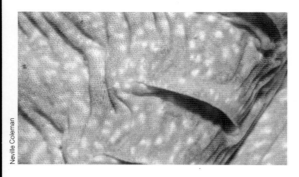

elongated gill filaments. Thin, plate-like secondary lamellae extend at right angles to the filaments. Blood flows across these lamellae in the opposite direction to the flow of water in a countercurrent flow that makes the uptake of oxygen and dumping of carbon dioxide more efficient.

The gills open to the outside through slits – usually five, sometimes six or seven. It is not known why some species have a greater number of gill slits, but these are generally more primitive sharks. Water enters mainly through the mouth, passes over the gills and exits through the gill slits. Some species pump water over the gills by rhythmically contracting muscles that open and close the valves at the entrance and exit of the system: these species are mainly sluggish bottom-living forms such as the catsharks and wobbegongs. Other species employ ram-jet ventilation, which uses the forward motion of the shark to move water backwards over the gills.

The highly active mackerel sharks, for example, rely entirely on ram-jet ventilation and must keep swimming to breathe. Between these extremes species such as the grey nurse (*Eugomphodus taurus*) and the piked dogfish are able to switch from respiratory pumping when at rest to ram-jet ventilation at cruising speeds, thereby saving energy.

In the bony fishes, the gills of the highly active species (such as tuna) that employ ram-jet ventilation are greatly strengthened and fused. However, the majority of both highly active and less active sharks have considerably strengthened gills suited to the cruising or intermittent cruising lifestyles typical of most species. Ancestral sharks may have had similarly strengthened gills; such a pre-adaptation to a swift oceanic lifestyle could have expedited the evolution of the highly active mackerel sharks.

◄ Active pelagic or open-ocean sharks often employ ram-jet respiration, relying on forward movement to force water through their gills. Relatively sluggish benthic sharks, on the other hand, have more muscular gills that must be able to supply oxygen while the animal is resting on the bottom.

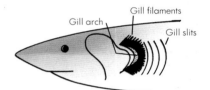

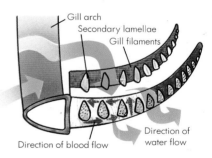

▲ The structure of a shark's gills, showing the countercurrent flow of water and blood. *(After Hughes and Morgan 1973)*

◄ The sand tiger or grey nurse spends much of its time cruising slowly at a variety of depths. There are many cases of sand tigers providing themselves with a simple and effective form of neutral buoyancy by gulping air at the surface and then adjusting their position in the water column by emitting bubbles from the cloaca.

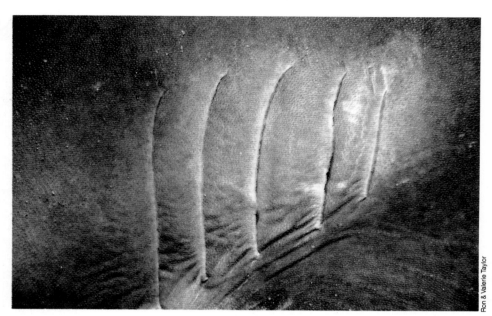

▲ The Port Jackson shark *(Heterodontus portusjacksoni)* has been observed pumping water into its gills through the first gill slit and out through the others, enabling the shark to chew its food — mainly molluscs and sea urchins — without having to take water in through the mouth and risking food being lost through the gill slits.

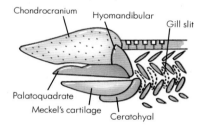

Chondrocranium   Hyomandibular
                                    Gill slit
Palatoquadrate
Meckel's cartilage   Ceratohyal

▲ Jaw suspension in an ancestral shark. The upper jaw (palatoquadrate) is bound tightly to the braincase or chondrocranium. The modified second gill arch (hyomandibular and ceratohyol) braces the jaws from behind. *(After Moss 1984).*

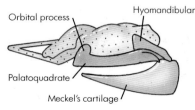

Orbital process   Hyomandibular
Palatoquadrate
    Meckel's cartilage

▲ Jaw suspension in a modern whaler shark. The upper jaw is only loosely attached to the braincase by ligaments from the orbital process. *(After Moss 1972)*

Not surprisingly, mackerel sharks have larger gill areas than other species; however, the gill area of the fairly active blue shark is similar to those of relatively sluggish or bottom-living species. Ram-jet ventilation may allow the gill area to be smaller than if the species relies solely on pump ventilation.

The oxygen-carrying capacity of blood is a function of the number of red blood cells and the amount of hemoglobin in these cells. Typical whaler sharks have a hematocrit (percentage of red cells to total blood volume) of 20 to 25 per cent and a hemoglobin content of around six grams per hundred millilitres. These values are much the same in hammerheads, but are lower in deep-water or benthic species. In contrast, mackerel sharks have much higher hematocrits (33 to 39 per cent) and hemoglobin contents (fourteen grams per hundred millilitres) that are close to those found in mammals, birds and warm-bodied tuna. High hemoglobin levels in both mackerel sharks and tuna are probably needed to maintain elevated body temperatures.

More active species of mammals have larger hearts than less active ones. However, the hearts of most sharks weigh much the same in proportion to their body weight, irrespective of their habits. For example, the hearts of both the relatively active whaler sharks and the sluggish, bottom-living smallspotted catshark are 0.1 per cent of body weight. Only the mackerel sharks have relatively large hearts, ranging from around about 0.2 per cent of body weight in the mako and white shark to 0.3 and 0.4 per cent in the porbeagle and salmon shark *(Lamna ditropis)*. The heavier heart of the mackerel sharks is associated with their elevated body temperature: the extra weight comes from the unusually thick, muscular ventricle, which has a relatively much smaller volume than in other pelagic species. This combination enables the higher ventricular pressures typical of endotherms

(animals whose body temperatures are usually above that of their environment.)

THE JAWS

Energy for activities such as swimming must ultimately come from food, and sharks owe much of their success to the efficiency and diversity of their feeding mechanisms.

The jaws of ancestral sharks seem to have been derived from a modification of the first gill arch. In the most primitive of known sharks, the cladodonts, the mouth was terminal (at the front of the head) rather then ventral (underslung) and the long jaws consisted of a single upper and lower jaw cartilage. The upper jaw was bound tightly to the cranium by ligaments, which allowed little independent movement, and was braced from behind (like the lower jaw) by the cartilages of the second gill arch. Cladodont sharks were probably active pelagic predators, but their long jaws and pointed teeth were an adaptation to seizing and tearing prey rather than to cutting or sawing as in modern forms. Among living species the jaw of the frilled shark still fairly closely resembles the primitive jaw.

In the hybodont sharks that succeeded the cladodonts the jaw shortened (allowing the bite to be more powerful) and the teeth became modified for both cutting and crushing, which enabled hybodonts to exploit such prey as molluscs and other invertebrates. Similar species still exist today in the Port Jackson sharks (Heterodontiformes).

The most important development in jaw design was the freeing of the upper jaw from the cranium. This made the upper jaw more mobile and enabled the shark to protrude its jaws. The ventral position of the jaws of modern sharks resulted from further shortening of the jaws together with expansion of the snout, which was then able to take on a sensory function. The flattened ventral surface of the head was also able to function as a planing surface, providing additional lift in swimming.

The success of this design is best seen in a whaler shark feeding on prey too large to be eaten in one or two bites. As the shark approaches, it tilts its head back and the lower jaw makes contact first with the prey. The teeth of the lower jaw are often prong-like, so they can gain an initial purchase. The upper jaw then moves forward and down; the upper teeth are sunk into the prey and the head is moved in a sawing motion that scoops a chunk out of the prey. The biting force of a two to three metre whaler shark has been measured at three tonnes per square centimetre. Such a powerful bite imposes considerable forces on the body, and to counteract this, the dorsal and ventral processes have been expanded to protect the spine and to improve its stability. This improved shock-absorber system also makes the body muscles more effective during swimming.

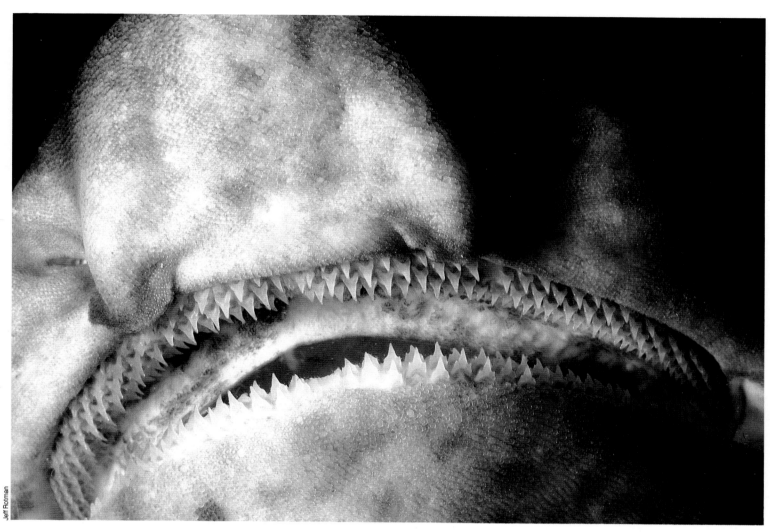

Jeff Rotman

TEETH AND DIET

One unusual and highly successful feature of sharks is their teeth, which are continuously replaced through life. The teeth are not attached directly to the jaw cartilage but instead are embedded in a membrane called a tooth bed. Teeth are formed in a groove on the inside of the jaw cartilage and move progressively forward on the tooth bed; eventually they erupt through the soft tissue overlying the replacement teeth to fold into place in the functional row. Measurement of replacement rates in whaler sharks shows that each tooth is replaced every eight to fifteen days during the first year of life. Because the bite is so powerful, teeth become blunt and are often broken. Replacement overcomes this problem and also allows the teeth to grow along with the shark.

The popular belief that sharks are scavengers, eating anything and everything, is far from the truth. Most species are very selective about what they eat. Pelagic whaler sharks, for example, feed mainly on small fish and squid, Port Jackson sharks (*Heterodontus* spp.) largely on echinoderms (especially sea urchins) and shellfish and gummy sharks (*Mustelus* spp.) on crustaceans. The sicklefin weasel shark (*Hemigaleus microstoma*) is a very specialised feeder: of stomachs examined from Australian specimens, 99 per cent contained cephalopods, mostly octopus.

Not all sharks are so specialised in their diet, and many will take other food if their usual prey is scarce. The diet of some species changes as they grow. Shortfin mako sharks weighing less than around 150 kilograms feed mainly on small fish and cephalopods, for which they are equipped with long, pointed teeth. Larger specimens have broader, more blade-like teeth, which they use for cutting up large prey such as swordfish, marlin and dolphins or porpoises. Small great white sharks have quite pointed teeth like a small mako and feed mainly on fish, while larger individuals have triangular cutting teeth for dealing with their prey – mainly marine mammals such as seals, sea lions and dolphins. The tiger shark (*Galeocerdo cuvier*) is one of the more omnivorous species, which is partly why it can be dangerous to humans. Juveniles have a liking for sea snakes and adults for seabirds and turtles, which they are able to cut up with their massive jaws and cockscomb-shaped teeth.

From the ancestral feeding mode of seizing and swallowing, sharks have developed an

▲ The metre-long swellshark (*Cephaloscyllium ventriosum*) – a sluggish, nocturnal bottom-dwelling species – has a huge mouth but relatively small, pointed teeth that apparently help it capture its prey of crustaceans and dead or living (but sleeping) fish. Broken teeth are replaced throughout the animal's life.

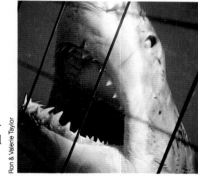

Ron & Valerie Taylor

▲ The great white shark is a superbly evolved predator, capable of converting almost anything it encounters into food. Its teeth are triangular and minutely serrated, enabling it to handle relatively tough mammals, such as seals, as well as fish. Its eyes roll back during a feeding lunge to provide extra protection.

► The bizarre cookiecutter shark (*Isistius brasiliensis*) feeds on squid or attaches itself to whale sharks, basking and megamouth sharks, tuna and marlin or whales and dolphins, using its suction cuplike lips and muscular pharynx for a tight grip

David Doublet

bizarre feeding modes. The cookiecutter uses its sucking lips to attach itself to the bodies of large fish such as marlin or sharks or whales. It then 'bores' out a plug of flesh with its teeth: this shark has even optimistically attacked the rubber-coated sonar domes of nuclear submarines. The cookiecutter is luminescent, perhaps to attract smaller prey or would-be predators, which it then attacks. A second species, the largetooth cookiecutter (*I. plutodus*), which grows to around 40 centimetres, has proportionately larger teeth than any other species (around twice the tooth height to body length ratio of the great white shark).

The bottom-living nurse shark utilises suction feeding to extract prey from holes and crevices: its thick lips create a seal and by rapidly expanding its muscular pharyngeal cavity, the shark produces a suction pressure of up to 1 kilogram per square centimetre, equivalent to one atmosphere of pressure at sea level.

One of the most spectacular specialisations is the planktonic filter-feeding seen in the basking, whale and megamouth sharks. These species have

enormous range of feeding mechanisms: the gouging of the whalers and the crushing of the gummy and Port Jackson sharks have already been mentioned. Some of the dogfish sharks, such as the piked dogfish, have blade-like teeth that overlap to form a continuous cutting edge ideal for slicing fish and squid into pieces small enough to swallow.

A small deepwater dogfish, the cookiecutter shark (*Isistius brasiliensis*) has one of the most

MUNCHING THEIR WAY THROUGH THE NIGHT

MARTY SNYDERMAN

Market squid (*Opalescens loligo*) play an important role in many oceanic food chains. These squid are heavily preyed on by pilot whales, sea lions and many other species that live in the open sea. Market squid, sometimes called common squid, are normally found far from shore in the open ocean off the coast of western North America, but when they mate the squid come into shallow water. A favourite mating site is the west end of Catalina Island, about 42 kilometres from the city of Los Angeles. Market squid live only a year or so, and have a very strong drive to mate before they perish. During heavy spawning, on moonless winter nights, the squid are literally present by the millions as they seek partners to perpetuate their species.

Because they are so preoccupied the squid are particularly vulnerable to predation when mating. After the mating ritual has been completed the females lay their eggs on the sandy bottom, and then both the males and females quickly deteriorate and die. In some places the bottom is several metres thick with dead and dying squid. It doesn't take long for a host of predators and scavengers to appear in order to feed on the live and dead squid and the eggs. Each squid egg-casing contains approximately 200 eggs and it is estimated that on average only one of the potential hatchlings will survive to complete the lifecycle and mate as an adult. Odds are that the remaining 199 will be devoured by a variety of sea creatures.

Blue sharks prey heavily on mating squid, especially at night when the concentrations of squid are at their highest. During those times the blue sharks simply swim, mouths agape, through the squid. The sharks continue to eat until their stomachs are

Marty Snyderman

totally distended, they have squid hanging out of their mouths and they simply cannot cram any more into their systems. At that point the sharks begin to vomit and create more room so they can once again begin to feed on the squid.

While that type of behaviour might seem obnoxious to you and me, we must remember that in the wilderness meals are never guaranteed. Blue sharks eat only when they can procure a meal and once the chance presents itself, they – like many predators – do all they can to take full advantage of the opportunity. That means the sharks take in as much nutrition as possible. In the final analysis, this voracious consumption plays a vital part in enabling these predators to survive from one meal to the next.

greatly reduced teeth; their gill rakers, situated on the inner sides of the gill arch, are modified into a straining apparatus and the mouth has moved forward to a nearly terminal position. Basking sharks cruise near the surface at around two knots with their mouths open wide; using this feeding method, large individuals filter more than a thousand tonnes of water an hour. The gill rakers, like the teeth, are shed periodically, which may explain why basking sharks apparently disappear in winter from the temperate waters in which they live. Possibly the rakers are lost during winter when there is not enough plankton in the water to sustain the shark's energy requirements, so during this time they hibernate on the bottom.

The whale shark supplements its diet of plankton with small fish. It has been seen rising vertically through a school of fish until its head is sufficiently clear of the water to drain its mouth, then sinking back with its mouth agape, allowing water and fish to pour in.

Some sharks use more than their mouths to catch food. Thresher sharks use their enormously elongated tails to stun fish; the vertebrae in the tip of the tail have expanded dorsal and ventral processes that make it an effective club. Sawsharks (Pristiophoridae) apparently use their toothed saw in a slashing action to cut and disable prey.

DIGESTION

Whatever the feeding method, prey passes to the stomach where it is acted on by the digestive juices. The products of digestion are absorbed in the intestine, which in sharks is called the spiral valve because its internal surface resembles a spiral staircase. This spiral arrangement provides maximum absorptive area in a small space, allowing more room for a large stomach and liver and, in females, for the development of live young.

Examination of the stomach contents of sharks shows that few have full stomachs. A study of shortfin mako sharks revealed that their average stomach capacity was 10 per cent of the body weight, while the amount of food in their stomachs averaged only 2.6 per cent of body weight. A mako weighing 63 kilograms would need to eat two kilograms of food a day; eleven and a half times its body weight a year. Young lemon sharks (*Negaprion brevirostris*) are reported to have a maintenance requirement – the amount of food needed just to maintain body weight, allowing none for growth – of 20 600 calories or 16.5 grams of food a day. For a 1 kilogram shark, this is equivalent to 1.7 per cent of its body weight per day.

Sharks in captivity consume between 3 and 14 per cent of their body weight a week, or 0.4 to 2 per cent a day. Sharks in captivity may stop feeding for several months, during which time they presumably live off reserves in the liver. Great white sharks are able to ingest large amounts of food at a time, and it has been calculated from

Ron & Valerie Taylor

◀ Active predators such as the grey reef shark (*Carcharhinus amblyrhynchos*) use the more pointed teeth in their lower jaws to grab and hold prey. The teeth of the upper jaw, which is tilted back during the first strike at food, then hold the prey and help to draw it into the mouth, while the lower jaw moves forward to gain further purchase.

Herwarth Voigtmann/Seaphot

▲ In the same way that antelope, for example, ignore lions when they are not hunting, reef fish pay little discernible attention to sharks that are simply patrolling. Many reef sharks will investigate anything novel – such as a diver – in their environment and their increased alertness will cause potential prey to move to a safe distance.

stomachs containing whale blubber that one meal could sustain the shark for up to two months. However, most sharks appear to eat at one or two day intervals, with an average meal weighing 3 to 5 per cent of their body weight.

Studies on lemon, sandbar (*C. plumbeus*) and blue sharks have shown that initial digestion of the meal is fairly rapid, taking around 24 hours, but that it takes three to four days for the meal to be completely voided. It may take longer when the water is colder: piked dogfish, for example, take five days to completely digest a meal of herring when the temperature is 10°C.

Mackerel sharks, in addition to having elevated muscle temperatures, also have a heat exchanger system in the blood vessels supplying the viscera. The warm gut of these highly active sharks presumably enables them to digest food more rapidly.

► The tope or school shark (*Galeorhinus galeus*), one of the most commercially important species of sharks, is widely distributed in cold and temperate waters in both hemispheres. It is ovoviviparous, giving birth to live young that hatch inside the uterus from eggs that are supplied by a yolk sac, and produces six to 52 young per litter.

Weldon Trannies

GROWTH RATE

In a unique bioenergetic study of young lemon sharks it was found that new tissue is produced slowly compared with predatory bony fish, and this was reflected in a slow rate of growth.

Lower growth rates in sharks may be a consequence of their slower digestion times and feeding rates. Newborn lemon sharks of 1.2 kilograms weigh 2.6 kilograms after a year; to achieve this weight gain they must eat six times their birth weight during this period. Fish grow fastest during the first few years, then slow as they age. Lemon sharks grow about 15 centimetres a year initially, but do not mature until around 240 centimetres, which means they may take fifteen years to reach maturity. However, lemon sharks kept in captivity and fed to satiation under ideal conditions can grow at ten times their natural growth rate.

Age and growth rates of sharks show considerable variation between species and sometimes even between different populations of the same species. The majority of sharks seem to have a maximum life span of 20 to 30 years: the Atlantic sharpnose shark (*Rhizoprionodon terraenovae*) and the starspotted smooth-hound (*Mustelus manazo*), both fairly small sharks that grow to just over a metre, have relatively short life spans of around ten to fifteen years respectively. The piked dogfish currently holds the longevity record, with a maximum age of at least 70, and possibly closer to 100 for north Pacific specimens. The Australian school shark (*Galeorhinus galeus*) is also a long-lived species: the recapture of a tagged individual after 33 years indicates that this shark could live to around fifty.

Nor surprisingly, the longest-lived species grow the most slowly. The piked dogfish grows at around four centimetres a year to sexual maturity which, in females, may not be reached for 20 years. While the Atlantic sharpnose shark and starspotted smoothhound can reach maturity in two or three years, most sharks do not mature until they are six or seven years old. The fastest absolute growth rates are found in some of the large pelagic sharks such as the blue, mako and white, which grow about 30 centimetres a year to maturity.

REPRODUCTION

Most bony fishes produce very large numbers of small eggs, which are spawned into the water where they are fertilised externally by sperm liberated from the males. This tends to be a very wasteful process, with high initial mortality among the unprotected eggs and larvae, and widely fluctuating survival rates due to variations in environmental conditions. Sharks have opted for an alternative reproductive strategy: the eggs are fertilised internally and more energy is invested in producing fewer, but better protected young, with a consequently higher survival rate.

Sharks' reproductive methods range from oviparous forms that lay large, well-protected eggs

▼ Requiem sharks, such as these blacktip reef sharks (*Carcharhinus melanopterus*), are viviparous, producing live young nourished in the uterus by a placenta analogous to that of mammals. Most requiem sharks have a long gestation period – up to a year – and produce relatively small numbers of young, from one or two to a dozen.

Bill Wood

to viviparous species that give birth to living young nourished via a placenta analagous to our own.

Male sharks have a pair of claspers, cylindrical intromittent organs formed from modified pelvic fins. In immature sharks the claspers are short and soft, while in a mature individual they are elongate and rigid from calcification. During copulation, one clasper is inserted into the female genital opening and in some species (such as the sandbar shark) the tip spreads out, anchoring the clasper and holding the oviduct open to facilitate sperm passage. During copulation the sperm flows from the genital pore into a groove that runs along the clasper. Associated with the claspers are two muscular sacs that run forward under the skin of the belly; prior to copulation these fill with seawater which, during copulation, is squirted out to flush the sperm from the clasper into the female oviduct. Sperm is produced from paired testes and stored either in the collecting ducts or in accessory sperm sacs. In some species, such as the blue shark, the sperm is enclosed in protective packets called spermatophores.

Mating in smaller, flexible species such as the small-spotted catshark is accomplished by the male coiling around the female's body. In larger, stiffer-bodied forms such as the whaler sharks, the male is orientated parallel and head to head with the female. Whatever method is used, the clasper is rotated toward the front before insertion.

In a number of species 'love bites' or mating scars can been seen on the females; tooth nicks, slashes and semicircular jaw impressions on the flanks, the back, pectoral fins and above the gill area. Biting by the male serves to stimulate the female to copulate and, in species such as the whitetip reef shark (*Triaenodon obesus*) to hold on to the female's pectoral fin during mating.

▲ Female sharks are often larger than males but males (*foreground*) are readily identified by their claspers, modified fins that are introduced into the female's cloaca, or genital opening, during mating to guide the sperm. Only one clasper is used at a time and is rotated to face forward before being inserted into the cloaca.

◄ The claspers of this Australian swellshark (*Cephaloscyllium laticeps*) are modified from the inner edges of the pelvic fins and in many species open out like a flower, exposing cartilaginous hooks that anchor the tip of the clasper in the female's cloaca. Siphon sacs in the male's body pump seawater to aid the flow of semen.

◄ Most female sharks display mating scars caused by males grasping a female's back, or her pectoral or dorsal fins, during courtship behaviour. Biting is thought to stimulate copulation and many males sharks and rays have longer teeth as an adaptation for courtship; females have evolved thicker, tougher skin to protect them during mating.

► The Tasmanian spotted catshark (*Parascyllium multimaculatum*) is a small (less than one metre long), little-known temperate water shark restricted to waters around Tasmania. Its small, flanged egg case is equipped with prehensile tendrils that wind around seaweed and sea-lily 'stems' or underwater cables to anchor the egg case.

Neville Coleman

▲ Bullhead sharks (family Heterodontidae) produce eggs in unique spiral-flanged cases. The Port Jackson shark lays ten to sixteen eggs each year from late July to early October, favouring traditional sites and sometimes actively pushing the leathery egg cases into rock crevices. The young take nine to twelve months to hatch and are sustained by a large yolk sac.

▼ Four stages in the development of the swellshark (*Cephaloscyllium ventriosum*).
1 Eggs are laid in greenish-amber cases known as 'mermaid's purses' and take seven to ten months to hatch.
2 The large yolk sac is gradually reduced as the developing embryo uses its contents; by the time the shark is ready to hatch, the yolk sac has completely or almost disappeared.
3 The hatchling has a double row of enlarged denticles along its back that apparently act as an 'anti-slip' ratchet to help it force its way out of the egg case.
4 Newly hatched sharks are active, can swim strongly and are ready to search for food.

Although the male's biting action is partially inhibited during mating, wounds can still be severe, and the female blue shark has developed a relatively thicker skin for protection.

Mating normally precedes ovulation by around a month and sperm are stored for this period in the shell gland of the female: in some species, such as the blue shark, sperm may be stored in a viable condition for a year or more. Eggs are produced in the female either in paired ovaries (for example, the piked dogfish) or in a single functional right ovary (in whalers and hammerheads). The eggs are around five millimetres in diameter at the resting stage, but increase to 30 to 40 millimetres at ovulation, when they rupture out of the ovary and are swept down the oviducts to the shell gland, where the sperm are stored and where fertilisation takes place. The shell gland also secretes an egg membrane that is a tough, horny egg case in oviparous forms, but is reduced to a cellophane-like membrane enclosing

the embryo in viviparous species.

No pregnant females of the largest living shark, the whale shark, have ever been recorded. Their method of reproduction is a mystery: a single egg case measuring 30 centimetres by 14 centimetres has been found but it was so unusually thin that it is not clear whether the whale shark is oviparous or whether this egg was in fact aborted and the species is viviparous.

In oviparous species (mainly the catsharks, carpetsharks and Port Jackson sharks) the eggs are laid on the sea bottom, where they complete their development nourished by their yolk supply. In some species the egg cases are rectangular, with tendrils at each corner to anchor them in weed. In most of the Port Jackson sharks, the egg cases have spiral flanges that wedge them into crevices in rocks.

Eggs are usually laid in pairs and, in the case of the smallspotted catshark, twenty to 25 are laid each year. Hatching is dependent on water temperature, and is usually over a period of several months.

Viviparous sharks can be divided into those species in which the embryos are nourished solely by yolk reserves, such as the piked dogfish, and those in which additional food reserves are obtained from the mother. In the piked dogfish, several fertilised eggs are jointly enclosed by the egg membrane in the uterus, forming a thin egg case or 'candle'. The 'candle' ruptures after six months and each embryo develops in the uterus, living off its attached yolk sac, which is completely resorbed just before birth. Ten or so 25-centimetre-long pups are produced after a gestation period of 22 months, which is the longest known pregnancy of any shark.

A form of viviparity in which the embryo receives maternal nutrients, but not through a placenta, is most common in the rays and probably also occurs in the tiger shark. In this group the eggs are encased in a thin membrane within which the embryos complete their development inside the

A. Kerstitch/Seaphot

1

A. Kerstitch/Seaphot

2

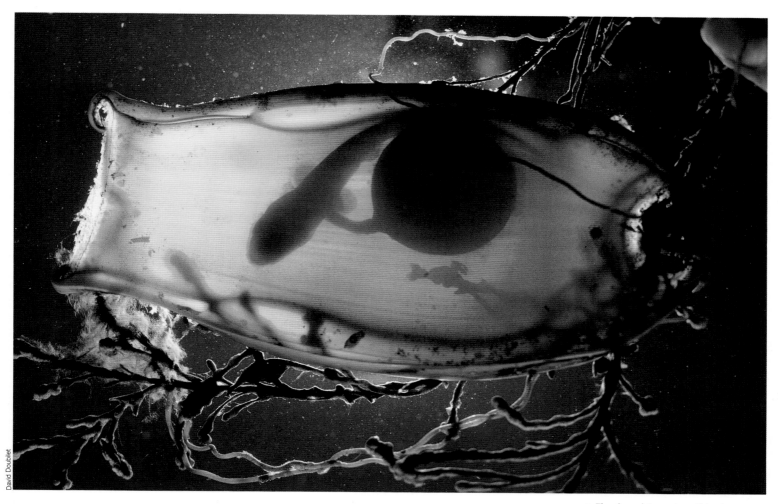

David Doubilet

uterus. Nutrients are apparently secreted by the uterus and absorbed by the embryo to supplement nutrients from the egg yolk itself. Tiger sharks produce between ten and eighty young, each 60 to 70 centimetres long.

In the whaler and hammerhead sharks the embryo initially takes up oxygen (and possibly additional nutrients) from the yolk sac and also through external gill tufts, which are later resorbed. During the third or fourth month of pregnancy the yolk sac is modified into a placenta that becomes attached to the uterus. Nutrients and oxygen are then passed from the mother across the placenta and through the umbilical stalk to the embryo; waste products go in the reverse direction.

In viviparous species the embryos are surrounded by the egg membrane and are contained within separate compartments in the uterus. Litter sizes vary from two in some species to more than a hundred in some blue sharks.

▲ The draughtboard swellshark (*Cephaloscyllium isabellum*) is common on rocky and sandy reefs off New Zealand, China and Japan. Its egg case is attached to the underwater forests of kelp and seaweed found in all these locations, providing the newborn sharks with ready access to their prey of crabs, worms, marine invertebrates and slow-moving fish.

A. Kerstitch/Seaphot

3

A. Kerstitch/Seaphot

4

Gestation periods are usually nine to twelve months.

Some species (such as the grey nurse, mako, porbeagle, threshers and probably the white and basking shark) practise a bizarre form of intra-uterine cannibalism known as oophagy. The ovaries of these sharks resemble those of bony fish, containing many thousands of very small eggs. The first group of embryos to hatch survive by feeding on the supply of successive batches of eggs, which the female continues to ovulate. During intermediate states of pregnancy, the embryos develop an enormously distended stomach full of yolk from these ingested eggs. Litter sizes are small, between two and sixteen.

Oophagy is taken one step further in the grey nurse, which produces only one large pup per uterus: in this shark, as well as feeding on the continual supply of eggs, one embryo from the initial batch of hatchlings in each uterus attacks and devours its siblings.

The great white and basking sharks pose an enigma, for while they are suspected of being oophagous no pregnant individuals have ever been reliably recorded. This is even more amazing in view of their large size, the curiosity which they arouse and the fact that there have been many commercial fisheries for basking sharks.

BREEDING CYCLES

Within their variety of reproductive methods sharks exhibit different breeding cycles. Some species reproduce throughout the year, while others have a distinctly seasonal cycle with mating, ovulation and birth occurring in certain months. In some species pregnant females have a batch of ova ripening in the ovary at the same time as embryos are developing. Soon after these 'pups' are born the female is ready to ovulate again, so a litter is produced each year. In other sharks only a

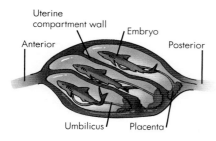

Uterine compartment wall · Embryo · Anterior · Posterior · Umbilicus · Placenta

▲ The uterus of a pregnant whaler shark showing uterine compartments, each containing an embryo, umbilicus and placenta. (After Baranes and Wendling 1981)

▼▶ Active and apparently more highly evolved sharks such as the lemon shark (*Negaprion brevirostris*) give birth to live young rather than laying eggs. Lemon shark litter sizes vary from four to seventeen, and newborn sharks remain close to where they were born for some time. In this series of photographs, a female lemon shark about 2.6 metres long was hooked off Bimini, in the Bahamas. The stress of capture may have caused her to give birth prematurely, though the baby sharks were well-developed, active (except for the last of the ten 'pups', which was stillborn) and about 60 centimetres long.

David Doubilet

David Doubilet

proportion of the mature females breed each year; the others enter a resting stage for a year or possibly longer. The sicklefin weasel shark is unusual in that mature females produce two litters each year after a gestation period of five to six months.

It appears that ancestral sharks had internal fertilisation and were oviparous, and that the trend has been toward the development of viviparity. Viviparity may be favoured because it allows production of larger, better-protected young, and because it does not impose habitat restrictions for egg laying, which is advantageous for wide-ranging pelagic species.

To protect the young from predation by other sharks of the same species and to avoid competition for food, most sharks show some form of sex and size segregation. Newborn young may be restricted to specific nursery areas separate from the adult population. In certain locations only mature males may be found, while in another area only mature females will occur.

Some sharks undertake extensive migrations, associated with their reproductive needs and feeding requirements. Tagging studies have demonstrated that blue sharks utilise currents to travel right around the north Atlantic, and even into the south Atlantic. Sharks tagged off southwest England have been recaptured off South America and New York, while specimens marked in the northeastern United States have been recovered off Europe. At the other extreme, tagging studies on Aldabra Atoll, in the Indian Ocean, have shown that blacktip reef sharks normally live in an area of only a few square kilometres.

The earliest sharks lived some 350 million years ago in the warm, shallow waters that covered most of what is now North America. Already large – some specimens were more than two metres long – they were streamlined and fast-swimming predators whose success is highlighted by the appearance of 'modern' sharks as much as 170 million years ago. Since then they have evolved to exploit a variety of marine (and even some freshwater) habitats, lifestyles and feeding methods that reflect the efficiency of their hydrodynamic design, reproductive biology and sophisticated sensory systems.

David Doubilet

David Doubilet

▲ ◄ As each of the pups was born, assisted from its mother's cloaca by a diver, it would rest briefly on the bottom of the shallow lagoon before swimming away and breaking the umbilical cord. Several small remoras that had accompanied the female shark, even after her capture, moved from their grip on her body and darted forward to consume each placenta as it was delivered.

THE SHARK'S SENSES

EDWARD S. HODGSON

Fascination and fear usually dominate human reactions to the behaviour of sharks. Both these reactions lead to questions about the senses of sharks. What 'triggers' a shark to feed or attack? How does a shark detect such a triggering stimulus? Can we, through understanding the sense organs involved, interfere with their functions and block shark behaviour that is hazardous to humans?

Early attempts to answer such questions concentrated upon the shark's sense of smell (olfaction). Nineteenth-century biologists plugged the nasal openings in the snouts of sharks and observed that the animals then failed to detect food. If only one nasal opening was blocked, the shark typically veered towards the normal unblocked side, swimming in circles. Dr George Parker of Harvard University, who did many of these experiments on 'circus movements', concluded that sharks tried to balance the amounts of chemical stimulation they detected on the two sides of the snout – a behaviour which would normally enable the swimming shark to home in on a source of odours, such as a bleeding fish. Sharks were viewed as 'swimming noses', with the other senses being of minor importance. More recent studies show that feeding and attack behaviours depend upon *several* important senses in sharks, including at least one that is absent or poorly understood in most other animals.

▼ Sharks were once thought to have poor eyesight, but research has demonstrated that many species can hunt by sight and, in fact, have excellent vision. In bottom-dwelling species, however, such as this Port Jackson shark, the eye is relatively small and vision is not as important as smell or electroreception for feeding or social behaviour.

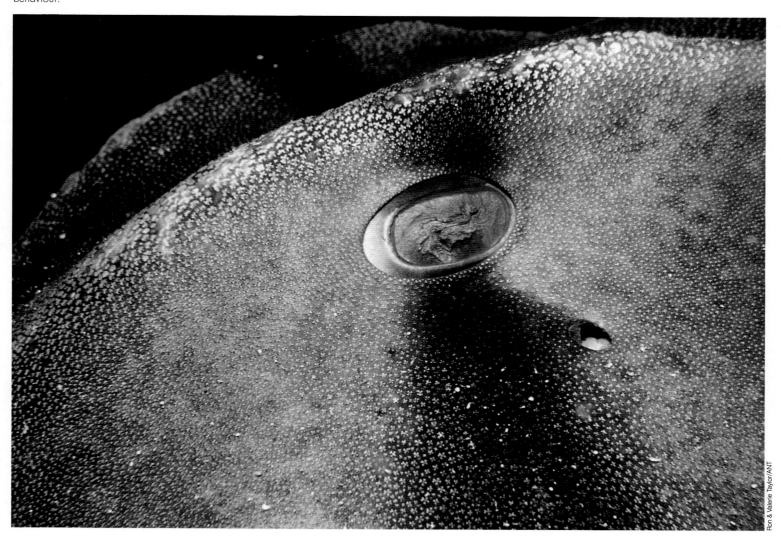

MECHANICAL AND ACOUSTIC SENSES

The senses of touch and hearing in sharks involve stimulation of specialised hairlike cells located in, or very near, the body surface. Most hair cells of sharks occur in pits, grooves or canals which make up the *lateral line*, extending along the shark's side and branching throughout the head. Mechanical strain on the largest hairlike projection from one of these sensory cells produces an electrical change within the cell. That electrical change stimulates an attached nerve fibre which passes the 'information' to the shark's central nervous system.

Since the information carried along nerves is in the form of brief electrical impulses, it has been possible to record that information by connecting amplifiers and oscilloscopes to the nerves. Such recordings made from lateral line nerves have shown that the hair cells detect the *direction* as well as the *amount* of movement in their fine projections (cilia). If the smaller cilia are bent towards the largest one, the hair cell is highly stimulated and many nerve impulses are sent to the brain. If the smaller cilia are bent away from the largest one, fewer nerve impulses go to the brain. It appears that the shark uses this characteristic of its hair cells to detect water currents, monitor its swimming direction or localise vibrations in the water.

The importance of the lateral line sensory system is indicated by the large number of nerve fibres running between it and the brain. Dr Barry Roberts, of the Plymouth Marine Laboratory in England, counted about 6000 sensory nerve fibres from the lateral line that fed into the brain of a dogfish shark (*Scyliorhinus*). Curiously, sharks also have nerves that carry impulses in the opposite direction, *towards* the hair cell sense organs. Impulses in these outgoing nerves inhibit the lateral line sense cells whenever the shark makes violent movements, as in escape or attack behaviour. Dr Roberts and his co-workers believe that this is a safety mechanism to prevent overloading and fatigue in the hair cell receptors. In

effect, the mechanical senses are kept in fully rested and responsive condition, ready to resume their usual jobs the instant that violent behaviour stops.

The ear of the shark is closely related to the lateral line system. Patches of hair cells lie within the inner ear, and are stimulated by vibrations having frequencies below a thousand cycles per second (1000 Hz). Field studies confirm that some sharks are attracted to sounds in the frequency range of 25 to 100 Hz, especially if the sounds are pulsed, like the low-frequency sounds made by struggling fish.

Traditional folk wisdom of Pacific Islanders recognises and exploits the shark's sensitivity to sound. Fishermen in the Society, Fiji, Tonga and Caroline islands, among others, commonly shake coconut shell rattles underwater to produce intermittent bursts of low-frequency sound that attracts sharks. There are also reports of Pacific Islanders *repelling* sharks with underwater sounds, but scientists have not yet been able to use sound to accomplish this consistently.

CHEMICAL SENSES (SMELL AND TASTE)

The sensitivity of sharks to chemicals is attested by many examples: the spearfisherman's loss of a freshly punctured catch to an attracted shark; the injured survivors of boating mishaps being circled or attacked by sharks; or the use of chum by fishermen and photographers to lure sharks within range of their hooks or lenses. Early experiments, mentioned above, ruled out visual

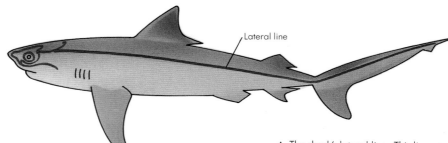

▲ The shark's lateral line. This line, which extends along the shark's side and branches throughout the head, marks the position of most of the specialised hair cell receptors which are central to the shark's sensory system. *(After Roberts 1978)*

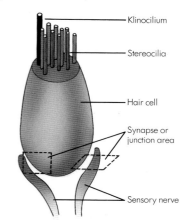

▲ Structure of a hair cell receptor from the lateral line. The klinocilium is the largest of the hair-like cell projections or stereocilia. Mechanical strain on the klinocilium produces an electrical change within the hair cell which is passed through the synapse to sensory nerve cells connecting with the shark's brain. *(After Roberts 1978)*

▼ One possible factor in shark attacks is that swimmers produce irregular, low-frequency vibrations — sounds — similar to those made by a struggling fish. Sharks' hearing is particularly sensitive to low-frequency vibrations, a fact exploited in New Ireland (*left*) and the Solomons (*below*) to attract them for capture by local fishermen.

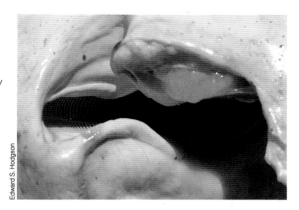

▶ Sharks can detect incredibly low concentrations of chemicals through the action of the nasal sacs — microscopically folded tissues arranged in rows — inside the nostrils, which are further equipped with a fleshy flap across the opening so that water flows in one side and out the other, providing a constant stream of water for testing.

▼ Bottom-dwelling species such as the Port Jackson shark hunt in darkness and often feed on animals that try to escape detection by burying themselves in sand. Their small eyes are of limited use and their nostrils have evolved into elaborately folded structures that expose the maximum surface area to water for detection of faint odours.

cues to the sharks in many of these cases. The olfactory sacs on the shark's snout are the location of greatest chemical sensitivity (smell), while gustatory (taste) receptors occur in the mouth and pharynx, enabling the shark to make a final discrimination of food before it is swallowed.

Modern investigations of the chemical senses of sharks generally use pure chemical stimuli, tested in precisely determined amounts under carefully controlled conditions. Since these test requirements are not easily achieved under field conditions, such work must be done

in laboratories. Electrical changes in olfactory organs, or in the brain, are recorded to detect responses of the shark's nervous system while chemicals are applied to the sense organs. As a follow-up, behaviour of unrestrained sharks may be studied in natural field conditions, using the same chemicals that were tested in the laboratory. Comparisons between observations in the laboratory and in the field have been particularly revealing. They show what kinds of chemicals have most powerful effects upon sense organs and upon behaviour, and how attractants and repellents differ in their effects upon the shark's sense organs.

The most extensive recent experiments of this kind were conducted at the Lerner Marine Laboratory in the Bahamas, as part of the United States Navy's research program on sharks. Wires were connected to smell organs or brains of lemon sharks (*Negaprion brevirostris*) and nurse sharks (*Ginglymostoma cirratum*) at the various positions marked in the diagram. While patterns of electrical activities at these sites were being monitored, chemicals mixed in sea water were allowed to flow through the olfactory sac. Chemicals that attract sharks produce characteristic changes in the olfactory organs and the front part of the shark's

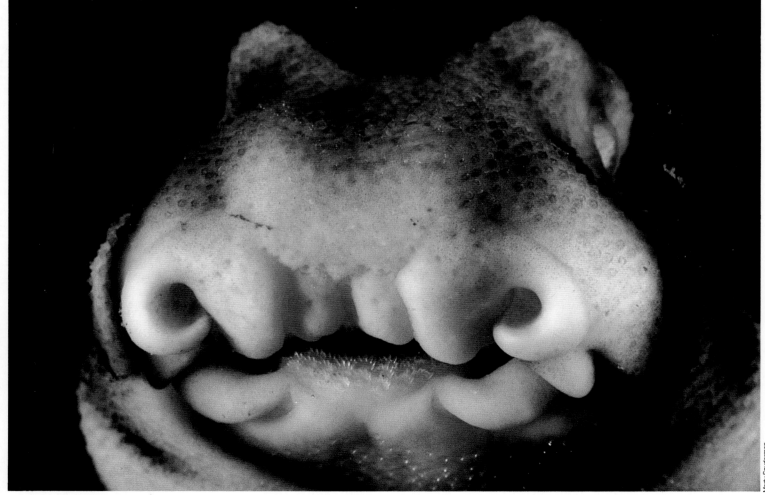

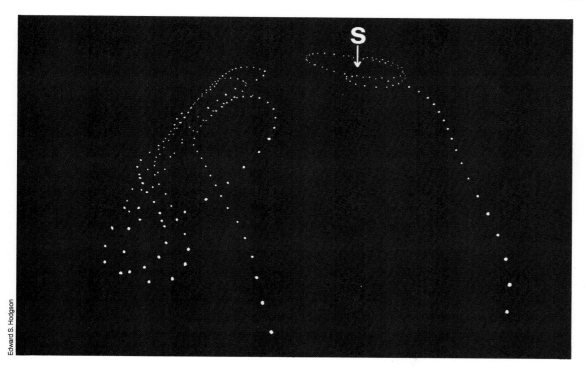

Edward S. Hodgson

◄ By photographing trails of blinker lights attached to sharks, scientists are able to monitor their responses to chemical stimuli. Here a lemon shark, originally swimming on the left side of the test enclosure, encounters an odour trail of glutamic acid (from S), swims directly to its source and circles it.

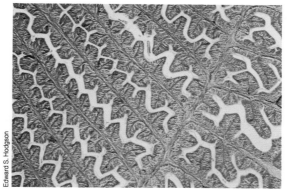

Edward S. Hodgson

◄ A microscopic view of a section of smell receptor tissue.

brain. Several components of meat (amino acids) and chemicals found in the skin or excretions of fish (betaine, trimethylamine), and components of blood (hemoglobin and serum albumen) produced changes in nerve activity, as well as eliciting approach and feeding reactions in free-swimming sharks. Unexpectedly, it was found that a more posterior part of the brain (medulla) also showed changes in nerve activity during stimulation; this proved to be a change in the nerve centres which control the contraction of gill muscles. When the shark first senses an attractive chemical stimulus, the gills give an extra 'beat', pumping extra water through the gill opening. Then, for several seconds while the shark lunges ahead, the gills are closed down against the body, apparently an advantage in providing maximum streamlining during the first few seconds of pursuit or attack.

Behaviour of free-swimming sharks was studied at Bimini by photographing the trails of blinker lights attached to sharks, or by using underwater television to monitor shark activities in the open ocean. Fortunately, there was good correlation between the types of chemicals (amino acids and amines) that produced the greatest changes in a shark's brain activity in the laboratory and those chemicals that triggered orientation and approach behaviour in the sea. The actual orientation mechanisms used by sharks to approach chemical stimuli, however, were found to differ. Nurse sharks (*Ginglymostoma*) home in on the stimulus by swimming criss-cross through the 'olfactory corridor' toward the greater concentration of chemical. Lemon sharks (*Negaprion*), and closely related species, react to chemical stimuli by swimming into the strongest

water current and using that current as their main 'guide' until they are near the chemical source. Under normal circumstances, either method works to bring the shark near its prey.

Some of the most stimulating chemical attractants, components of meat or blood, may affect a shark's brain activity and behaviour at concentrations as low as one-millionth part of a molar solution in sea water. To explain how such low thresholds could possibly stimulate olfactory receptors, some biologists have suggested that chemicals might become bound to the nasal sac lining and thereby reach higher accumulated amounts. However, when radioactive chemical stimuli were injected into the shark's nasal sac, and the densely packed receptor cells were examined for radioactive accumulation, nothing of the sort was found. Evidently the stimuli flow freely through the smell organs, exciting the smell receptors in no more than a few thousandths of a second, and then pass out of the nasal sac.

When stronger concentrations of effective chemical stimuli are encountered, sharks generally attempt to bite anything visible in their immediate

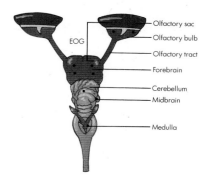

Olfactory sac
Olfactory bulb
Olfactory tract
Forebrain
Cerebellum
Midbrain
Medulla

EOG

▲ The brain of a lemon shark, showing the positions where electrical activities were recorded in the Lerner Marine Laboratory experiments on chemical stimulants.

Edward S. Hodgson

▲ Scientists at the Lerner Marine Laboratory, where much of the most important experimental work on sharks has been conducted, anesthetise a dusky shark (*Carcharhinus obscurus*) by pumping a diluted solution of anesthetic into the mouth so that it will flow into the gills and inhibit the shark's respiration.

▼ A group of lemon sharks (*Negaprion brevirostris*) engages in social circling in the shark testing pool at the Lerner Marine Laboratory. Intensive study of captive and free-ranging lemon sharks has shown that they are highly social and cover a range of around 300 square kilometres, perhaps guided by their inbuilt geomagnetic sense.

area. Such a case is shown in the photograph where a large lemon shark, after stimulation with an invisible amine and amino acid mixture, is making a frenzied attack upon air bubbles at the ocean surface. Plastic bottles containing mixtures of amino acids and amines which are allowed to diffuse slowly in the water may be attacked by sharks passing nearby on coral reefs. This is another confirmation of the relevance of laboratory findings to the understanding of shark behaviour in natural surroundings.

Attempts to find an 'ultimate' chemical repellent have now largely been abandoned. Instead attention has shifted to naturally occurring repellents. These are found in various animals which *appear* to have no defence against predators, but which are not attacked by other fish or sharks.

One of the earliest recognised natural repellents is holothurin, found in sea cucumbers (*Actinopyga agassizi*), relatives of the beche-de-mer used in some oriental soups. When a shark attempts to grasp a living sea cucumber – an event that happens rarely – the cucumber is quickly ejected from the mouth and is not disturbed again. Both the shark's smell and taste receptors are affected by the sea cucumber's protective

secretion. In the laboratory, nerve recordings show that holothurin disrupts, and later blocks, chemoreceptor responses. A dilution of one part in 600 000 of holothurin can kill a 20-kilogram shark in a tank, but in the open ocean any shark is likely to swim away before receiving such a toxic dose of the repellent.

A similar case involves the relatively immobile fish *Pardachirus marmoratus*, the 'Moses sole' from the Red Sea. A milky secretion, which is retained in the mucus covering of the fish's skin, deters sharks from biting this sole. The repellent is an acidic protein that reduces water surface tension and upsets the crucial stability of receptor cell membranes.

Still more effective natural repellents may be found in the large numbers of relatively slow-moving invertebrate animals in many marine environments such as coral reefs. If they deter attacks by sharks, and if the repellents can be chemically identified and synthesised in sufficient volume, some of these natural products may yet produce helpful shark repellents. Scientists today, remembering the lessons learned from Shark Chaser and similar products, proceed with caution in evaluating claims for potential repellents.

Edward S. Hodgson

EYES AND VISION

The eyes of sharks are basically similar to those found in many backboned animals, with a rigid eyeball enclosing a light-sensitive receptor area (retina). Shark retinas are populated largely by rod cells (functioning in dim light), but they also include cone cells (functioning in bright light). Dr Samuel Gruber of the University of Miami, who devised a behavioural test for colour vision in sharks, reported that at least one species appears to be capable of responding to colour cues. Many shark species have been shown capable of

◄ In a test of the olfactory sensitivity of free-ranging lemon sharks at Bimini Atoll in the Bahamas, a flask of trimethylamine oxide (a chemical excreted by fish) proved irresistible to this species, which demonstrated its hunting method by swimming into the strongest current of chemical and following the chemical 'bait' to its source.

Edward S. Hodgson

◄ Unlike lemon sharks, nurse sharks (*Ginglymostoma cirratum*) track down chemical stimuli by crisscrossing through the 'olfactory corridor' towards the source. A high concentration may even stimulate this normally placid species into a feeding frenzy like that often demonstrated by active and aggressive grey reef sharks.

▼ An invisible but, to the shark, potent mixture of amino acids and amines — components, respectively, of meat and fish skin or excretions — has stimulated this lemon shark into a frenzied attack on air bubbles at the ocean surface, confirming in field conditions results obtained in laboratory experiments.

distinguishing between different intensities of light and between different shapes of test patterns.

Although there have been few surprises from studies on the eyes of sharks, an interesting assortment of anatomical variations, related to the particular habitats or behaviour of various species, has been revealed. Eye size and position, for example, vary over a wide range. Relatively inactive sharks inhabiting shallow waters – such as hornsharks and carpetsharks – have eyes that usually measure less than 1 per cent of the body length, suggesting that they rely far less upon vision than other senses. More active, midwater predatory species have larger eyes. Extreme eye enlargement is found in the big-eyed thresher sharks which inhabit deep water. They have upwardly directed eyes that may be as large as one-fifth the size of the head. Extremely large eye size is typical of deep-dwelling fishes, and the upward aim of the thresher shark's eyes may provide it with a better view of prey that it is attacking with the elongated upper lobe of its tail.

The eyes of most sharks are rimmed with

Edward S. Hodgson

Ron & Valerie Taylor

▲ Active, fast-moving sharks that live in the open ocean make use of sight for hunting and have much larger eyes than bottom-dwelling species. Many, such as this pelagic blue shark (*Prionace glauca*) have eyes equipped with a tapetum – a layer of mirror-like cells on the retina that reflect light back to receptor cells.

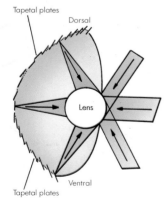

▲ Orientation of the tapetal plates behind the retina in a shark's eye. The tapetal plates function like mirrors. They are positioned so that light reflects back to the front of the eye, with some passing out through the lens to produce 'eyeshine' similar to that of cats. (*After Gruber 1978*)

immovable eyelids. However, some (particularly the carcharhinid sharks) have the lower lid folded into a nictitating membrane. This tough, movable membrane closes over the eye during feeding and protects it from damage. There is no need for eyelids to close and lubricate the eye or to reduce the amount of light that enters. Opening and contracting the pupil of the shark's eye regulate light admitted, especially in those species that are active during daytime.

Perhaps the most remarkable feature of the shark's eye is a series of reflecting plates (tapetum) just behind the retina. The tapetal plates function like mirrors, reflecting up to 90 per cent of certain colours of light back into the light receptor cells of the eye. This increases the sensitivity of the eye and produces 'eyeshine' similar to that seen in cats. Sharks that live in brightly lit shallow waters can darken the tapetum with movable pigments, much as a curtain might be pulled across a mirror. All these eye specialisations clearly refute the old assumption that vision plays only a minor part in the shark's sensitivity to its environment!

ELECTRICAL AND MAGNETIC SENSES
The most unusual senses used by sharks allow them to detect weak electrical voltages. Such

electrical cues may emanate from prey animals or be produced by currents flowing through the earth's magnetic field. Sharks may employ their 'electrical sense' in ordinary daily orientation, during long-distance migration and in locating nearby prey. Experiments that reveal these abilities and analyse the operation of the sense organs which make them possible are among the most exciting in the modern study of sense organs.

Since the 1930s, there have been reports that dogfish sharks (*Scyliorhinus*), as well as skates and other relatives of sharks, are very sensitive to metallic objects in the water. Drs Dijkgraaf and Kalmijn, working in the Netherlands, found that skates could detect voltage gradients as low as 0.01 microvolt per centimetre, the greatest electrical sensitivity known in the whole animal kingdom! They showed that the sense organs detecting these weak electric fields are the 'ampullae of Lorenzini', delicate jelly-filled canals connected to pores in the skin of the shark's or skate's snout.

In an ingenious extension of laboratory tests to events in the open sea, Kalmijn recently tested the responses of the dogfish shark (*Mustelus canis*) to underwater electrical stimuli off the coast of Massachusetts, USA. Two electrodes were fastened to an underwater cable and energised from an electric stimulator in a rubber raft that floated above the test area. A fish extract was allowed to flow out of a chumming tube, also fastened to the underwater cable. When the fish odour attracted sharks into the area, Kalmijn observed their behaviour through a glass-bottomed viewing box next to the raft. He describes typical dogfish behaviour as follows: 'After entering the test area, the dogfish began randomly searching the sand, evidently trying to locate the odour source . . . when nearing the underwater setup, the animals did not bite at the opening of the chumming tube, but turned sharply toward the current electrodes from distances up to 25 cm, viciously attacking the electrically stimulated prey.' On the basis of several hundred observations of shark attacks on the sources of electric current, Kalmijn concluded that odour stimuli attracted the sharks from a distance but at close range the electrical fields were much more compelling to the animals.

An intriguing possibility is that sharks may have an inbuilt electromagnetic compass sense that they can use for orientation. When swimming through the earth's magnetic field, a shark induces electric fields that depend upon the direction of the shark's movement. Experiments on the leopard shark (*Triakis semifasciata*) and also on stingrays, related to sharks, show that these animals change their swimming directions when the earth's normal magnetic field in their area is changed by energising a nearby induction coil. In fact, when the earth's magnetic field was approximately neutralised, the animals appeared to lose their sense of position and moved randomly! These observations open up questions of enormous importance for understanding shark behaviour. They also suggest that we have a long way to go in research before claiming even an approximate understanding of the shark's total sensory world.

INTEGRATION OF THE SENSES IN BEHAVIOUR

Human imagination is inevitably strained whenever attempting to comprehend the total sensory input that influences a shark's behaviour at any given moment. It is most unlikely that a shark ever relies upon one type of sense organ alone; the animal's brain presumably integrates the nerve impulses from thousands of receptor cells which, more or less simultaneously, signal detection of mechanical, chemical, visual and electric stimuli. Different sensory systems may temporarily dominate during the various stages of behavioural patterns, such as the feeding or attack patterns.

As a final illustration, consider a shark that orients toward a potential food source and eventually eats it. Underwater sounds (the struggles of an injured fish, or some similar low-frequency vibrations) can attract the shark from a great distance. Approaching the sound source, the shark may cross an odour corridor (from a wound, an

Neville Coleman

excretion, etc.). The smell may trigger a more precise orientation that will depend upon the shark species – some will home in by criss-crossing the odour trail; others will simply swim upstream against the odour-carrying current. Once close to the potential food, electrical potentials from the prey's heartbeat or muscle contractions may provide cues for a more precise aim. The shark may obtain further information visually, while circling the prey, or get tactile information by bumping the prey with the snout. The actual attack will be a superbly integrated affair with nictitating membranes closed over the eyes and gill movements giving an extra 'charge' of oxygen and then maximum streamlining even as the jaw begins to open and close.

No one pattern will fit all sharks, for the sense organs and sensory worlds of each species are somewhat different. In every case, however, we can be sure that both sense organs and the behaviour they influence are superbly adapted to the habitat and needs of the species – one of the chief reasons sharks have been successful for some 200 million years!

▲ The shark's sensitive electroreceptor system is based on delicate jelly-filled canals called the ampullae of Lorenzini, connected to pores on the surface of the skin. The electric organs of many skates and rays may have evolved to provide a burst of current that 'jams' a predatory shark's electroreceptors, confusing its close-range detection of prey.

▼ Electroreceptors (ampullae of Lorenzini) and lateral line canals in the head of a shark. The lateral line canals are marked by heavy lines; the openings of electroreceptors are indicated by solid dots. *(After Kalmijn 1978)*

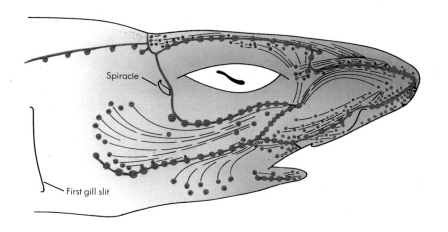

Spiracle

First gill slit

SHARK BEHAVIOUR

ARTHUR A. MYRBERG JR

▲ When a number of sharks (especially the highly social grey reef shark) feed together, the sheer volume of sensory input – from smell to sight, vibration and electrosense – builds to a crescendo that sometimes overwhelms normal inhibitions. 'Social facilitation' results – a 'feeding frenzy' that is the equivalent of violent mob behaviour in humans.

The remarkable senses of sharks are discussed in Chapter Five. However, their behaviour is inextricably linked with their efficient olfactory, chemical, electrical and visual senses – senses that influence every aspect of their lives and may be responsible for what seems to humans to be erratic or dangerous behaviour. The longstanding myth that sharks are mindless, destructive automatons has been well and truly exploded by studies that show them to be sophisticated and remarkably intelligent animals, capable of learning and possessing subtle social systems.

Shark lore has existed throughout history whenever sharks have directly influenced human endeavour. Tropic islanders, for example, have long been acquainted with the habits and movements of sharks and can predict when and where they can be found. Interest in sharks was minimal, however, in the great population centres of the world even through the first third of the twentieth century. Human–shark interactions were not only rarely and sporadically reported, but relatively little public news media existed to disseminate information rapidly to outlying regions. Science also had little interest in the ways of sharks; supposedly knowledgeable experts even questioned the impact of sharks upon any human interest.

Coastal fishermen were often highly interested in sharks, however, since they were familiar not only with the reduced catches due to such predators but also the reasonable prices paid for sharks in certain regions. That interest, in turn, generated sporadic investigations by fishery scientists from several countries between the early 1920s and mid-1960s, particularly in the United States, England and Australia.

Progress in understanding shark behaviour accelerated following the establishment of the Shark Research Panel by the American Institute of Biological Sciences in 1958. The panel, supported in large measure by the United States Navy's Office of Naval Research, was concerned with all aspects of the biology of elasmobranch fishes but emphasis was directed at the shark hazard problem. Although that problem had long been recognised in certain regions of the world prior to World War II, little concern existed elsewhere until that war brought about global use of the world's oceans. The problem continued despite the end to hostilities because of the ever-increasing importance of the oceans for recreational purposes.

A REMARKABLE SENSORY WORLD

Sharks use smell, taste, and the 'common chemical sense' provided by specialised cells in the lateral line to detect chemicals in their environment and, presumably, to aid them in social behaviour as well as hunting. The sense of smell can detect chemicals in extremely low concentrations and is especially acute in sharks. For example, two common species found along the coast of the southeastern United States, the Atlantic lemon shark (*Negaprion brevirostris*) and the nurse shark (*Ginglymostoma cirratum*) are sensitive to many chemical compounds at concentrations as low as approximately 1 part per million, particularly electrolytes and amino acids – the structural units of animal protein. These same sharks can also distinguish waters of differing salinity, an ability that

might assist them in locating different water masses during daily seasonal movements, in maintaining the segregation of the sexes shown by various species and in locating appropriate pupping areas. Another remarkable ability, chemically based recognition of the members of one's own species, has been shown by the catshark (*Scyliorhinus stellaris*), and male Pacific grey reef sharks (*Carcharhinus amblyrhynchos*) have been observed moving along apparent odour trails produced by females.

The visual systems of many sharks are, contrary to popular belief, highly developed. The abundance of low light photoreceptors found in the eyes of all species points to the importance of night time and twilight for these animals, but there is no question that sharks will feed during the day if given the opportunity. Brightly coloured objects seem to be especially attractive: survival gear painted yellow has been shown to attract ranging sharks, while the same gear painted black is ignored. In one experiment, however, silky sharks (*Carcharhinus falciformis*) avoided bait on a fluorescent orange globe but readily removed bait from a black globe.

Sharks are also well endowed for sensing mechanical disturbances. Not only do they have specialised stretch receptors in the deep layers of their skin and muscle masses, they also have well-developed inner ears (similar to those found in all vertebrates) as well as thousands of hair cells, called neuromasts, in specialised canals along the sides and on the head – the lateral lines. The inner ears and neuromasts are sensitive to underwater vibrations and probably play an important role in sensing water movements close to the body and aiding the co-ordination of swimming. A shark's inner ears are especially sensitive to vibrations from some distance away. Studies of a number of species show they can hear sounds as low as 10 Hertz (cycles per second) and as high as 800 Hertz: in other words from about 1.5 octaves below the frequency of the lowest key on a piano to that of G_5, just below high C. Since adult human hearing extends from about 25 Hertz to around 16 000 Hertz, humans hear many sounds sharks cannot: on the other hand, sharks can detect certain very low frequencies unheard by humans.

Many species of sharks will move rapidly to specific sources of vibration, explaining why nearby sharks often appear shortly after a speared or hooked fish begins struggling. Low frequency, irregularly pulsed, broad-band vibrations are also produced by the strumming of cables and set lines – and by humans when struggling in the water.

ELECTRORECEPTION

Electroreception is a profoundly important dimension of the sensory world of sharks, but one that we cannot easily identify with, since humans possess no comparable system. The significance of the electrical sensitivity of sharks first became evident when they were observed to 'home in' on bioelectrical fields measured at 0.005 microvolts per centimetre – the highest known electrical sensitivity in the animal kingdom! The ampullae of Lorenzini, small sac-like structures beneath the skin of the head, provide sharks with their astonishingly sensitive electroreception system, and field experiments on the shallow water dogfish (*Mustelus canis*), the oceanic blue shark (*Prionace glauca*) and the swell shark (*Cephaloscyllium ventriosum*) have all demonstrated that these animals indeed detect and take prey by the use of electroreception. Fortunately, the strength of a bioelectrical field falls off very steeply over distance and even in the case of a human body the field is

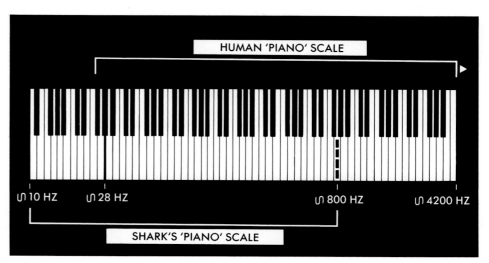

undetectable by a shark beyond a distance of one or two metres.

Other tiny electrical fields, well within the dynamic range of sharks and their relatives, include not only those generated by ocean currents as they flow through the earth's magnetic field, but also those created by a shark's own body as it swims through that same electrical field. As the shark moves, it induces a tiny electrical field whose strength depends on the direction in which it is heading. The ampullae of Lorenzini are also sensitive to these tiny changes, endowing sharks with their own built-in geomagnetic compass sense. Exacting experiments have shown that the round stingray (*Urolophus halleri*) is fully capable of geomagnetic orientation, and whenever animals travel long distances through a medium as featureless as water, it is strongly possible that they are somehow directing their attention to the earth's magnetic field. Based on what we already know, it is reasonable to assume that the long travels recorded for many sharks are the result not of lost and aimlessly wandering animals, but of well-oriented individuals moving to distant regions for their own reasons.

The popular belief that sharks are automatons incapable of learning is simply untrue. Experiments seeking to establish just how sensitive members of a species are to a particular visual object, a specific sound or a particular electrical field, have almost invariably required subjects to

▲ Although sharks and humans can detect some low-frequency vibrations in common, a shark's hearing has evolved for the detection of very low frequency sounds such as a struggling fish might make. Sharks can hear from 10 Hertz (cycles per second) to 800Hz; humans from 25Hz to 16 000Hz. (After Myrberg, 1986)

Arthur A. Myrberg Jr

▲ Silky sharks (*Carcharhinus falciformis*) approach a hydrophone broadcasting low-frequency sounds at a depth of 20 metres. This species is a fast and relatively aggressive open-ocean feeder whose superb hearing enables it to detect prey – primarily schools of mackerel, ocean mullet, tuna and squid – at great distances.

▼ The shark's compass sense. Swimming through the earth's magnetic field induces electrical fields that give the shark the basis for an electromagnetic compass sense. (After Kalmijn 1978)

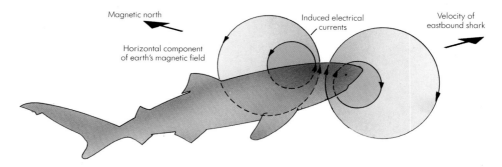

Magnetic north

Horizontal component of earth's magnetic field

Induced electrical currents

Velocity of eastbound shark

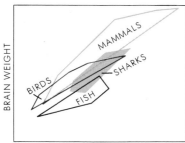

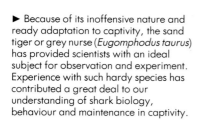
▲ Brain weight compared with body weight in four major groups of vertebrates. Sharks' brains, represented by the shaded area, are surprisingly large in relation to their body weight out of water and demonstrate the fallacy of the traditional view of sharks as 'mindless killers' incapable of learning. (*After Northcutt, 1978*)

learn a specific task to demonstrate their sensitivity. The success of such studies has shown that sharks can indeed learn through experience: a capability that may explain behavioural differences between juvenile and adult sharks. Juveniles generally appear to be more aggressive and clearly more inquisitive than adults. Their activity levels are often higher and their actions are often more erratic and unpredictable than those of adults of the same species. Such youthful high spirits – clearly ill-suited for a long and healthy life – change as individuals grow to maturity through these learning experiences, not unlike those of many other young animals on their way to adulthood.

Since we are now aware that sharks and their relatives possess many of the attributes ascribed to the so-called higher vertebrates, it is only fitting that another truth about them be debunked. Sharks were long considered insatiable feeding machines, driven only by primitive instincts. Given such an attitude it was not unreasonable to assume that they must have only pea-sized brains. Fortunately, that myth is no longer with us: scientists have recently demonstrated that many sharks and rays have brains comparable in size with those of many birds and mammals.

SHARKS IN CAPTIVITY
A 1963 review of the distribution and longevity of sharks in captivity around the world, showed that more than fifty species had been held in aquaria for at least several months. Nevertheless, until recently only a few hardy benthic species – hornsharks (*Heterodontus* spp.), leopard (*Triakis* spp.) and catsharks (*Scyliorhinus* spp.), the sand tiger shark (*Eugomphodus taurus*) and the Atlantic nurse shark –

consistently survived under such conditions up to one year or more. Despite these few successes, the consensus has been that most sharks are not only difficult to collect and transport but, once in captivity, often refuse to feed and therefore die. Severe hematological changes can readily occur also in sharks during and after capture, and important research findings may actually have been based on abnormal animals. Increasing knowledge on the maintenance of good health in captive sharks has now resulted in many species – even the larger and more pelagic species (for example, requiem sharks of the genus *Carcharhinus*) – being kept in large public aquaria for periods far exceeding one year. Proven techniques for transporting sharks to distant locations are now available, as are the means for maintaining high water quality during captivity. Sufficient space for unimpeded movement, prophylaxis and the use of supplements to correct dietary deficiencies are just a few of the practices that are now used to keep sharks at a level of health comparable with that found under natural conditions.

Although knowledge about the factors that control feeding behaviour could be considered critical for the health of sharks in captivity, surprisingly few studies have been directed at such factors. Also, since food is often the reward for appropriate behaviour in learning tasks, trainers and scientists must rely on control of feeding motivation: control that can best be maintained through understanding the *ad libitum* ('as much as one desires') rate of feeding. A 15-day peak in food intake has been suggested for juvenile lemon sharks, while a recirculating water system with precise control over light, temperature, salinity and

▶ Because of its inoffensive nature and ready adaptation to captivity, the sand tiger or grey nurse (*Eugomphodus taurus*) has provided scientists with an ideal subject for observation and experiment. Experience with such hardy species has contributed a great deal to our understanding of shark biology, behaviour and maintenance in captivity.

Ben Cropp

flow rate found a consistent 3.5 to four-day peak in food intake in the same species, with an additional but uncertain peak at 28 days. The four-day peak was generally preceded by a gradual two to three-day rise and was followed by a precipitous drop, suggesting that after an animal is sated several days are needed for its appetite to sharpen again.

The natural feeding behaviour of sharks has rarely been observed during the day. This strongly suggests that twilight and darkness are the most important times for feeding in the majority of these predators. Such cycles of activity would not come as a surprise, since sharks are certainly no exception to the universality of rhythms of activities in biological systems. The few experiments that have been conducted demonstrate clear rhythms around a 24-hour period (even in total darkness). Daily rhythms appear to be directly related to feeding.

HUMAN–SHARK INTERACTIONS

Much has been written about the dangers posed to humans by sharks, and most of the early literature maintained the view that shark attack is motivated by hunger. That view was initially challenged in 1969, when American researchers Baldridge and Williams noted consistent peculiarities in cases listed in the international Shark Attack File. These cases often involved severe wounding but little or no loss of flesh. The wounds appeared to have been caused solely by the teeth of the upper jaw during an apparent bite-and-run or slashing attack: wounds that were inconsistent with the idea that hunger was the underlying motivation for the attack. As Baldridge and Williams pointed out, 'If hunger motivated [such] attacks, then the shark or sharks involved were certainly inefficient feeders'.

Other attacks apparently motivated by factors other than feeding involve the Pacific grey reef shark, and are unique in that a highly stereotyped pattern, termed the exaggerated swimming display, precedes the attacks. The display varies in intensity; the maximum is when a shark is approached closely and especially if it is cornered and cannot escape. The display, though not normally seen during feeding, resembles the actions of the body and the head during an exaggerated bite and is apparently derived from the feeding act itself. Although only the Pacific grey reef shark performs the full display, components are shown by Galapagos sharks (*Carcharhinus galapagensis*), silky sharks, blacknose sharks (*C. acronotus*) and bonnethead sharks (*Sphyrna tiburo*).

Since these displays are neither dependent on location nor related to feeding, their significance remains unclear. However, I remember reading a recommendation to swim rapidly towards an approaching shark, since such behaviour on the part of potential prey (you or me) would probably confuse the shark, causing it to break off the attack and retreat. Based on what we now know about

what may happen when one approaches a shark too closely – and who but the shark knows that critical distance? – I certainly won't heed that recommendation, since it might well move me into a far more dangerous position!

That Pacific grey reef sharks are so aggressive despite their relatively small size (usually one to 1.5 metres long) stands in contrast with the behaviour of other sharks. Overt aggression, attacks, chasing or apparent threat are rarely observed. Even during active feeding, including the infamous 'feeding frenzies', sharks seem interested only in getting the food (sometimes biting one another apparently by mistake) rather than competing with each other.

Ron & Valerie Taylor

▲ Increasing knowledge of the dietary, spatial and social needs of sharks means that even such delicate pelagic species as the oceanic blue shark can be captured, transported and kept in good health for long periods.

▼ When persistently approached or startled by unusual sounds or rapid movements, grey reef sharks perform a threat display that consists of an exaggerated swimming pattern in which the shark wags its head and tail in broad sweeps, arches its back, lifts its head, depresses its pectoral fins and sometimes swims in a horizontal spiral or a series of figure-eight loops that bring it closer to the source of its anxiety. (*After Johnson and Nelson, 1973*)

DISPLAY   **NON-DISPLAY**

Ron & Valerie Taylor

▲▼ Stimulated by blood and bait in the water, more than a dozen grey reef sharks gather and their behaviour becomes increasingly aggressive until they are involved in a feeding frenzy. In a bizarre and savage climax, one shark that had been bitten accidentally during the frenzy is followed, attacked and killed by a larger comrade.

Aggressive behaviour could be expected if sharks defended exclusive areas, but there is no evidence to suggest that any sharks are truly territorial. Such aggressive behaviour may simply be the result of individuals attempting to maintain a position of relative dominance in specific areas. Recent evidence suggests that female grey reef sharks show elevated aggression and exaggerated swimming displays in pupping areas: perhaps they are simply defending themselves from possible predation. Defence of such a 'personal sphere' is well documented for other animals.

SOCIAL BEHAVIOUR

The classic view of the shark is that of a solitary hunter, ranging the oceans in search of food. Although this is true or probable for large species such as the great white shark and the tiger shark, many other species move in groups, at least during part of their lives. One of the most spectacular instances of such behaviour is that of the scalloped hammerhead (*Sphyrna lewini*). Daytime schools of more than a hundred scalloped hammerheads gather near islands and seamounts in the Sea of Cortez, between Baja California and the western coast of Mexico.

Unfortunately, little information exists about the social behaviour of these or other species of sharks, though dominant–subordinate associations (social hierarchies) have been reported *between* different species. Oceanic whitetip sharks (*Carcharhinus longimanus*) dominate silky sharks of comparable size when both species are feeding. Silvertip sharks (*Carcharhinus albimarginatus*) dominate Galapagos sharks, while both dominate blacktip sharks (*C. limbatus*). Such interactions,

Ron & Valerie Taylor

however, may actually reflect anti-predatory behaviour on the part of the subordinate species. Social hierarchies among members of the same species have also been reported and in bonnethead sharks at least, females tend to shy away from males, regardless of size. The reason for such shyness is unclear, but the harassment and bites that males of many species of sharks inflict on females during mating may explain why females give them such a wide berth. It should be mentioned, however, that such biting is not solely the 'domain' of males: females inflict such bites on other females during non-feeding periods and even males occasionally show similar wounds.

The social hierarchies noted among members of a given species – be they dogfish, bonnetheads, silvertips or great white sharks – are clearly

◀ The popular image of the shark as a lone hunter is shaken by the spectacular and mystifying congregations of scalloped hammerheads (*Sphyrna lewini*) that occur near seamounts in the Sea of Cortez, off western Mexico. The function of these gatherings – often of hundreds of individuals – is unknown, but may be related to mating.

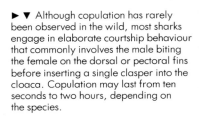 ▶ ▼ Although copulation has rarely been observed in the wild, most sharks engage in elaborate courtship behaviour that commonly involves the male biting the female on the dorsal or pectoral fins before inserting a single clasper into the cloaca. Copulation may last from ten seconds to two hours, depending on the species.

size-dependent; that is, smaller individuals move away from larger individuals. Although this might suggest that anti-predatory mechanisms are operating, such an organisation is typical of many fishes.

One might actually question why adult sharks would move about in packs or schools at any time. It's easy to understand why small sharks might do so, since a tight aggregation would reduce the chance of any given individual being eaten. Such an argument wanes in importance, however, as individuals become large enough for the risk of predation to be reduced. Perhaps the answer rests with the fact that food often occurs in widely separated patches and individuals may be able to take advantage of the extended sensory capabilities of the group. That advantage disappears if there isn't enough food to support a group; thus, apart from the mating season (when aggregations form for purposes of reproduction) the size of a shark pack may indicate the abundance of prey.

The ultimate social activity in sexually reproducing animals is mating. The scarcity of observations of mating in sharks indicates that it either occurs rarely or that it occurs primarily at night: the relatively few cases observed during daylight show that unrelated species demonstrate

strong similarities in position and activities by the mating pairs. Mating behaviour has been observed in catsharks (*Scyliorhinus canicula* and *S. torazame*), the hornshark (*Heterodontus francisci*), the blackfin reef shark (*Carcharhinus melanopterus*), the Atlantic nurse shark and the whitetip reef shark (*Triaenodon obesus*). All occurred on the ocean floor, except for one report of Atlantic lemon sharks copulating at the surface. In most instances, the male maintains a bite-hold on one of the pectoral fins of the female during copulation, no doubt to assist the placement of the clasper in the female's genital opening.

Future studies on the social behaviour of sharks will likely take advantage of the fact that animals often perform distinctive and relatively stereotyped acts: the exaggerated swimming display by the Pacific grey reef shark signifies threat, as do the 'hunch' displays of the bonnethead sharks, the silkies and the blacknose sharks. Certain specific acts by male scalloped hammerheads appear directed solely at females of the same species, suggesting a form of courtship.

BEHAVIOURAL ECOLOGY

Sharks are not only relatively rare in many areas, they are also wide-ranging, shy (in most instances), fragile (in terms of capture and transport) and can become dangerous. These limitations must be overcome before significant advance can be made in our knowledge of the ecology of these animals. One important advance in that regard has been the use of ultrasonic underwater telemetry. Other tools include small one or two-man submersibles, underwater television, stereophotography, specially designed boats, even tethered balloons. Through the use of such instrumentation and ideas inspired by ethology and behavioural ecology, our knowledge will surely continue to grow. This is especially so with regard to one major void in our knowledge about sharks. We are well aware that sharks can intercept a variety of visual, chemical, mechanical and electrical signs from their prey and use them for their own purposes. However, we are almost totally ignorant about the ways sharks use signals to communicate with each other. Is it possible that certain sharks might even attempt to communicate with their prey, using deceptive signals? If we knew something about the communication processes they use, we might be closer to understanding important aspects of their behaviour.

Body markings, for example, are used throughout the animal kingdom for communication. Is it possible that the distinctive body markings of sharks are used also for such purposes? Markings such as those possessed by the angelsharks are used as camouflage. However, many sharks show specific regions of pigmentation – such as along the edges and the tips of fins – that do not suggest functional camouflage. Might such

markings have a communication function?

As I have dived among sharks I have been constantly intrigued by the variety of their body markings, and I would like to advance an idea about one likely function for the white fin markings of a species found throughout the world's tropical and subtropical oceans – the oceanic whitetip shark (*Carcharhinus longimanus*). Although the idea centres on communication, it is not concerned with providing information between members of that particular species: instead, it concerns another type of communication – providing deceptive information to prey for the benefit of the shark itself.

While conducting acoustical experiments on oceanic sharks over the deep waters of the Bahamas during the mid-1970s, we often encountered oceanic whitetips. These sharks moved slowly, almost lethargically; their movements appeared uncommonly effortless compared with other sharks we had observed over the years. The slow movements were deceptive, however: oceanic whitetips can move with astounding speed over distances of more than 30 metres. Attaining such high speeds could explain, at least in part, something long known about these sharks – their prey includes some of the fastest moving oceanic fishes; tuna, mackerel, dolphinfish and even white marlin. It is highly unlikely that this shark could overtake such fast moving prey from behind, nor is it likely that it could sneak up on them in clear, open water. One suggestion has been advanced to answer this intriguing problem: oceanic whitetips move into surface schools of small fishes when these schools are being preyed on by tuna, mackerel or marlin. As the predators leap about feeding on their prey, they literally jump into the open mouths of the sharks. I can't help but wonder, however, what the chances are that a shark could position itself precisely at the end of the trajectory of a speeding leaping fish.

My own suggestion is based on a visual effect I have often experienced while observing oceanic whitetips; other divers have confirmed the same effect. As long as whitetips remain close by, their body shape is unmistakable. As they move to the limit of visibility however, the eyes are constantly drawn to their white-tipped fins, with the result that the sharks' greyish, countershaded bodies become indistinct: indeed, the shark seems to disappear unless one concentrates on it. And when that form becomes indistinct, attention focuses on the three to five white fin spots moving in close formation. Occasionally, when two whitetips move closely together at such distances, a 'school' of white spots can be seen moving through the clear water. The effect of this optical illusion is particularly striking during periods of moderate or low light, since in these conditions the spots stand out in far greater contrast to the background light.

Now comes the speculation. If the eyes of a

Neville Coleman

▲ Colouration and body markings in many species of sharks seem to play a part in enabling members of the same species to recognise each other. The blacktip reef shark (*Carcharhinus limbatus*) has strongly marked dorsal, pectoral, anal and tail fins that may serve to regulate 'schooling' behaviour in this highly social tropical species.

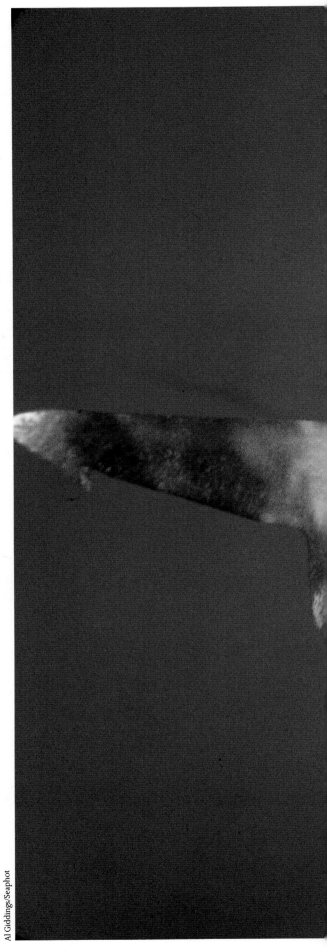

human and those of the fishes mentioned are not too dissimilar in terms of their general levels of sensitivity, the perceptual change that occurs – that is, the white-tipped fins of a shark becoming a 'school' of white spots – holds the explanation for how such fishes are caught by oceanic whitetip sharks. If the white spots are considered, at a distance, to be a small school of appropriately sized prey, rapidly moving predatory fishes might as well move toward such 'prey' and, if they were to reach a point where the sudden acceleration of the oceanic whitetip could overcome their attempts to escape, they could become the unexpected prey of the 'spots'. The white spots of the oceanic whitetip shark might well be species-recognition marks. However, they appear to possess another function as well – they are lures for attracting fast-moving fishes that hunt by sight. This may also explain why the first dorsal and the pectoral fins of this shark are so conspicuously large that they are often called 'paddles'. One way to improve the effectiveness of any lure is to increase its size so that it can be seen over a larger area, increasing the probability of prey being attracted. The large pectoral 'paddles' play an important role in the effortless gliding movements of such sharks and the large median dorsal fin adds stabilisation to sudden, rapid forward movement; nevertheless, whatever forces initiated the increase in fin size, the spots seem to have *benefited* since their increasing size could lure prey from ever greater distances.

Much of our knowledge about the behaviour of sharks is based on observations of precious few species. Yet that knowledge is vastly greater than what was available only a few years ago. Facts have replaced the speculations and myths that were so intimately associated with these animals for so many years. The number of scientists working on the behaviour of sharks has always been small, but even that number appears now to be dwindling. Sharks are inherently difficult to study: they are wide-ranging and inhabit a concealing medium, they are relatively swift swimmers and often move alone or in very small groups. Many species of interest can be found only in remote locations. Members of most species are fragile, requiring careful capture and transport, large holding facilities, highest water quality and an appropriate diet. Finally, many of the most interesting species, from the standpoint of human interest, are formidable and dangerous. Whenever observers must enter the water in their vicinity, severe safety measures must be taken. These and other considerations mean behavioural and ecological studies must be long-term in nature, with information accumulating often too slowly for many of today's scrutineers of science. Important advances in our knowledge of shark behaviour remain for the future, so long as scientists aren't deterred by the very difficulties that have made our present level of understanding so long in appearing.

▶ An intriguing explanation for the white-spotted dorsal and pectoral fins of the oceanic whitetip (*Carcharhinus longimanus*) involves an optical effect whereby the neutral grey of the shark's body can barely be seen in low light: the white spots may appear to predators (themselves prey for this species) like a school of small, edible fishes.

Al Giddings/Seaphot

Marty Snyderman

DO SEA LIONS EAT SHARKS?

MARTY SNYDERMAN

Our boat, the *Sand Dollar*, was drifting well out of sight of land about 30 kilometres off the coast of San Diego, California, over a bottom that is several hundred metres deep. As I looked over the side I could see at least a dozen blue sharks and four mako sharks cruising in and out of the chum line created by our bait. Most blue sharks – the most commonly encountered open-ocean sharks off the coast of southern California – are sleek and graceful animals, while makos look like torpedoes whose teeth do not fit into their mouths. Blue sharks can generally be baited in at any time throughout the year, but makos are much more common in summer and autumn.

At the time I was working on a documentary film about sharks for Survival Anglia with Stan Waterman and Howard Hall. Howard and I had worked with blue sharks and mako sharks for several years, and we considered ourselves to be rather well versed in their behaviour. Stan is acknowledged as a superb underwater cimematographer. Several accredited scientists were also aboard as part of the film crew.

Most of the sharks had been on the scene for several hours and all were obviously interested in the chunks of fish we were throwing in the water. To that point our day had been routine. We began baiting early in the morning and the sharks had begun to gather around the boat as soon as the wind had picked up and spread the chum line. The mixture of blues and makos was typical for summer and conditions were near perfect for a good day of film work.

We were refilling our tanks between dives when a medium-sized California sea lion suddenly appeared at the bait basket. For a moment we stared in utter amazement as the sea lion swam among the sharks. Then our professional training overtook us and we hurriedly suited up so that we could get into

the water and film a sea lion being attacked by sharks, an event we thought was certain to occur. This type of animal behaviour is precisely what documentary filmmakers pray for.

Cameras running, we jumped into the water; but we were not prepared for the sequence of events that took place before our eyes. The sea lion constantly stole our bait from the sharks. Whenever a shark moved closer to the mammal than it cared for, the sea lion would manoeuvre to a position behind and above the shark, and then swoop down and bite it on the top of its body just in front of the tail. Try as they might, none of the sharks could turn the game on the sea lion.

As the scene unfolded, the sea lion simply outmanoeuvred each and every shark every time we placed a bait in the water. Several of the blue sharks and all the makos became so annoyed at being bitten by the sea lion that they departed. The sea lion remained behind and feasted on our bait, making it impossible to film any 'marauding' sharks.

Needless to say, all of us – filmmakers and scientists alike – were completely surprised that the expected pattern of events had been reversed. Since that dive I have witnessed many similar situations and every time the results have been the same: the sea lions were able to outmanoeuvre the sharks and compete successfully with them for the bait.

Do sea lions eat sharks? Obviously not. But certainly all sharks, even large ones, don't have an easy time preying upon sea lions. While many species of seals are known to have been taken by sharks, very few examples have been reported of sharks successfully preying on sea lions. Three cases of sea lions being taken by great white sharks have been documented. Great whites are known to prey heavily on a variety of seals but sea lions, being better swimmers are, therefore, much more demanding prey.

SHARK ECOLOGY

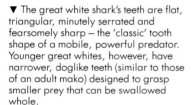

▲ Although modern sharks share many characteristics with their ancestors, most notably general body shape and a predatory lifestyle, variations in the style of predation have seen extensive changes in anatomy. The Port Jackson shark, for example, has teeth modified for crushing hard-shelled prey such as oysters, sea urchins and crustaceans.

▼ The great white shark's teeth are flat, triangular, minutely serrated and fearsomely sharp — the 'classic' tooth shape of a mobile, powerful predator. Younger great whites, however, have narrower, doglike teeth (similar to those of an adult mako) designed to grasp smaller prey that can be swallowed whole.

TIMOTHY C. TRICAS

Sharks are prominent members of almost all marine ecosystems. They occur in shallow bays and estuaries, cold waters of rocky coastlines, tropical coral reefs, in the centre of oceans and abyssal plains of the deep. Each shark species is well adapted to the physical conditions and biological assemblages that characterise its environment.

Sharks are among the top predators in most marine communities and are the marine equivalents of large carnivores in terrestrial ecosystems. Studies in shark ecology encompass many aspects of the relationships between sharks and their environment. These include factors that influence the numbers and distribution of sharks, links between sharks, their predators and prey, and ways in which they compete with other species for food and space. Because they range over large areas and live in an environment that limits prolonged observation and experimental study, sharks present marine ecologists with unique challenges. Our understanding of their roles in marine ecosystems is still surprisingly limited and much research remains to be done.

The most obvious variations between different shark species are in the shape of the head and tail, the articulation of the jaw and head, and the shape of the teeth: variations that can be explained as adaptations to the differing environments in which species must feed, avoid predators, and reproduce. An ecological approach to the study of sharks helps us better to understand the dynamics of marine communities and the environmental factors that shape patterns of shark evolution.

This chapter is divided into two main sections. The first deals with the feeding habits and the environmental adaptations that allow sharks to feed efficiently on their prey. The second looks at the structure of the shark community on a typical Pacific coral reef and provides insights into how sharks of different species may coexist within the same ecosystem.

FEEDING ECOLOGY

One of the most remarkable features of living sharks is the large number of characteristics they share with their ancestors, which inhabited the oceans more than 300 million years ago. Most notable is the striking similarity of body form found in species of vastly different sizes and lifestyles. For example, the whale shark (*Rhincodon typus*) reaches lengths of more than fifteen metres and feeds in tropical seas by straining plankton and small fishes through its gill rakers. This large species has a body plan very similar to that of the cookiecutter shark (*Isistius brasiliensis*), which reaches a maximum length of less than half a metre and is a parasite that feeds by biting small pieces of flesh from tunas, marlins, porpoises and whales. The retention of this basically similar body form by sharks in widely differing environments suggests that they developed characteristics early in their evolutionary history that make them successful predators.

On closer examination of individual species, distinct morphological (physical and anatomic)

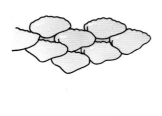

A

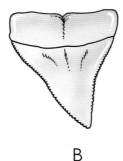

B

C

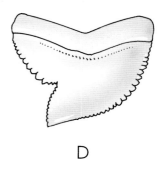

D

differences that relate to their feeding become apparent. Perhaps the most marked differences are in tooth shapes, which in most species seem well adapted to prey that is available to them.

Some bottom-dwelling species, such as the horn sharks (*Heterodontus* spp.) and smooth dogfishes (*Mustelus* spp.) have teeth modified for crushing hard-shelled invertebrate prey such as crustaceans (crabs and lobsters) and molluscs (clams). Other species have flat, triangular teeth

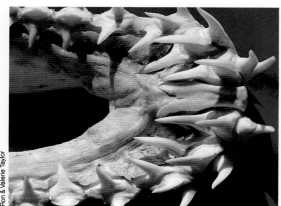

Ron & Valerie Taylor

with sharp serrated edges for cutting prey. This latter tooth structure is found in many species, including the requiem or whaler (family Carcharhinidae), great white (family Lamnidae) and hammerhead (family Sphyrnidae) sharks. These species feed heavily on fishes and cephalopods and are found in a variety of marine communities. A third general tooth class is long and narrow in profile, double-edged and without serrations. It is best suited for grasping fish prey, which is usually swallowed whole. This tooth structure is found in the bottom-dwelling sand tiger (family Odontaspididae) and the oceanic porbeagle and mako (family Lamnidae) sharks. Many additional tooth forms exist, some of which are unique to particular species. For example, the tiger shark (*Galeocerdo cuvier*) has a flat, highly serrated, triangular tooth with a large primary notch on the outer margin. This configuration functions well to cut through the hard shell of turtles and to take bites out of very large prey items such as tropical marine mammals and other sharks.

The importance of tooth shape to feeding habits is illustrated by the dynamic changes in dietary patterns that can occur during the lifetime of a shark. For example, great white sharks (*Carcharodon carcharias*) less than around three metres long feed on small fish, which they usually swallow whole. Larger white sharks feed primarily on large marine mammals, which they consume in pieces. Small white sharks have very narrow teeth that are very similar to those of adult mako sharks and are best suited to grasping small fish. (Captured young white sharks are often mistaken for makos because of their tooth shape!) In contrast, when white sharks grow longer than around three metres they develop triangular serrated teeth best suited to gouging and cutting prey too large to swallow whole. Thus, the feeding habits and predatory success of the white shark are intimately related to its tooth structure. Changing tooth morphologies in association with shark growth have also been reported for requiem and hammerhead sharks, but the function in relation to their feeding remains to be demonstrated.

Australian Picture Library

Similarities and contrasts in ecological adaptations are found among species that frequent the same habitats. The blue shark (*Prionace glauca*) is common in the surface waters of the northeast Pacific and north Atlantic oceans. It planes gracefully through the water on broad pectoral fins by slow, sinuous undulations of its long body and tail. It feeds primarily upon small fishes such as anchovies and sardines, and small squid that migrate from deep water to the surface at night. Blue sharks have small mouths and small serrated

▲ General tooth shapes common to sharks with similar feeding ecologies. Note the large primary notch to facilitate the cutting of prey.
A Crushing teeth from the upper jaw of the smooth dogfish (*Mustelus canis*).
B Serrated triangular tooth from the upper jaw of the oceanic whitetip shark (*Carcharhinus longimanus*).
C Elongate tooth from the upper jaw of the mako.
D Subtriangular tooth of the tiger shark (*Galeocerdo cuvier*).

◄ Bottom-dwelling and relatively sluggish sand tiger or grey nurse sharks have teeth similar in shape to those of fast-moving oceanic predators such as makos and porbeagles. In both cases, this tooth shape is superbly evolved to hold fish (and in the case of makos, pelagic squid) that do not have to be bitten into smaller pieces.

◄ Requiem sharks — members of the family Carcharhinidae — are opportunistic feeders that will take advantage of almost any food resource, from fish and crustaceans to seabirds, turtles and carrion. Their teeth are designed to cope with a variety of textures, and are replaced constantly through the shark's life as they wear or are broken.

▲ Tropical reefs support a range of shark species, some of which are active in daylight hours while others, which rest in crevices and coral caves during the day, hunt at night. The remora accompanying this small requiem shark (*Carcharhinus* sp.) does not feed on scraps, but cleans parasites from the skin and gill chambers of its host.

triangular teeth for feeding on small prey. A summer visitor to the same waters is the shortfin mako (*Isurus oxyrinchus*). This species has short, stout pectoral fins, a fusiform body, and a tail with upper and lower lobes of almost equal length. In contrast to the blue shark, it is adapted to swim extremely fast and feeds on schools of mackerel and other fishes. It has long needle-like teeth for grasping its prey. In spite of their morphological differences, these two sharks are remarkably similar in colour. Both have dark blue backs that are countershaded by a white undersurface. This colour pattern serves to make both species blend into their open-water environment, and to render them virtually invisible to their prey (and predators) at a distance. Thus, while species may exhibit different specialisations, they may also share adaptations that maximise their success in a particular habitat.

SHARK COMMUNITIES ON PACIFIC REEFS

Most islands and coral atolls in the central Pacific have a submarine reef profile similar to that shown in the accompanying diagram. There is usually a shallow reef flat that separates the seaward reef from shallow backwaters or a large lagoon. The reef flat is often exposed at low tide, and is frequented by large fish only when flooded. The back reef, or lagoon, area is usually scattered with patch reefs of living coral across a sandy bottom. On the seaward side of the reef crest is the fore-reef area, which rapidly falls off into deeper waters. The seaward and back regions of the reef are usually connected by a series of deep channels that cut through the reef flat.

The species composition and distribution of sharks on different tropical reefs in the Pacific are remarkably similar. The most common visitor to the reef flat during flood tide is the blacktip reef shark (*Carcharhinus melanopterus*). Juvenile and adult sharks of this species often frequent waters so shallow that their dorsal fins are completely exposed above the surface. This relatively small shark grows to an average length of around 1.5 metres and feeds upon a broad range of small fishes, crustaceans and cephalopods that inhabit the reef flat and adjacent shallow waters. It is an active species, capable of quick and rapid turns, and often moves about the reef flat in large aggregations and exhibits high levels of excitement when feeding. Its relatively small size permits it to forage efficiently for prey over shallow areas that are less accessible to larger sharks. Although the blacktip is the most common visitor to the shallow reef flat, it is also found in shallow waters – usually less than fifteen metres deep – on both sides of the reef flat. Telemetry and conventional tagging studies indicate that blackfin reef sharks have a limited home range, frequent the same areas of the reef, and forage for food mainly at night.

Another shark common to most Pacific reefs is the whitetip reef shark (*Triaenodon obesus*). This species is slightly larger than the blacktip reef shark and reaches a maximum length of around two metres. It has a slender, flexible body and swims close to the bottom where it moves among reef crevices and caves in search of food. Whitetip sharks are usually most abundant between depths of five and 40 metres but appear to prefer habitats with high vertical relief and abundant reef interstices. Only rarely are they observed on the reef flat or very shallow waters. Their diet includes a wide variety of reef fishes, octopuses, and crustaceans. During the day, they often rest (sometimes in groups) in caves or on the open reef with mouths open and oriented upstream, taking advantage of water currents to ventilate the gills. Various telemetry and tagging studies show that individual whitetip sharks are strongly attached to specific geographical areas of the reef, and individuals can be observed in the same area over periods of many years. Although daytime feeding by this species is reported, activity increases during the night and indicates hunting may be more intense then. Although it is well known that olfaction is used by whitetip sharks during hunting, their ability to detect the electric fields of prey by use of electroreceptor organs on the snout (the ampullae of Lorenzini) may be especially important for this species while hunting in caves and crevices.

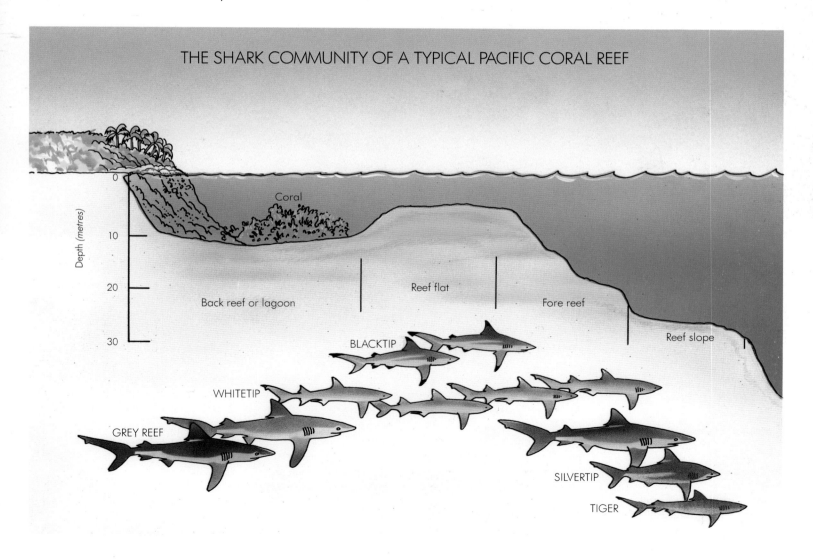

THE SHARK COMMUNITY OF A TYPICAL PACIFIC CORAL REEF

Depth (metres)

Coral

Back reef or lagoon

Reef flat

Fore reef

Reef slope

BLACKTIP

WHITETIP

GREY REEF

SILVERTIP

TIGER

▲ Tagging studies of the whitetip reef shark (*Triaenodon obesus*) indicate that this species is most active at night and at slack tides. Whitetips spend most of the day resting in caves; individuals favour particular caves and have narrow home ranges.

The shark most familiar to divers in deep waters of central Pacific reefs is the grey reef shark (*Carcharhinus amblyrhynchos*). It is slightly larger than the whitetip, reaching lengths of more than two metres. Its distribution overlaps considerably with that of the whitetip reef shark, but it is more abundant in deep areas on the seaward side of the reef flat and also in deep areas of the backreef or lagoon. Particularly large aggregations of grey reef sharks are reported in deep passes and channels that transect fringing reefs. Their diet consists primarily of reef fishes and cephalopods. At Enewetak Atoll, grey reef sharks will strike rubber squid lures during the daytime, a good indication that they feed naturally at that time. Apparently this species (like most other reef sharks) does not feed every day, since a great majority of the stomachs examined by the author were empty. Its behaviour

is well studied. It is best known for its threat display, which is characterised by an exaggerated swimming motion with back arched, pectoral fins depressed, and snout lifted. This behaviour can be elicited if grey reef sharks are cornered on the reef by divers and often precedes an attack. Sometimes, however, they are extremely aggressive to divers without apparent provocation. This unique behaviour may function in more natural situations as a means of defending a territory or personal space against other sharks, or perhaps as a defence against large predators such as tiger sharks. Its importance in spacing individuals of the same or different species, however, remains to be investigated.

A large shark commonly encountered on the seaward reef is the silvertip (*Carcharhinus albimarginatus*). This species is larger than the grey reef shark, and adults typically inhabit waters below 25 metres. It feeds largely on small fishes, squid, and octopuses associated with the reef. Other sharks found on the outer reef, but less well studied, are the blacktip shark (*C. limbatus*) bull shark (*C. leucas*) and hammerheads (*Sphyrna* spp.). Relatively little is known about the ecology of these species on Pacific reefs and the factors that influence their distributions and abundance.

The largest shark on most Pacific reefs is the tiger shark (*Galeocerdo cuvier*), which can grow to more than five metres. It has a blunt snout, very large mouth, and the flat, triangular, serrated teeth described earlier. Tiger sharks feed on a wide variety of prey items from many habitats and have perhaps the most diverse diet of all sharks. They usually occur in deep water on the seaward side of the reef flat, but also frequent deep channels and passes. Individuals will enter shallow waters adjacent to the reef flat to feed on sea birds at rest on the water surface. Smaller prey such as bottom-dwelling crustaceans, cephalopods and small fishes are also commonly taken, probably in

deeper waters near the reef. This species is also a voracious predator on large stingrays and other sharks. Because of its large size and wide-ranging habits, little is known about its movement patterns. A 4-metre female tracked with ultrasonic telemetry by the author and associates for two days on a reef in Hawaii moved a distance of around 80 kilometres per day and covered an area of around 100 square kilometres. That particular shark also made deep excursions during the night along the steep reef slope, where it presumably fed on fishes or invertebrate prey.

The distribution and abundance of sharks in marine communities is strongly influenced by the morphological and behavioural adaptations of each species to its physical environment and to its prey. We have looked at one particular environment, but similar adaptations determine the feeding ecologies and predatory success of shark species in other habitats. A great deal of work still remains to be done to extend our knowledge of the role of sharks as predators in marine ecosystems throughout the world.

▼ The grey reef shark (*Carcharhinus amblyrhynchos*) shares reef habitats with the smaller blacktip reef shark (*C. melanopterus*), but prefers deeper waters on the seaward side of the reef. The blacktip is usually found on shallow sand flats inside lagoons.

Marty Snyderman

WHEN SHARKS AND DOLPHINS CROSS PATHS

MARTY SNYDERMAN

Many of us know of instances where sharks have been killed by dolphins when the animals were together in captivity. Those who have witnessed such events report that the dolphins kill the sharks by repeatedly ramming the sharks' soft underbellies with their snouts.

But what happens when sharks and dolphins encounter one another in the wild? Do fierce fights occur? Do the animals simply swim their separate ways? I am not sure that anyone can claim to be an expert in this matter, but I will never forget one night when I watched dolphins and sharks swimming side by side as they fed on flying fish.

I was aboard the *Ambar II* at Socorro Island, just over 300 kilometres south of Land's End at the southern tip of Mexico's Baja Peninsula. Our diving day had ended, and we were sitting on deck an hour or so after sunset watching the squid that were attracted by the lights of our boat. Several flying fish had landed on deck, and the water around the boat was rapidly becoming populated with them. We were shooting a film about sharks for the television series 'Wild Kingdom'. We had seen plenty of sharks during our dives – hammerheads, duskies, blacktips and silvertips – so it was no surprise when several duskies showed up that evening to feed on the squid and flying fish.

In order to catch a flying fish, a dusky would single one out and then swim at it from behind until the flying fish was only 30 centimetres or so directly in front of the shark's snout. As the shark closed in, the flying fish would move off to its side. Then the dusky would 'thrust' its head to the side and snare the flying fish. I watched the sharks repeatedly pursue the flying fish in this manner, and to my utter amazement the duskies never missed their prey.

After I had been watching the sharks for about 45 minutes, a dozen bottlenose dolphins appeared in the lights under the boat. They too were interested in feeding on the flying fish, though they were not nearly as successful as the dusky sharks. It seemed as if the flying fish were able to detect the dolphins' sonar and were often able to avoid the dolphins because of this early warning.

The dolphins and sharks swam in close proximity to one another throughout the night without a single incident of aggression. Both groups fed on the flying fish, but competition was not evident even when sharks and dolphins were within a few metres of one another. In short, it was a case of 'You go your way and I'll go mine'. In captivity where close quarters might lead to conflict the situation might have been different, but in the open sea on the night in question the dolphins and sharks simply left each other alone.

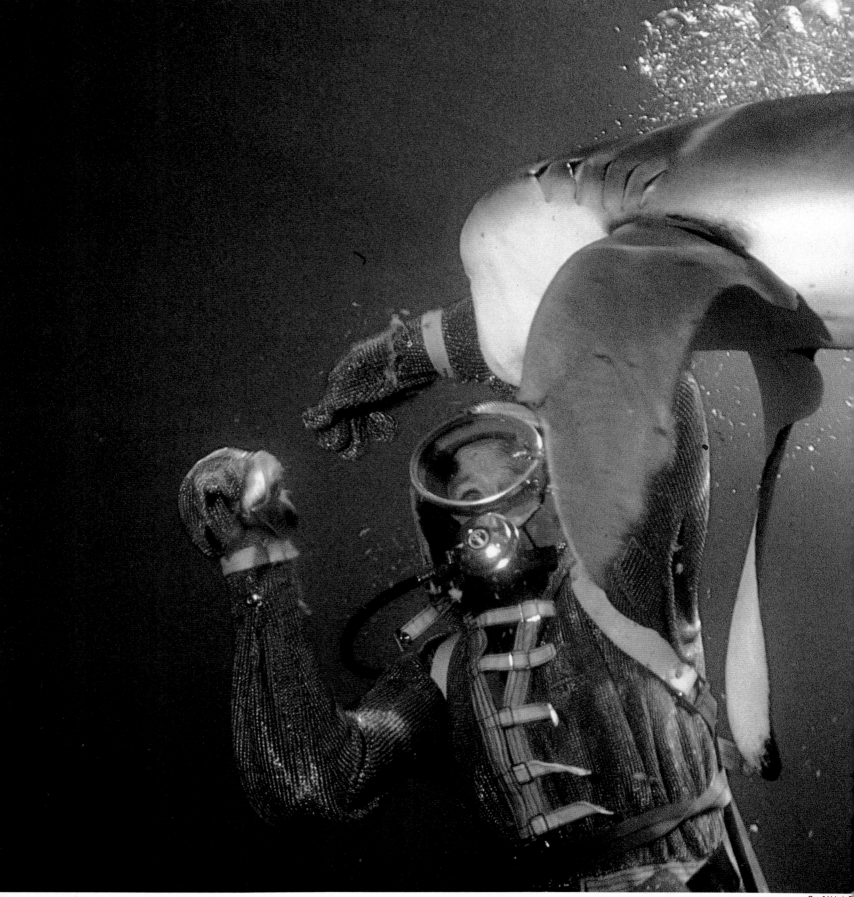

▲ Protected by a unique suit of stainless 'chain mail', Australian diver Valerie Taylor provokes an attack by a blue shark.

SHARK ATTACK

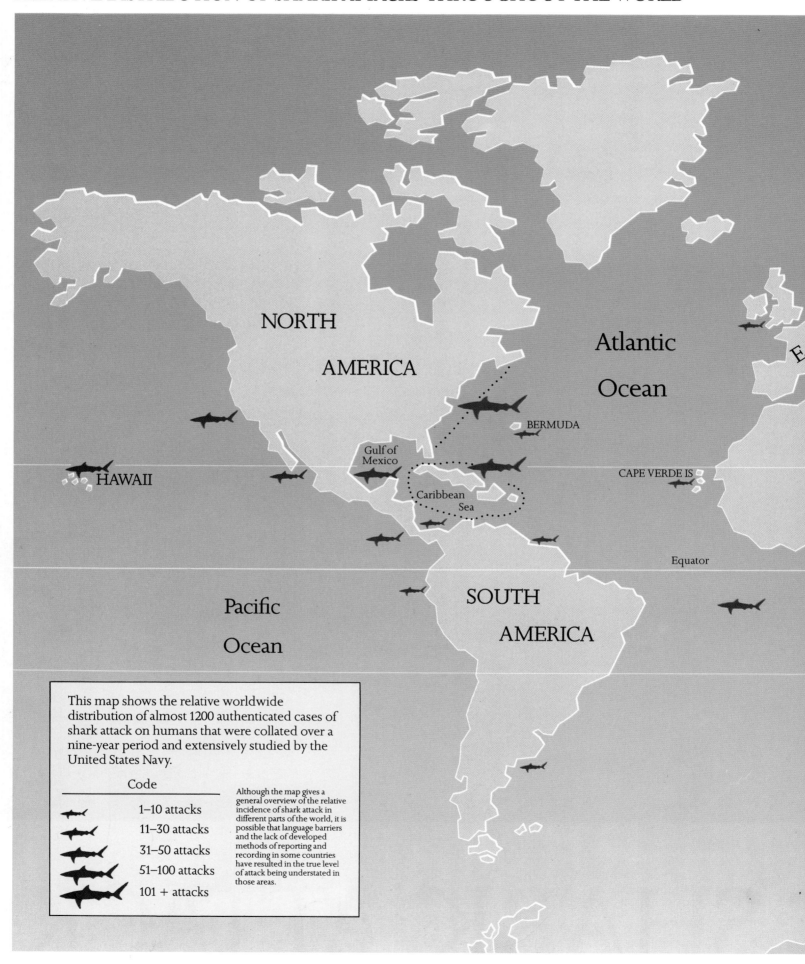

NORTH

AMERICA

Atlantic

Ocean

E

BERMUDA

Gulf of
Mexico

HAWAII

CAPE VERDE IS

Caribbean
Sea

Equator

Pacific

SOUTH

Ocean

AMERICA

This map shows the relative worldwide
distribution of almost 1200 authenticated cases of
shark attack on humans that were collated over a
nine-year period and extensively studied by the
United States Navy.

Code

	1–10 attacks
	11–30 attacks
	31–50 attacks
	51–100 attacks
	101 + attacks

Although the map gives a
general overview of the relative
incidence of shark attack in
different parts of the world, it is
possible that language barriers
and the lack of developed
methods of reporting and
recording in some countries
have resulted in the true level
of attack being understated in
those areas.

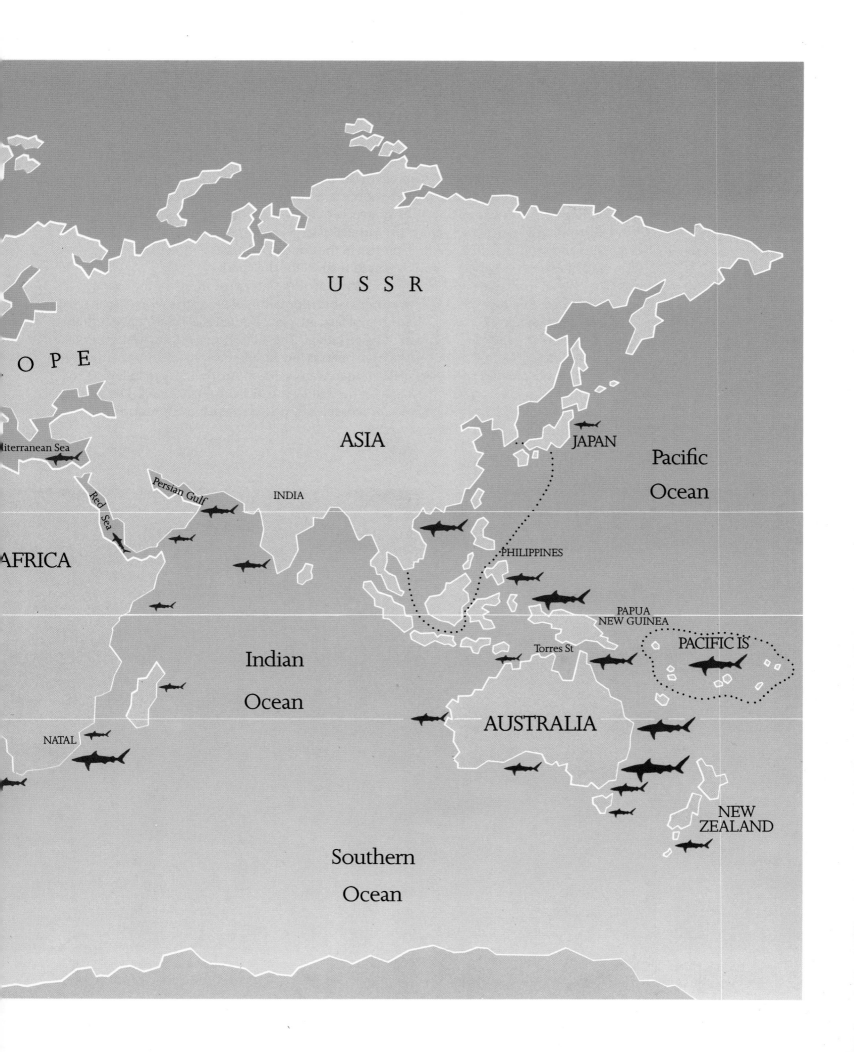

USSR

OPE

ASIA

JAPAN

Pacific

Ocean

iterranean Sea

Persian Gulf

INDIA

Red Sea

PHILIPPINES

AFRICA

PAPUA
NEW GUINEA

PACIFIC IS

Indian

Torres St

Ocean

AUSTRALIA

NATAL

NEW
ZEALAND

Southern

Ocean

SHARK ATTACK IN AUSTRALIAN WATERS

▲ An angry great white shark attacks a boat's fender. Great whites will often inspect divers out of curiosity, but they are capable of aggressive and sustained attacks. In 1984, a Tasmanian abalone diver was pinned to the ocean floor for more than an hour while a 6-metre great white attempted to prise him out of a crevice.

▼ The great white defies the popular misconception that shark attacks are linked to warmer water temperatures. The truth is that there are simply more people in the water during the warmer months, and that sharks are attracted to the noise and splashing of swimmers, whose activities may fatally resemble those of injured fish.

ROLAND HUGHES

Thanks to the worldwide success of the box office hit movie *Jaws*, the mere mention of the word shark is enough to conjure up images of a maneater on some horrific killing spree. Whether on the busy streets of New York or London, or on a beach in Australia, the reaction is always the same. But to give Australians credit, their love of the surf and sand and their abiding interest in the continent's vast marine playground have led, if ever so slowly, to a sophisticated respect for the shark.

It's an undisputed fact that before the introduction of meshing on the eastern seaboard, Australia's seas had the unenviable reputation of being the worst in the world for shark attacks. Recently, a number of fatal attacks off Australia's coast have refuelled the popular belief that sharks are savage killers. The facts, however, suggest otherwise. Since records began in 1901 there have been as few as 250 shark attacks and a little over a hundred fatalities recorded in Australian waters. More Australians are killed on the country's roads each month than have died this century from shark attack. Despite this, many people still imagine that sharks ceaselessly prowl the sea in some sort of programmed search for human prey.

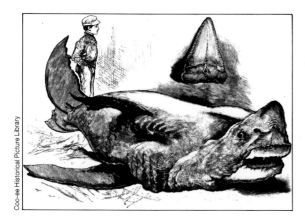

EARLY SHARK ATTACKS

Rock carvings and paintings indicate that Aborigines were familiar with several kinds of sharks and rays. We will, of course, never know how many Aboriginal people were attacked by sharks while swimming or fishing. Early European navigators, too, quickly became familiar with the sharks of Australian waters. In 1623 the Dutch sailor Jan Carstensz noted the presence of 'sharks, sword-fishes, and the like unnatural monsters' in the ocean near Cape York, Queensland. Shark Bay in Western Australia was named by the English explorer William Dampier in 1699, reportedly because his men had killed and eaten a shark there.

The first Australian shark tragedy was recorded by François Peron, a naturalist with Louis Baudin's exploratory expedition to Western Australia. In March 1803 Peron noted:

The eastern side of Faure Island is infested with sharks remarkable for their size and voracity. One of these monsters almost devoured Lefevre, who had saved my life at the Josephine Islands. He was already knocked over: the terrible shark was about to swallow him, when three other sailors, running up at his shouts, managed to rescue him from the jaws of the animal. Furious at thus being deprived of its prey, the shark hurled itself several times at the sailor, succeeding in tearing off part of his clothing, and only retired when it had received five wounds.

Although swimming was not a particularly popular pastime among the early European convicts and settlers in eastern Australia, a fear of sharks was nevertheless apparent in the colony from its earliest days. Prisoners were isolated on Pinchgut Island in Sydney Harbour and at Port Arthur in Tasmania because their fear of sharks was a strong deterrent to escape. The *Sydney Gazette* of 26 February 1804 mentions a shark attacking a boat in Port Jackson and two years later the newspaper issued 'A Caution to Parents' to keep their children away from the hospital wharf where a large shark had been sighted.

The first recorded fatal attack in eastern Australia occurred on 17 January 1837 when Alfred Australia Howe, aged twelve, was taken in the Macleay River in northern New South Wales. Ironically, the boy had been rescued eight years earlier from a boating capsize in Sydney Harbour in which his father, the government printer, had been drowned.

COPPLESON'S RESEARCH

It is surprising that, given the significant tally of shark attacks already registered in Australian waters, there is no local full-time research being undertaken on what actually provokes sharks to attack humans. The only comprehensive study of shark attack ever attempted in Australia was completed in 1958 by Dr Victor Coppleson.

▲ While there has been an incredible increase in the number of people using the ocean for sailing, swimming and diving, there is no evidence to suggest a comparable increase in the number of shark attacks. Human attitudes, it seems, have changed more than the behaviour of sharks: in the nineteenth century, when these illustrations were published, sharks were recognised as dangerous and predatory animals but were regarded more as curiosities than monstrous killing machines.

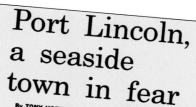

Port Lincoln, a seaside town in fear

BY TONY HORWITZ

The setting is a small and scenic seaside town. A young woman is attacked in shallow water by a great white shark of mythic proportions. Only limbs — or, in this case, flippers — escape the shark.

And now, sadly, to complete the *Jaws* analogy, the bereaved town takes to the seas to hunt the killer.

"The shark has to be captured and killed," says Mr Brian Wood, treasurer of the Port Lincoln Game Fishing Club, which is co-ordinating the shark hunt.

"It's had a taste of human flesh and it may come back again for more easy prey."

Police are combing the beaches for remains of the body. Offshore, fishing boats ply the waters with nets and bait, hoping to lure the shark back to the scene of Sunday's crime.

The 14 volunteers on board are armed with hooks, oil drums to weigh down and tire a hooked shark, and high-powered rifles to finish off the six-metre monster if its blunt nose appears above water.

An old friend of the victim's

THE VICTIM: Mrs Shirley Durdin, 33.

THE HUNTER: Graham Bauer with the bullet he intends to use on the shark.

THE TOWN: Port Lincoln, where a shark threatens tourism.

◄ Today's media coverage only encourages a hysterical response to shark attack, complete with gun-toting vigilantes bent on avenging the death of Shirley Anne Durdin in 1985. 'It's had a taste of human flesh and it may come back again for more,' said one of the hunters. The great white shark responsible has never been sighted since the attack.

▲ Wiseman's beach, Port Lincoln.

A REVIEW OF SHARK ATTACKS IN AUSTRALIAN WATERS

In 1950 Dr Victor Coppleson published, in the *Medical Journal of Australia,* preliminary results of his analysis of recorded shark attacks in Australian waters. His research was more fully documented in his 1958 publication, *Shark Attack.* Coppleson's findings are illustrated below.

TIME OF ATTACK (104 cases)

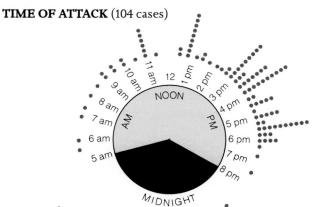

Most attacks occur
in the afternoon, usually between 2 pm and 6 pm.

DEPTH OF WATER (27 cases)

Depth of water (centimetres)	Number of attacks
shallow; depth unknown	2
0	2
60	6
90	10
120	2
150	
deep; depth unknown	2
360	
	3
600	

MONTH OF ATTACK (58 cases)

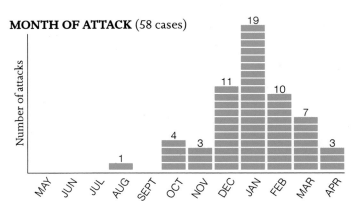

Attacks are most common between December and March. This, of course, is at least partly explained by the warm summer weather which attracts large numbers of people into the water. In Sydney and Newcastle, all but one of the 40 recorded cases occurred between 14 December and 14 April.

Based on more detailed study, Coppleson was able to draw up a timetable for shark attacks in Australia:

North of Tropic of Capricorn . . . . .all year
Southern Queensland . . . . .November–May
Newcastle . . . . .December–April
Sydney . . . . .December–April
Adelaide . . . . .December–March
Melbourne . . . . .January–March
Bass Strait and Tasmania . . . . .January

NUMBER OF PEOPLE SWIMMING (25 cases)

Number of people	Number of attacks
swimming alone	5
2–10	10
11–20	3
21–30	2
31–40	2
41–70	1
several hundred	2

DISTANCE FROM SHORE (41 cases)

Number of attacks 11 14 5 11

Distance (metres) 10 50 100 600

Coppleson concluded that the swimmer attacked by a shark is usually either a lone bather, part of a small group or on the edge of a large group. Shark attacks can occur in all kinds of weather, on dull days and fine days, at high, medium or low tides, in clear, muddy or even brackish water. Usually only one person is attacked; typically the shark will make two or three attacks on the victim, ignoring nearby swimmers.

Rich Mula/Ocean Images

Although they were made nearly thirty years ago, most of Coppleson's findings still apply today, even if the interpretations he put on those findings are sometimes now disputed. One of his major discoveries was that most attacks occurred between two and six o'clock in the afternoon and that weather, tides and water clarity were not factors that influenced the attacks. Coppleson's investigations also confirmed that the majority of Australian attacks were made by lone sharks and that only in a few instances were shark packs involved. He found in many cases the shark would strike the same victim a couple of times while completely ignoring other swimmers nearby. This was the case with a shark attack that occurred off Wiseman's Beach near Port Lincoln in South Australia on Sunday 3 March 1985.

Shirley Anne Durdin and her husband Barry were snorkelling for scallops in two metres of water, 50 metres from the shore. Nearby, a fisherman trailed a line from the side of a small dinghy and two men and a woman were frolicking in the water with three children and a dog. At 1.30pm, Shirley Durdin was struck below the waist by a 6-metre white shark. Eyewitnesses said there was a big spray of red froth and bubbles and that one man started yelling, 'Help, help, help, she's gone, she's gone.' When one of the larger boats in the vicinity rushed over to the scene of the attack to help, the shark resurfaced and made off with the remains of Mrs Durdin's body. Local fishermen reported that a 'monster' white shark had been feeding in the area for four weeks and blamed rotten bait and burley that had been thrown into the bay for a local fishing competition for attracting it.

THE 'ROGUE' SHARK THEORY

Coppleson was a strong advocate of the 'rogue' shark theory. He found that places that had been free of attack for years would suddenly within a short period become the scene of two, three or even more attacks. Then, just as suddenly as they began, the attacks would cease and the area would enjoy a long period of freedom from shark attack. This pattern, Coppleson claimed, recurred far too often to be a matter of simple coincidence. He blamed individual sharks, which he called 'rogues', for the occurrence. One of Australia's most horrific series of shark attacks is attributed to a 5-metre 'rogue' tiger shark.

On 26 July 1983 Ray Boundy told how over the preceding 36 hours he had watched helplessly as a large shark first took a young crewman then came back for the female cook, after his 14-metre trawler, the New Venture, capsized and sank 100 kilometres northeast of Townsville. After managing to escape from the sinking boat Mr Boundy and the crew, 24-year-old Dennis Murphy and 21-year-old Linda Horton, took a surfboard, lifering and piece of foam from the wreckage and decided to paddle toward Lodestone Reef where they knew help could be found. They set off at 1pm on Monday 25 July and it wasn't until after dark that evening that the shark first appeared. On spotting the swimmers, the shark began to follow their progress, surfacing occasionally and pushing at the

► The serrated cutting teeth of the tiger shark.

Ben Cropp

pieces of foam, lifering and surfboard to which they were clinging. By this time the three crew were only eight kilometres from Lodestone Reef and tried to ignore the harassing shark in the hope it would eventually leave them alone.

However, their wish was not fulfilled. On one of its many passes the shark suddenly turned and lunged at Ray Boundy, grabbing his leg. In a split-second reaction Ray drove the shark off with an almighty kick. 'He got such a fright we thought he had gone,' Ray said later. Ten minutes after the first attack, the shark reappeared and seized Dennis Murphy's leg, pulling him under several times. When the shark let go Dennis told the others he had lost his leg and that he had no hope. He persuaded them that with the shark's attention on him their opportunity had come to escape. Acting under the brave crewman's advice Ray Boundy and Linda Horton paddled off, leaving Dennis Murphy

to deal with the shark. 'We heard a lot of screaming and kicking and punching, then saw the shark lift his body upside down out of the water and eat it,' Ray Boundy said.

Two hours later, while Linda Horton was sitting in the sling of the lifering with her feet up on the foam and with Ray beside her, the shark struck again. Grabbing Linda around the arms and chest, the shark shook her three or four times then disappeared under the water with her body. Terrified, Ray immediately grabbed two remaining pieces of foam for support and paddled as fast as he could for the reef. It wasn't until after daylight that the shark returned and began circling Ray Boundy. By this time the outer reef, offering safety, was in sight and Ray made a last-ditch effort to reach the reef in one piece. His desperate progress was watched by the shark as it zigzagged behind him.

Once Ray had made it to the reef edge, the shark turned and disappeared. Not long afterwards Ray was spotted and rescued by a surveillance helicopter.

Although Ray Boundy did not recognise the species of shark responsible, evidence suggests that it was almost certainly a tiger shark. Following the multiple attack, local fishermen landed a number of large tiger sharks in the area but as the culprit was never proved caught, it was not properly identified. This is a very common problem with shark attacks as positive identification of maneaters can only be made if tooth fragments are found in the victim. More importantly, while some people have speculated that the 'rogue' shark had particularly set its sights on the three *New Venture* crew, no one knows just what triggered the attack. Clearly

► Influential Australian shark researcher Dr Victor Coppleson was a strong advocate of the 'rogue shark' theory, which holds that individual sharks may develop a taste for attack, if not human flesh, and that a single shark may be responsible for several attacks in one area. The notion is given some support by the horrifying deaths of two crew members from the trawler *New Venture*, which sank northeast of Townsville, Queensland. Ray Boundy, owner of the *New Venture*, watched helplessly as a 5-metre shark — identified from his description as a tiger shark — tore the body of crewman Dennis Murphy to pieces before returning some hours later to take Linda Horton. Boundy was followed by the same shark as he swam desperately for the safety of Lodestone Reef.

Ben Cropp

THE SHARK ARM MURDER CASE

Record books around the world abound with bizarre cases and fascinating tales of shark attack, but none has managed to top what is known internationally as the 'Shark arm murder' case. On 18 April 1935, Albert Hobson set off in his boat to a point off Coogee Beach in Sydney where he had left a line bait. Pulling up the line, Albert was struck dumb with amazement, for he had not only hooked a small half-eaten shark but had also snared a 4.5-metre tiger shark, entangled in the line but still very much alive. Albert secured the giant shark and towed it to the beach. Once there he decided to turn the prize shark over to the Coogee Aquarium for exhibition. Albert's find soon had Sydneysiders flocking to the aquarium to see the 'monster'. For several days the tiger shark slowly cruised around its new home, happily eating all the fish thrown to it. Then, on 25 April, having not taken food during the morning and early afternoon the shark, according to observers, went 'crazy' and began bumping into the aquarium walls and turning in circles. After twenty minutes of this behaviour the shark suddenly startled onlookers by regurgitating a human arm. The shocked aquarium owners immediately called the police and Dr Victor Coppleson was asked to examine the arm in the Sydney morgue. According to police, the arm was that of a very muscular man. On the forearm was a slightly faded tattoo of two boxers shaping up to each other.

Coppleson reported that in his opinion the arm had not been bitten from the body by a shark because it was so cleanly separated at the shoulder joint. He also stressed that a surgeon had not performed the task because the usual skin flaps a doctor would leave were not present. On learning this the police decided to publicise the incident in the hope of solving the mystery. They issued a photograph and description of the tattoo and it wasn't long before a man came forward to identify the arm as that of his brother, 45-year-old James Smith.

Within a short time police had arrested Patrick Brady for murder and questioned another man, Reginald Holmes. Several days after being questioned Holmes was found dead in his car near the Sydney Harbour Bridge. He had a bullet in his head. Smith had last been seen alive on 8 April at 6pm in a Cronulla hotel, and police decided that James Smith, Patrick Brady and Reginald Holmes had been involved in standover tactics, murder threats, forgery and conspiracy to defraud an insurance company. A series of murder trials followed, with the Crown alleging that Brady and Holmes had murdered Smith on the night he had last been seen alive. They believed that Smith's body had been cut up, stuffed into a tin trunk and dumped in the ocean. As the arm could not be forced into the trunk, the men decided to tie it to a rope attached to a heavy weight and sink it to the sea bottom beside the trunk. The police conjectured that the shark must have seized the arm sometime between the night of 8 April and 17 April, when it was caught off Coogee. Surprisingly, the arm remained intact for another eight days in the shark's stomach until it was dramatically disgorged on 25 April.

Three sensational trials later, John Brady was finally acquitted through lack of evidence; he lived a free man until his death in 1965. As to the tiger shark, it became very sick a couple of days after disgorging the arm and the aquarium owners had to kill it. When police performed an autopsy they found that the tiger shark's stomach contained a portion of the other shark and some fish bones but no further human remains.

much more research needs to be undertaken if biologists are to understand the reasons for shark attacks.

KINDS OF ATTACK

Research into recorded attacks in Australian waters indicates that shark aggression generally falls into seven categories. Writing in 1963, Gilbert Whitley reported some 390 cases of sharks attacking human beings, horses, dogs, boats and surf skis. Of these, about 118 people were killed; many others were badly wounded while some received only minor injuries.

Whitley recorded 184 cases of attacks on swimmers, including surfers, spearfishermen and people falling from boats and piers. There were another 83 cases of attacks on Aborigines, Torres Strait Islanders and Malayan or Japanese pearl

divers. In 21 instances shipwrecked or drowned people had been attacked – including those cases where human remains were found in sharks although no attack had been witnessed. Another 21 cases were doubtful and included missing persons assumed to have been taken by sharks but possibly murdered. There were 31 'accidental' attacks on people netting or cleaning fish, handling live sharks or emptying nets and traps. In 46 cases sharks attacked boats, rafts, canoes, floats or surf skis. There were only seven recorded attacks on horses and dogs but many more were undoubtedly unreported.

Pearl divers along the Great Barrier Reef figured significantly in Whitley's list, particularly native 'swim divers' who worked without specialised diving equipment or helmets. Iona Asai was one such diver who had a remarkable

▲ Meshing is regarded as the most effective practicable method of protecting large numbers of swimmers from sharks, but it is so expensive to establish and maintain that only restricted areas may be netted. In many places, such as Botany Bay south of Sydney, authorities can do no more than warn swimmers of potential danger.

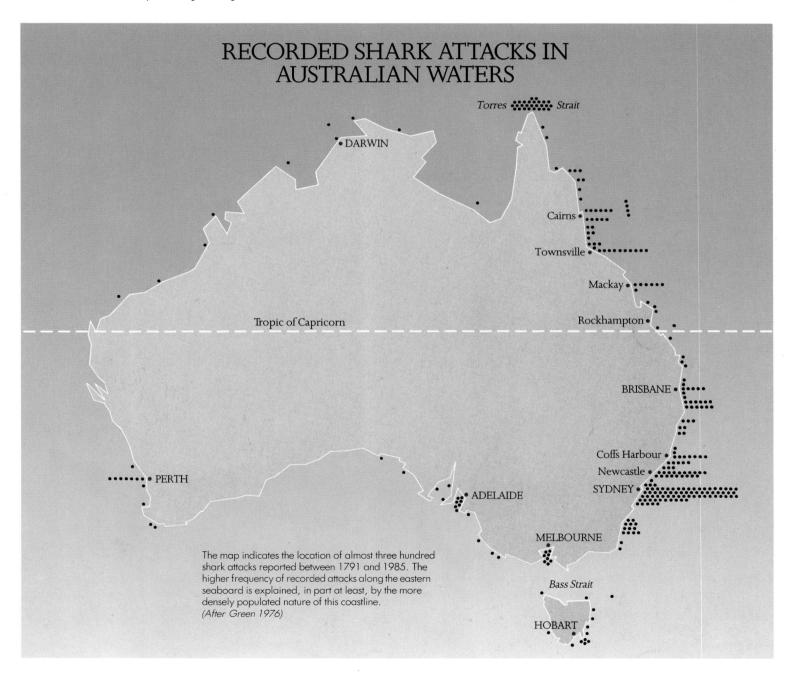

RECORDED SHARK ATTACKS IN AUSTRALIAN WATERS

The map indicates the location of almost three hundred shark attacks reported between 1791 and 1985. The higher frequency of recorded attacks along the eastern seaboard is explained, in part at least, by the more densely populated nature of this coastline.
(After Green 1976)

POTENTIALLY DANGEROUS SHARKS OF AUSTRALIAN WATERS

GREAT WHITE SHARK
Carcharodon carcharias

Primarily a coastal and offshore species of continental and insular shelves, the great white grows to about 6 metres and is regarded as second only to the orca, or killer whale, as a marine predator. It has been identified in attacks on humans off California, southern Australia, New Zealand and South Africa. California has the highest recorded rate of attacks, with an average of 1.3 per year from 1950 to 1982. Despite its reputation, many cases have been reported of great whites inspecting divers without attacking.

TIGER SHARK
Galeocerdo cuvier

Regarded as the most dangerous shark in tropical waters, the tiger shares with the great white and bull sharks membership of the 'unholy trinity' of proven maneaters. It grows to about 6 metres and is responsible for repeated attacks on swimmers, divers and boats. The tiger shark is one of the very few species that actually consumes human prey – though it also has a reputation as a 'garbage can with fins' and will eat bony fishes, other sharks (including tiger sharks), rays, turtles, seabirds, sea snakes, carrion and garbage from ships.

COPPER SHARK
OR BRONZE WHALER
Carcharhinus brachyurus

Common in warm temperate waters from Japan and the Mediterranean to New Zealand and Argentina, the copper shark (known as the bronze whaler in Australia and as the narrowtooth shark in the United States) occurs from the surfline to depths of at least 100 metres. This species has been implicated in a number of attacks on surfers and bathers, but may have been blamed for attacks by the more aggressive bull or Zambezi shark (*C. leucas*), which shares a similar distribution. The copper shark is a slender species that grows to a maximum of about 2.3 metres.

BLUE SHARK
Prionace glauca

Like the copper and tiger sharks, the blue shark belongs to the family Carcharhinidae, which includes most of those species known to attack humans. It is found around the world in temperate and tropical waters and grows to at least 3.8 metres. The blue shark is a fast and aggressive predator of the open oceans and has attacked people and boats. Victims of plane crashes and ship sinkings are especially in danger of attack from blue sharks, if only from injury caused by 'test-feeding'.

BULL OR ZAMBEZI SHARK
Carcharhinus leucas

Because it is less physically impressive than great white or tiger sharks, the bull shark's reputation as a danger to humans has been underemphasised. However, it is abundant in tropical and subtropical seas, estuaries and even freshwater rivers (specimens have been collected 3700 kilometres from the sea in the Peruvian Amazon). It frequents shallow water near beaches, and is a versatile and opportunistic feeder that will attack without provocation. The bull shark is a stout to heavy-bodied species that grows to 3.4 metres in length, and is now known to be the culprit in attacks formerly blamed on the elusive Ganges shark (*Glyphis gangeticus*).

SHORTFIN MAKO
Isurus oxyrinchus

A common, active offshore and pelagic species of temperate and tropical waters around the world, the shortfin mako is famed as the game fish that can leap several metres in a single bound above the water and is capable of high-speed dashes when hooked or in pursuit of prey. The shortfin mako grows to around four metres in length and has been identified in attacks on boats; game fishermen who find themselves sharing a boat with an aroused mako have been known to jump into the water to avoid its anger! The mako's power, aggressiveness and wickedly sharp teeth, in combination with speed so great that defensive weapons may be ineffective, make it a real danger to divers.

HAMMERHEAD SHARKS
Sphyrna spp.

The unique lateral wings that give these warm temperate and tropical sharks their name may provide increased manoeuvrability and sensory capacities. Of the nine species of hammerheads, only the scalloped hammerhead (*S. lewini*), great hammerhead (*S. mokarran*) and smooth hammerhead (*S. zygaena*) are regarded as dangerous to humans mainly due to their size – respectively 4.2 metres, 6.1 metres and 4 metres. However, most provoked or unprovoked attacks have been attributed only to 'hammerheads' and none of these species is aggressive; indeed, while all will approach divers and occasionally steal speared fish from them, they have a reputation for timidity that belies their size, power and effective dentition.

► Despite appearances, the grey nurse is not an aggressive shark and will not attack humans unless provoked.

Ron & Valerie Taylor

encounter with a shark. A Torres Strait Islander, Asai was diving from a lugger into just four metres of water when he was attacked by a tiger shark. He told of the attack in his own words:

On the year 1937, day Friday just about 11 o'clock in the morning, the third time I dive and walked in the bottom. I went behind a little high place. The shark was on the other side. I never saw him and he never saw me. I saw a stone like a pearl shell on the north side and when I turned I saw the shark six feet away from me. He opened his mouth. Already I have no chance of escape from him. Then he came and bite me on the head. He felt it was too strong so he swallow my head and put his teeth

round my neck. Then he bite me.

When I felt his teeth go into my flesh I put my hands round his head and squeeze his eyes until he let go me and I make for the boat. The captain pulled me into the boat and I fainted. They got some medicines from Jervis Island school teacher.

WATER TEMPERATURE AND SHARK ATTACK

One popular misconception is that shark attacks are directly linked to water temperature. Because most Australian attacks have been recorded in summer when the sea is at its warmest, some researchers claim that shark aggression toward humans runs on a set timetable: north of the Tropic

On 15 October 1984 a Tasmanian abalone diver reported that he was pinned to the ocean floor for more than an hour as a 6-metre white shark tried to prise him out of a crevice. Two months earlier, on 13 August, two Perth fishermen reported an attack on their fishing boat by a 'monster' 7-metre white shark. Their evidence was the smashed boat and the many shark teeth still embedded in the woodwork. No doubt, with more than 300 000 Australians already qualified as scuba divers and many thousands more snorkelling all year round, the number of shark attacks will increase.

Ron & Valerie Taylor

▲ The blue shark is an efficient open-ocean predator and has been implicated in attacks on humans.

SHARK ATTACK AND FEEDING

According to Coppleson and other shark experts, one of the most common misconceptions about sharks is that they attack people in order to eat them. Analysis of 1000 recent shark attacks throughout the world shows that well over 50 per cent of these attacks had no direct relationship with feeding. More than 75 per cent of victims were struck only once or twice and less than 30 per cent of attacks were fatal. In fact, a study of wound patterns made on shark attack survivors supports biologists' claims that these sharks were not trying to remove large portions of flesh from their victims. The sharks were not attacking for food because, despite large amounts of blood and tissue in the water, they rarely pressed home their attack after the initial strike.

SHARKS' THREAT BEHAVIOUR

Work by American researchers on reef sharks' reactions to divers has added considerably to our knowledge on shark attack. Reef sharks, notably the grey reef shark, *Carcharhinus amblyrhynchos*, compete with each other as well as with other sharks for food and have developed a ritualised threat display. Marine biologists have found that

of Capricorn, all the months of the year are deemed dangerous; in southern Queensland the risky months are noted as November to May; for Newcastle, Sydney and Perth the danger period is from December to April; for Adelaide it is from December to March; Melbourne is most dangerous between January and March; for Bass Strait and Tasmania January is the problem month. Of course as the summer months are obviously the time when most people are in the water and therefore have more chance of being attacked by sharks, one wonders how reliable this timetable is. Even more serious doubts are raised by the fact that white sharks have often defied this attack pattern theory.

Ben Cropp

▶ There have been 250 shark attacks in Australian waters since 1901: a fraction of the number of humans killed by motor vehicles or by other people. While sharks will always elicit feelings of revulsion, they should be regarded in the same way as lions, tigers and bears: as dangerous, predatory but nonetheless magnificent animals.

many of the attacks made on divers by this particular species came about because the shark was cornered and had no means of escape. In every case of shark attack investigated, the shark performed its threat display before it attacked. The reef shark's threat display consists of an S-shaped swimming pattern followed by a figure of eight as it moves closer to the 'threatening' skindiver. As the shark swims, it twists and turns in an exaggerated fashion with its pectoral fins depressed, snout

raised, jaws slightly open and back arched. On its direct approach it appears rigid. It frequently breaks off the attack within a metre of contact and repeats the procedure until the offending diver leaves the water. Marine biologists believe this ritualised behaviour is connected with courtship displays and territorial defence.

Wide-ranging migratory sharks may have threat responses that are very different from those of the reef sharks. These sharks may be stimulated to attack after swimmers or divers make what the sharks consider to be aggressive incursions into their 'living space' as opposed to their geographical territory. While much more work needs to be carried out on this aspect of sharks' behaviour, the evidence suggests most shark attacks are aggressive threat reactions to people's presence in the water. The fact that the type of wounds found on victims are often similar to those sharks inflict on each other when they fight supports this explanation.

Another behaviour pattern that is often highly sensationalised is the frenzy some sharks display when, in the presence of food, they appear to lose all control and attack anything in their path. But while this behaviour is known to occur, especially among reef sharks, statistics show that it is not relevant to the majority of attacks that take place off Australia.

Attacks by great whites may be more directly

THE TRAGEDY OF MARCIA HATHAWAY

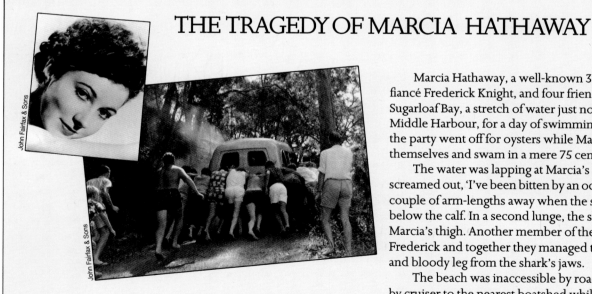

John Fairfax & Sons

John Fairfax & Sons

One of the most tragic shark attacks to occur in Sydney waters occurred on the Australia Day holiday of 1963. It was a humid, overcast day and ironically a headline in that morning's *Sydney Morning Herald* read 'Australia Day Surfers Warned of Sharks.'

Marcia Hathaway, a well-known 32-year-old actress, her fiancé Frederick Knight, and four friends came by boat to Sugarloaf Bay, a stretch of water just north of Balmoral Beach in Middle Harbour, for a day of swimming and picnicking. Two of the party went off for oysters while Marcia and Frederick cooled themselves and swam in a mere 75 centimetres of water.

The water was lapping at Marcia's hips when suddenly she screamed out, 'I've been bitten by an octopus!' Knight was only a couple of arm-lengths away when the shark seized her right leg below the calf. In a second lunge, the shark's teeth were fixed in Marcia's thigh. Another member of the party rushed to assist Frederick and together they managed to release the girl's torn and bloody leg from the shark's jaws.

The beach was inaccessible by road. Marcia was taken back by cruiser to the nearest boatshed while Frederick dived into the water and swam to the nearest house for help. An ambulance was waiting when Marcia's boat drew up. As it started the slippery climb from the water's edge, the tyres skidded and the clutch burnt out. Volunteers strained as they tried to push the ambulance up the hill. A second ambulance was called but Marcia Hathaway had suffered enormous blood loss and was dead on arrival at hospital, less than half an hour after the attack.

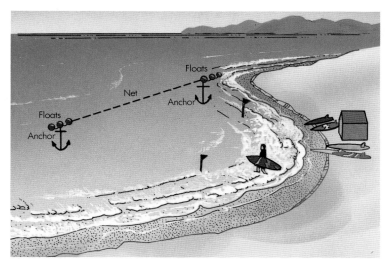

▲ How shark nets are positioned to protect a New South Wales surfing beach. In recent years up to 350 sharks have been caught per annum, the most common of which are hammerheads. A shark netting program has also been established in Queensland. *(After Coppleson 1976)*

▲ A shark net in place. Each end of the 150-metre net is secured by a 14-kilogram anchor and its position marked by glass floats, which also help to hold the net upright. The loosely hanging nets, about six metres deep, are set by trawler in the late afternoon and usually hauled in the next morning. The frequency of meshing for each beach is determined by a quota system and therefore not all beaches in the program are protected at any one time. *(After Coppleson 1976)*

Ben Cropp

▲ Meshing of Sydney beaches began in 1936, and in the period from October 1937 to February 1939, 1500 sharks (including 900 potential maneaters) were caught. Since then the number has continued to decline, reflecting a relatively steady decrease in the population of potentially dangerous sharks.

related to feeding than attacks by most other species. This is because it habitually preys on marine mammals. White sharks' behaviour is different from that of every other shark. Many fishermen report this shark's spine-chilling habit of quietly raising its head out of the water to investigate anything unusual. Marine biologists believe that this most unsharklike action results from the white shark's search for seals basking on the rocks along the shore. Victorian and South Australian fishermen operating around Phillip and Kangaroo islands claim to have seen white sharks lift their bodies clear of the water to seize a sleeping seal from the rocks.

COPING WITH SHARKS

Mesh netting of beaches is by far the most effective method of reducing shark attack on swimmers. Shark experts advise bathers that if they see a shark while they are in the water they should assume it to be dangerous and head straight for the beach or boat as quickly and quietly as possible. Kicking wildly and thrashing with the arms in a panic to escape is the worst thing a person can do. It only sends vibrations to the shark that suggest the person is a fish in trouble, and therefore easy prey. Probably the best method of stopping a shark once it has decided to attack is to put on a show of aggression and kick or pummel it when it rushes in. For divers separated from their boats it is best to retreat to the sea bottom and wait patiently for the shark to move on. Divers should avoid entering the water with white sharks, tigers, whalers, hammerheads and mako sharks.

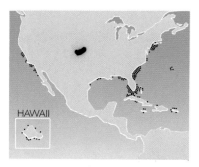

HAWAII

Attacks by UNIDENTIFIED SHARKS

SHARK ATTACK IN THE UNITED STATES

GUIDO DINGERKUS

Shark attacks in the United States can be divided into two categories: unprovoked attacks and provoked attacks. Every year in the whole of the United States there are fewer than twelve shark attacks and usually only one or two are fatal. In 1984–85 about 600 people were struck by lightning throughout the country. The risk of being attacked by a shark is, then, some fifty times lower than that of being struck by lightning, and is far smaller than the likelihood of being involved in a car or plane crash.

Unprovoked shark attacks are only occasionally due to feeding behaviour of sharks. Sharks are large, predatory animals. At least to the larger species, humans fall within the acceptable size limits of a food object. If a person swims into the feeding territory of a hungry shark, an attack may occur. The same would happen with any large predator, such as a lion or tiger. Sharks, however, do not actively seek out humans to feed upon as do maneating tigers, which seem to acquire a preference for the taste of human flesh.

WHERE SHARKS ATTACK

A study of shark attack records in the United States shows that most attacks are on bathers swimming in depths of between one and a half and three metres during the middle of the afternoon in summer. This reflects not so much where most sharks are as where the most bathers are! The more people who are in the water, the higher the chance that someone will swim into the feeding territory of a large shark. Also, people who are wounded or

▲ A shark swimming in shallow water inspires fear but represents far less danger than being struck by lightning. Almost all of the 350-odd species of sharks are harmless; even those considered dangerous will usually attack only when provoked.

bleeding or who are splashing about noisily in the water are more prone to shark attacks. Sharks, like wolves or lions, tend to feed on weak or wounded animals and these people are, therefore, the most likely to attract a shark. Similarly, divers with speared fish are carrying an attractive lure for sharks and are thus more prone than other divers to shark attacks.

In the United States the majority of attacks occur in southern California and Florida. As mentioned above this is due more to the fact that the warmer water in these areas attracts a greater number of bathers and divers than to a greater preponderance of potentially dangerous sharks. Indeed, feeding studies and observations on captive individuals of two potentially lethal species – sleeper sharks (*Somniosus* species) and sixgill sharks (*Hexanchus griseus*) – show them to be highly predatory and voracious sharks that feed on seals and large fishes and that could easily kill and eat humans. They are also quite common and will often feed very close to shore. However, probably because they inhabit very cold water, either far north or at great depth, unprovoked attack on a person by either of these species has never been recorded.

IDENTIFYING SHARKS THAT ATTACK

In many cases of shark attack the species of shark involved is never positively identified. Only if the shark is captured, or if pieces of the teeth are left in the victim, can identification be certain. In the absence of such evidence identification of the shark is dependent on descriptions given by the victims or witnesses; and these are usually vague, or at least lack the amount of detail that would allow the species to be identified. Very often the shark is labelled as a 'sand shark' – a catch-all term applied to any shark about two metres that is in shallow water and is a darkish colour. The term 'sand shark' has been applied to many small requiem, or carcharhinid, shark species, including smooth dogfish sharks (species of the genus *Mustelus*) and the sand tiger shark (*Eugomphodus taurus*). The sand tiger shark is frequently found in shallow

Marty Snyderman

Jeff Rotman

water, is a dark brown colour, and reaches a maximum size of about three metres. Its long, thin teeth, which stick out of its mouth and give it a 'vicious' look, may explain its popularity in aquariums. However, this appearance is misleading as the sand tiger is usually quite docile and uses its long, thin teeth to catch small fishes that it eats whole. As the teeth are not designed for biting pieces out of larger prey, it rarely attacks larger animals. Indeed in United States waters there has never been a reported case of a sand tiger making an unprovoked attack on a human.

DANGEROUS SPECIES

Let us now examine some of the species of sharks definitely known to be involved in unprovoked attacks on humans, as well as species that are also suspected of being involved.

One of the most dangerous sharks, and in tropical waters unquestionably the most dangerous, is the tiger shark (*Galeocerdo cuvier*). It commonly reaches four to five and a half metres in length and there have been many reports of individuals above six metres. It is often nicknamed the 'garbage can shark' because it seems in part to be a general scavenger, swallowing almost anything it encounters in the water. There are many

accounts of indigestible items – including car licence plates, paint cans, rolls of tar paper and shoes – being found in tiger sharks' stomachs. However, the presence of food items such as whole fish (including smaller sharks), sea lions, spiny lobsters, sea birds and sea turtles in the stomachs of other tiger sharks, clearly shows that as well as a scavenger it also is a formidable predator. In the stomachs of approximately three-quarters of the tiger sharks caught off the coasts of New Jersey and Long Island, parts of sea turtles have been found. A confirmed maneater, it is probably responsible for more human deaths than are actually attributed to it. The tiger shark is fairly common along the southern coasts of the United States and it is also probably the largest species of shark that regularly comes to feed in quite shallow water. In summer it will come as far north along the Atlantic coast as Massachusetts. Off Bimini, in the Bahamas, the author has caught six of these sharks, ranging in length from four to five metres, in only one or two metres of water. It is, therefore, a species that poses a serious threat to bathers in shallow, warm waters. Possessing uniquely shaped jagged teeth, it usually leaves distinctive curved, irregular and readily identifiable wounds on its victims.

▲ The shock and surprise of a shark attack often mean that the animal responsible is never positively identified. The sand tiger (*Eugomphodus taurus*) has frequently been blamed for attacks in the United States and Australia. Although its ragged, projecting teeth fit the image of a vicious shark, there has never been a verified attack by a sand tiger on a human being.

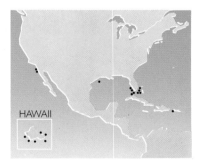

Attacks by TIGER SHARKS, *Galeocerdo cuvier*

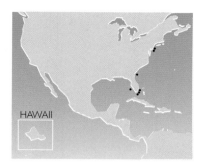

Attacks by BULL SHARKS,
Carcharhinus leucas

Possible attacks by HAMMERHEAD SHARKS,
Sphyrna spp.

The bull shark, *Carcharhinus leucas*, is probably the next most dangerous shark in warm waters. Averaging two and a half to almost four metres in length, it is said to reach five metres. Similar to the tiger shark in behaviour, it is known to be a scavenger as well as a very active predator. Coming into shallow water, it will feed on almost anything it encounters, swallowing smaller prey whole and using its razor-sharp teeth to bite circular chunks out of larger prey. It is probably the only species to enter pure fresh water, and has been caught as far as 3200 kilometres upstream in the Amazon River. It is especially aggressive in fresh water, where apparently it comes mainly to feed. In Lake Nicaragua many human deaths have been caused by this shark.

All of these factors probably mean that the bull shark comes into close association with humans quite frequently. A confirmed maneater like the tiger shark, it too has probably caused many more human deaths than have definitely been attributed to it. Usually dusky brown, grey, or black in colour, it fits perfectly the 'sand shark' description given by many attack victims and witnesses.

Its triangular, finely serrated teeth can easily be misidentified as belonging to a great white, which also has triangular teeth, though with much coarser serrations. The great white shark has triangular teeth in both the upper and the lower jaws, whereas only the upper teeth are triangular in the bull shark (the lower teeth are dagger-like). It was probably because of its teeth that a killer shark off the New Jersey coast in 1916 was identified as a great white. This shark, over two and a half metres long, killed several people and attacked others over a period of about one week. However most of

these attacks occurred in rivers or creeks, some several kilometres upstream from the ocean. Great whites never enter brackish or fresh water, and usually prefer to be further offshore in deep water. The evidence tends to indicate that this shark was a bull shark, and not a great white.

Hammerhead sharks are relatively easy to identify due to the distinct broad heads from which they derive their name. Several species are fairly common around the United States: the scalloped hammerhead shark (*Sphyrna lewini*), the smooth hammerhead shark (*S. zygaena*) and the great hammerhead shark (*S. mokarran*). The great hammerhead commonly reaches between four and four and a half metres in length, and can grow to over five metres. Living mainly in deeper water, these species will come into shallow water to feed. They seem to feed mostly on fishes, including stingrays and other sharks.

Another species of hammerhead, the bonnethead shark (*Sphyrna tiburo*) is a much smaller species that rarely exceeds one and a half metres in length. It is quite common on shallow flats, such as in the Florida Keys, where it feeds upon the schools of fishes there. Probably because of its small size and fish feeding habits, it has never been implicated in an unprovoked attack upon humans.

The three larger species of hammerheads have been implicated in unprovoked attacks on humans but the reliability and accuracy of the evidence supporting such implications has been questioned by some scientists.

The lemon shark (*Negaprion brevirostris*) receives its name from the yellowish colour on its back and sides. Quite common in tropical waters, it

▶ Possibly the most dangerous shark in the world — in tropical waters, at least — the tiger shark (*Galeocerdo cuvier*) has a justified reputation as a maneater. It is an indiscriminate feeder, using its uniquely shaped, jagged teeth to tear irregular chunks of flesh from almost anything it encounters.

Ron & Valerie Taylor

usually reaches two and a half to three metres in length and can exceed three and a half metres. It usually lives in shallow water and often enters brackish water. Feeding mainly upon fishes, it also eats stingrays and other sharks. Indeed the author has caught several lemon sharks – in the Florida Keys and off Bimini, in the Bahamas – with stingray spines embedded in their jaws.

In aquariums lemon sharks are known to become quite aggressive toward divers, and at least at Marineland of Florida and the New England Aquarium have had to be removed from the tanks because of this aggressiveness. With this propensity for aggression and the fact that they feed in quite shallow water (often so shallow that their dorsal fins stick up out of the water) it seems likely that they would come into frequent contact with bathers and hence be responsible for many attacks, especially in Florida waters where both they and bathers are very common. However, less than ten documented unprovoked attacks have been attributed to this species. Perhaps their aggressiveness in captivity is artificial, and in the wild they prefer to avoid larger animals and only pursue smaller animals (mainly fishes) as prey.

The dusky shark (*Carcharhinus obscurus*) receives its name from its dusky grey to black colouration. Averaging two and a half to three metres in length, individuals have been reported to exceed four metres. Feeding mainly on fishes, it usually lives in deeper water but is known to come occasionally into shallow water to feed. Being a typical requiem shark of the genus *Carcharhinus*, many of whose species look very similar, it is difficult to positively identify as the perpetrator of an attack unless the shark is caught or its teeth remain in the victim. However, there are at least two cases where the dusky shark was positively identified as the attacking species. Because of its size, it must definitely be classed as a dangerous species. But since it is usually found in deeper water and seems to feed primarily on smaller fishes, it is probably involved in only a very small percentage of attacks upon humans.

There are several other species of requiem sharks that, like the dusky shark, may be involved in attacks upon humans. These are: the sandbar shark (*Carcharhinus plumbeus*), the blacktip shark (*C. limbatus*), the Caribbean reef shark (*C. perezi*), and the spinner shark (*C. brevipinna*). All these species

▲ The great hammerhead (*Sphyrna mokarran*) like its relatives the scalloped and smooth hammerheads, has been implicated in unprovoked attacks on humans. Most attacks seem to have occurred in very shallow water, when hammerheads (which are usually deepwater sharks) are hunting for food.

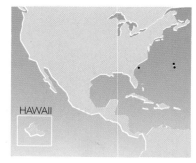

Attacks by DUSKY SHARKS, *Carcharhinus obscurus*

reach from two to two and a half metres, with individuals reported up to three metres. Primarily fish eaters living in deeper water, they are all known to come into shallower water to feed. They have all been implicated in unprovoked attacks on humans, though they have not been positively identified as perpetrators. Because these species are so similar, they could only be positively identified by catching the individual, or by teeth left in the victim. As all of them are dark in colour they could all fit the 'sand shark' description so often applied to attacking sharks. Although large enough to pose a danger, these species are still relatively small in size and come only occasionally into shallow water in order to feed, primarily on smaller fishes. If they are involved at all, it is probably in only a very small fraction of unprovoked shark attacks.

The blue shark (*Prionace glauca*) and the oceanic whitetip shark (*Carcharhinus longimanus*) are both tropical pelagic species with wide distributions. They rarely come into shallow water, and prefer water 30 metres or more in depth. Both reach between two and a half and three metres in length, and there have been reports of individuals growing to more than four metres. Primarily fish-eating species, they are also known to feed on marine mammals, sea turtles and sea birds. The blue shark has aroused the hatred of whalers because of its habit of descending, often in dozens, on the bleeding carcasses of harpooned whales, sometimes leaving very little for the whalers. Divers have reported both species as being very aggressive in the open water, and their sizes make both of them definitely dangerous to humans. Because they live far out to sea, they do not pose a threat to shore bathers. However, open water swimmers and divers in deep water are susceptible to attacks by these species, though there have been few reports of such attacks – a possible reflection on the scarcity of swimmers and divers in such deep water. The greatest threat posed by these sharks is to victims of plane crashes and boating mishaps who find themselves in the open ocean. With wounded and bleeding people in the water, these sharks may rapidly be attracted. Under these conditions there have been several cases of people being attacked and killed by either blue or oceanic whitetip sharks.

THE GREAT WHITE

In temperate waters, the most dangerous species of shark is unquestionably the great white shark, *Carcharodon carcharias*. Averaging between three and a half and five and a half metres, it may reach six metres in length. Reported lengths of up to eleven metres have so far been shown to be exaggerations or misidentifications of basking sharks. This shark's propensity to attack and kill humans is well known, and indeed in many areas it is known by the local names of 'maneater' and 'white death'. Preferring

◄ ▲ At the site of a plane or ship disaster, blue sharks stimulated by blood in the water will sometimes attack without hesitation, and spearfishing divers have had to defend themselves from excited and curious sharks. Although blue sharks are not usually aggressive they are not particularly timid and divers are advised to treat them with great caution.

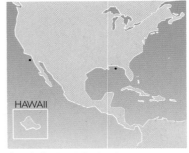

Attacks by BLUE SHARKS, *Prionace glauca*

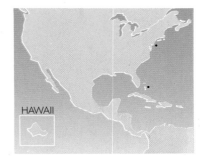

Possible attacks by SANDBAR SHARKS, *Carcharhinus plumbeus*

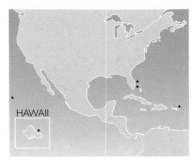

Attacks by OCEANIC WHITETIP SHARKS, *Carcharhinus longimanus*

127

▲ Tiger sharks are justifiably feared predators of tropical waters. A tiger shark such as this is large enough to kill and consume a human being and may only be safely approached when it is drugged or, preferably, dead.

Attacks by GREAT WHITE SHARKS, *Carcharodon carcharias*

► Although the attack rate in United States waters (primarily northern central California) by great white sharks remains steady at around 1.3 attacks per year, the number of divers meeting great whites underwater is increasing. More and more divers are reporting 'inspections' by great whites, which then depart without attacking.

cooler water, it is found in United States waters from California to Alaska along the Pacific coast and from New Jersey to Maine along the Atlantic coast. Occasionally during winter it has been recorded in more southern localities, such as Florida.

Recent studies show that the great white feeds primarily on marine mammals, though it will also feed on fishes, sea turtles and sea birds. Dr John McCosker of Steinhart Aquarium believes that when great whites attack swimmers, divers, and surfboarders, they are really mistaking them for marine mammals. Indeed a human in the water, with arms and legs sticking out, does look from beneath like a seal, porpoise or small whale.

McCosker also hypothesises that the feeding strategy of the great white is to make an initial attack on its prey, then retreat and wait for the prey to die from blood loss, thus avoiding any danger to itself, before coming back to feed.

Quite often the victims of attacks by great whites will die as a result of blood loss, organ damage or shock, but the fact remains that great whites rarely eat the humans they attack. Perhaps they should better be nicknamed 'manbiters' rather than 'maneaters'.

Great whites seem to prefer water deeper than 30 metres. Along the Atlantic coast where the

bottom drops off very slowly and one needs to go out several kilometres before reaching the 30 metre depth, they are found far offshore. Along the Pacific coast of the United States, however, the bottom drops off very rapidly and so great whites can be seen here very close to shore. It is not surprising, then, that very few great white attacks occur along the Atlantic coast, whereas an average of three to four attacks on swimmers, divers, and surfboarders occur every year along the Pacific coast. If indeed these attacks are occurring because great whites mistake humans for sea mammals, many of them could probably be prevented if we could devise a way to look less like marine mammals from underwater. At present, however, the great white definitely poses the greatest shark danger to humans in temperate waters; overall, the danger it presents is rivalled, or perhaps surpassed, only by the tiger shark in tropical waters.

OTHER SPECIES FOUND IN TEMPERATE WATERS

There are several species of temperate water sharks which, as they grow to three metres in length, are large enough to be dangerous to humans. However they are almost exclusively fish eaters that live in deep water and rarely come close to shore. These

are the mako shark (*Isurus oxyrinchus*), porbeagle shark (*Lamna nasus*), thresher sharks (*Alopias* species) and the salmon shark (*Lamna ditropis*). To date there have been no documented unprovoked attacks on humans by these species, but attacks on open-water or deepwater divers and plane or boat accident victims in temperate waters are very possible.

Along the coasts of the United States there are many smaller species of sharks, less than two metres in length, that have never been implicated in unprovoked attacks upon humans. These are either fish eaters or bottom feeders that feed upon crustaceans and molluscs. Although they are common in shallow waters, they do not pose a threat because of their preference for small food items and their small size. Indeed they would tend to consider a larger animal, such as a human, as a possible predator and hence to flee it rather than attack it. Species in this group would include the smooth dogfish sharks (species of the genus *Mustelus*), angelsharks (*Squatina* species), the blacknose shark (*Carcharhinus acronotus*), sharpnose sharks (*Rhizoprionodon* species), the horn shark (*Heterodontus francisci*), the swell shark (*Cephaloscyllium ventriosum*) and the leopard shark (*Triakis semifasciata*).

PROVOKED SHARK ATTACK

Any animal will defend itself when it feels threatened. The size and strength of many sharks make them among the most dangerous of animals when provoked. Many more people are bitten in provoked than in unprovoked shark attacks.

By far the largest numbers of provoked shark attacks happen to people who are catching sharks. In part because of their primitive nervous systems, sharks are very difficult to kill. It is not unusual for fishermen who have clubbed a shark over the head, or shot numerous bullets into its body to have their 'dead' shark suddenly 'come back to life', thrashing about wildly and viciously snapping its jaws. This has sometimes resulted in the loss of an arm or leg. The author has known cases where large sharks were still actively swimming around, showing no signs of drowsiness, half an hour after being injected with an anesthetic dose large enough to kill three or four adult humans of the same total weight. All the species discussed above, including those usually considered harmless, have been known to bite humans while they were being caught.

The next largest group of provoked shark attacks involves divers. Some divers, seeing a shark resting on the bottom, decide it would be fun to wrestle or ride it. Grabbing the shark either by the fins or the tail, many are surprised when the enraged shark quickly overpowers and bites them, sometimes fatally. Even the nurse shark (*Ginglymostoma cirratum*), usually a docile, bottom dweller that feeds on crustaceans and

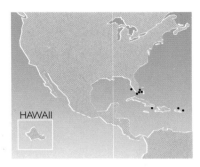

Attacks on divers by NURSE SHARKS, *Ginglymostoma cirratum* (all provoked)

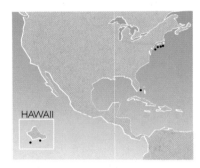

Attacks on FISHERMEN

◄ The nurse shark (*Ginglymostoma cirratum*) like the sand tiger, spends a great deal of time resting on the sea floor. Generally regarded as a lazy and unaggressive species, it may retaliate if harassed. Though its teeth are small, its powerful jaws can grip so tightly that assistance may be necessary to break its hold on an arm or leg.

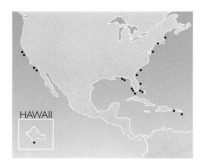

Attacks on DIVERS CARRYING FISH

Attacks at PLANE or BOAT CRASHES, *species unknown*

▶ Found in tropical and warm temperate seas round the globe, the whale shark (*Rhiniodon typus*) is, at nearly fourteen metres, the world's largest fish. It is a filter feeder, with gill rakers modified to strain out plankton and krill, and a favourite with underwater photographers. It will often approach divers to examine them.

molluscs, will viciously attack a human if it is harassed. For this type of feeding a nurse shark does not have long, thin teeth; it has low, broad, molar-like teeth with which it crushes and chews its prey. When it attacks a diver in response to provocation, it does not bite off a chunk of flesh but rather grabs and tenaciously holds on to and shakes its victim. Often the jaws have to be cut open because the shark will not let go. There have been cases where harassing skin divers have drowned because nurse sharks have held them on the bottom and not allowed them to surface for air.

Basking sharks (*Cetorhinus maximus*) and whale sharks (*Rhincodon typus*), both of which average over nine metres in length and can grow to twelve and eighteen metres respectively, are favourites for divers to hitch rides on. Being filter feeders and having very minute teeth, they are very docile and do not seem to mind being ridden. However even these sharks can be dangerous to ride. All sharks have dermal denticles which cover and protect their skin; if the diver is not wearing proper protection (gloves, wetsuit, etc) these denticles can cause severe lacerations. Again, an accidental blow from a fin or the tail of one of these massive animals carries enough power to stun or kill a diver.

Divers often try to handfeed sharks in the wild. If due caution is not exercised, disaster can result; divers have lost fingers and hands while handfeeding blue sharks, lemon sharks, bull sharks and others. If a lot of food is in the water and many sharks are attracted, a feeding frenzy may occur. Feeding frenzies have cost divers arms, legs, and even their lives.

The most dangerous activity that divers engage in is to spear sharks underwater. Wounded and enraged sharks will turn and attack their aggressors, often with dire results. Divers, too, who carry speared fish are inviting sharks to attack. Excited by the smell of blood and other body fluids from the speared fish, a shark will follow the scent and will attack the first object it encounters. A diver who is carrying speared fish should have them on a long line that trails behind. In this way a shark will encounter the fish before it comes upon the diver.

The least common types of provoked shark attack occurs when a bather steps on a shark. Many of the smaller species, such as angelsharks, swell sharks, horn sharks, leopard sharks and smooth dogfish, will spend time sitting on the bottom. Some even camouflage into the bottom and wait for prey to come swimming by. If a bather or wader inadvertently steps on one of these sharks a bite on the foot or leg may result. As the sharks are small the wounds they inflict are usually only superficial cuts. Bathers can avoid such bites by sliding their feet along the bottom rather than taking regular steps. In this way sharks sitting on the bottom will be 'stirred up' and will most likely swim away.

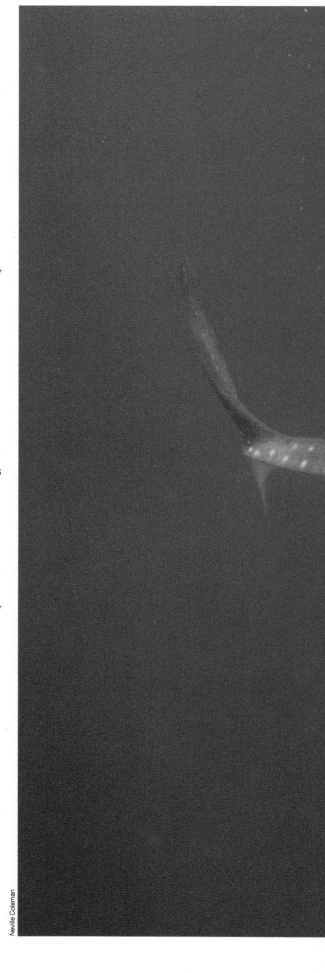

Neville Coleman

SHARK ATTACK IN SOUTH AFRICA

LEONARD J.V. COMPAGNO

The South African coastline, from the mouth of the Orange River in the eastern South Atlantic to the Mozambique border in the southwestern Indian Ocean, stretches for only 2954 kilometres, yet includes in or adjacent to its boundaries approximately 100 species of sharks. All eight of the major groups or orders of sharks occur here, and most of the families. There is every likelihood that several additional species will be found in South African waters, especially from northeastern incursions of tropical species and discoveries of deepwater and oceanic species.

The South African shark fauna is very diverse, and includes oceanic, continental shelf and continental slope species, wide-ranging circumtropical and circumtemperate sharks, local endemic species found nowhere else in the world, cold temperate sharks, warm temperate sharks, and tropical–subtropical sharks. The interaction of two great current systems on the trapezoidal landmass of South Africa constrains and strongly influences many of these sharks and makes for a great variety of habitats compressed into a coastline which, when compared with that of Australia or the United States, is relatively short. The cold Benguela current sweeps the west coast of South Africa and supports a coldwater shark and bony fish fauna roughly similar to that of northern California. The warm Agulhas current flows along the east coast of South Africa, warming the beaches of Natal, Transkei, and the eastern Cape and bringing with it many tropical Indo-west Pacific sharks and other fishes. These species extend their range for varying distances south, depending on their temperature tolerances and the fluctuations in warm-water masses. One warm-water species, the bull or Zambezi, shark (*Carcharhinus leucas*), readily penetrates into fresh water and highly saline bays in the area.

▼ South Africa's many swimming and surfing beaches present an idyllic picture-postcard scene. While it would hardly be true to say that danger and death lurk beneath the waves, South Africa shares with Australia an unenviable record for shark attack, though vigorous anti-shark measures have greatly reduced the risks to swimmers.

R. Udeist

Al Giddings/Ocean Images

SPECIES INVOLVED

Slightly less than a quarter of the shark species in South African waters are large or powerful enough to be considered dangerous. Potentially dangerous sharks are listed in the accompanying table. They include sharks that occur in waters readily accessible to people, but not the large deepwater sharks of the continental slopes that live beyond the range of normal human activities. Omitted also are the giant filter feeders, the whale (*Rhincodon typus*) and basking sharks (*Cetorhinus maximus*), and the three species of thresher sharks (*Alopias* spp.), which are normally harmless unless captured or harassed.

As with shark attacks worldwide, very few of the known shark attacks in South African waters can be attributed to particular species. This is because of the difficulty of identifying the attacker in most cases, and from the formerly confused state

of classification of the requiem shark family (Carcharhinidae), which contains most of the dangerous and potentially dangerous species. Of the species listed, five or so have actually been indicted in attacks that have resulted in human injury or death: spotted raggedtooth, great white shark, Zambezi (or bull) shark, oceanic whitetip shark, and tiger shark. Of these, the spotted raggedtooth is considered only minimally dangerous because of its sluggishness and because it is primarily a fisheater; attacks on people attributed to it usually result in little injury and are more likely to be the result of threat, mistaken identity, or accidental provocation than an attempt to feed on people.

The remaining four species are among the most dangerous living sharks. The Zambezi and great white sharks are the species most frequently indicted in South African attacks on swimmers and

▲ Despite their size, terrifying image and undoubted capacity to take any prey with ease, great white sharks tend to attack in a very inhibited fashion. It may be that they are merely 'taste-testing' swimmers, wetsuited divers or surfboard riders who look from below like seals — animals high on the list of the great white's favoured prey.

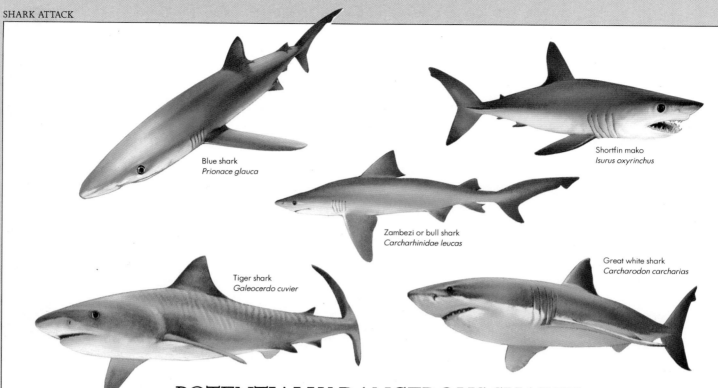

Blue shark
Prionace glauca

Shortfin mako
Isurus oxyrinchus

Zambezi or bull shark
Carcharhinidae leucas

Great white shark
Carcharodon carcharias

Tiger shark
Galeocerdo cuvier

POTENTIALLY DANGEROUS SHARKS IN SOUTH AFRICAN WATERS

TYPE	FAMILY	SCIENTIFIC NAME	COMMON NAME
sixgill and sevengill sharks	Hexanchidae	*Notorhynchus cepedianus*	spotted sevengill shark
nurse sharks	Ginglymostomatidae	*Nebrius ferrugineus*	giant sleepy shark
raggedtooth sharks	Odontaspididae	*Eugomphodus taurus*	spotted raggedtooth
mackerel sharks	Lamnidae	*Carcharodon carcharias*	great white shark
		Isurus oxyrinchus	shortfin mako
weasel sharks	Hemipristidae	*Hemipristis elongatus*	snaggletooth shark
requiem sharks	Carcharhinidae	*Carcharhinus albimarginatus*	silvertip shark
		C. amboiensis	Java shark
		C. brachyurus	copper shark or bronze whaler
		C. brevipinna	spinner shark
		C. leucas	Zambezi or bull shark
		C. limbatus	blacktip shark
		C. longimanus	oceanic whitetip shark
		C. obscurus	dusky shark
		C. wheeleri	blacktail reef shark
		Galeocerdo cuvier	tiger shark
		Negaprion acutidens	sharptooth lemon shark
		Prionace glauca	blue shark
		Triaenodon obesus	whitetip reef shark
hammerhead sharks	Sphyrnidae	*Sphyrna lewini*	scalloped or bronze hammerhead
		S. mokarran	great hammerhead
		S. zygaena	smooth or black hammerhead

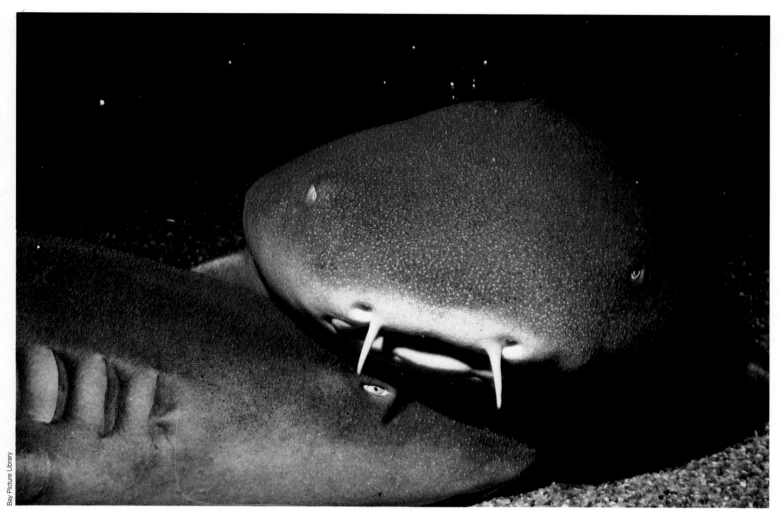

Bay Picture Library

▲ In South Africa, as in other countries, positive identification of sharks responsible for attacks on humans is rare. There may be an element of embarrassment in admitting that relatively harmless animals such as these nurse or giant sleepy sharks (*Nebrius ferrugineus*) were goaded into an attack after harassment by foolhardy divers.

divers. The oceanic whitetip shark does not visit bathing beaches and is not a problem except for offshore divers; however, it can pose a dramatic threat to people in the water after air-sea disasters far offshore, and was probably responsible for many fatalities after the troopship *Nova Scotia* was torpedoed off Natal in 1942. One or two (possibly more) attacks in South African waters can probably be attributed to the tiger shark. This is the least discriminating of living sharks, and is not averse to swallowing unusual items. Some writers rate it the most dangerous tropical shark.

There is documented evidence for several attacks on swimmers, divers and bathers by both Zambezi and great white sharks, validated by tooth fragments in wounds on the victims. At least some writers have thought the Zambezi shark the most dangerous species in the warm waters of Natal, and responsible for many attacks off bathing beaches there. In terms of relative abundance and habitat the Zambezi shark is, or was, more likely to come in contact with humans than the tiger and great white sharks, which also occur in the warm inshore waters of Natal. Although smaller than the other two, the Zambezi shark has very large teeth, massive jaws and heavy jaw muscles for its size, eats almost as wide a range of food as the tiger shark,

and occurs in a greater variety of inshore habitats than the other species.

In the Natal anti-shark nets the catch ratio of Zambezi, great white and tiger sharks averaged about 3.8 : 1.4 : 1.0 between 1966 and 1974. But between 1978 and 1984 the proportion of Zambezi sharks declined somewhat and, on average, the ratio was about 1.2 : 1.1 : 1.0. Yearly catches of Zambezi sharks, however, show a gradual increase in numbers from 25 in 1978 to 52 in 1984, possibly reflecting the steady increase of anti-shark nets and protected beaches off Natal. At least one South African authority, the late Tim Wallett, thought the reduction of the resident Zambezi shark population was itself one of the major contributing factors in the dramatic reduction of shark attacks off the Natal beaches. In contrast, tiger sharks and great white sharks, thought to be migratory transients off Natal, showed no such increase in total annual catches: an inexplicable increase in the number of Zambezi sharks netted in 1985 (a total of 83) is not matched by similar upsurges in the catches of great white and tiger sharks.

The formidable great white shark often attacks people in a seemingly inhibited fashion and so inflicts much less damage than it might. Much controversy has raged over why this is so.

Accumulating evidence from South African, as well as Californian and New Zealand sources, suggests that white sharks often approach divers underwater without attacking. Despite the media-created 'Jaws image', such 'close encounters of the white shark kind' may be much more frequent than actual attacks. The writer has interviewed several South African divers who were approached, investigated, but not attacked, by what were undoubtedly great white sharks. In some instances these divers were spearfishing and the sharks may have been attracted by injured fish; one diver lost a fish to an aggressive white shark. In other cases divers were engaged in non-fishing underwater operations, including archeological salvage, and were approached by white sharks without obvious signs of aggression.

Of the remaining sharks listed, the giant sleepy shark, shortfin mako, copper shark, spinner shark, blacktip shark, dusky shark, blacktail reef shark, sharptooth lemon shark, blue shark, whitetip reef shark and great hammerhead have been implicated in attacks in South Africa (as they have in other areas), though none of these species are perhaps as dangerous as the white, tiger, Zambezi and oceanic whitetip sharks. The snaggletooth shark, silvertip shark, Java shark, scalloped hammerhead and smooth hammerhead are considered potentially dangerous, though they have not been positively identified in attacks anywhere. The Java shark is easily confused with the Zambezi shark, and some attacks attributed to Zambezi sharks may have involved this little-known, large-toothed, big-jawed shark.

Giant sleepy sharks are docile tropical reef sharks that feed on small fishes and crustaceans, and are most likely to be involved in attacks after being accosted and provoked by foolhardy divers. Sharptooth lemon sharks occur in the same habitats as giant sleepy sharks, but are much more powerfully armed and can be very aggressive when provoked or disturbed. Sleepy and lemon sharks are almost never caught in the Natal shark nets and, it seems, seldom frequent beaches used by bathers.

Shortfin makos are offshore sharks that eat mainly bony fishes and squid, and are dangerous primarily when hooked or otherwise provoked by sportfishermen from boats. Most mako incidents occur when fishermen hook them or are landing bony fishes that the mako then attacks, but very few unprovoked attacks on swimmers and divers can be attributed to them. Small numbers of makos have been taken in the Natal shark nets, indicating occasional or regular incursions inshore.

As with oceanic whitetip sharks, blue sharks are abundant offshore and are a problem primarily to offshore divers and in air-sea disasters. Neither species figures in the Natal shark net catches. Blue sharks are noticeably more timid than oceanic whitetips when interacting with divers. The whitetip reef shark is a normally timid,

small-toothed, reef-loving species that is minimally dangerous. The snaggletooth shark is a rare, mainly fisheating species with impressive, almost mako-like impaling teeth. The spinner and blacktip sharks are fast-moving fisheating species that may be dangerous in conditions where food is present; they have sometimes accosted spearfishing divers or indulged in feeding frenzies. The copper, silvertip and dusky sharks and the three hammerheads all grow to a total length of between 2.4 and more than four metres and should be treated with caution; particularly the great hammerhead, silvertip and dusky shark. The blacktail reef shark is a small shark closely related to

Kevin Deacon/Auscape

the variably aggressive grey reef shark *(Carcharhinus amblyrhynchos)*, and like that species may direct non-feeding threat displays and attacks at divers who corner it or otherwise provoke it.

A number of other species – sevengill sharks, spotted raggedtooth sharks, great white sharks, blacktail reef sharks, blacktip sharks, copper sharks, Zambezi sharks, tiger sharks, hammerheads, and possibly spinner sharks and dusky sharks – have often approached spearfishing divers in South African waters, and have sometimes harassed them and stolen their catches without inflicting injuries. In many such cases the divers may have averted

injuries by defending themselves with their spearguns or other weapons.

Great white and mako sharks have been responsible for several unprovoked boat attacks in South African waters, mostly off the Cape province, usually but not always when fish were being caught from the boat. From 1936 to 1977 approximately 25 boat attacks occurred in Cape waters, mostly in the western Cape. Thirteen of these attacks occurred in the four-year period between 1974 and 1977. Of sixteen boat attacks where the shark could be identified, fourteen were by great white sharks and two by shortfin makos. At least eleven boat attacks, all by white sharks, have occurred in False Bay in

▲ Known as the spotted raggedtooth in South Africa, the sand tiger or grey nurse *(Eugomphodus taurus)* will approach spearfishing divers and on occasion steal their catches. The only 'attacks' in which it has been identified occur when divers attempt to defend their catches and are injured by the shark's formidable teeth or flailing tail.

the western Cape, which can apparently boast more attacks of this sort than any other place I know. On several occasions both white sharks and makos have severely damaged and even leapt into boats, sometimes causing injuries to the occupants.

There are a few recent cases of white shark attacks on surfboards in South African waters, which resemble similar cases in California.

PATTERNS OF SHARK ATTACK

The pattern of shark attack off South Africa, like the pattern throughout the world, may be correlated with temperature. No attacks on swimmers or divers have been recorded in the cold sector of the west coast from Cape Town to the Orange River mouth, though white shark attacks on divers are possible there. In the western and eastern Cape, between the Cape Peninsula and False Bay and off

▼ The growing popularity of skindiving, spearfishing and surfboard riding in South Africa has seen a parallel growth of human contact with sharks. On the other hand, increased awareness and effective anti-shark measures have reduced the danger of a fatal meeting with such a dangerous and aggressive species as the tiger shark.

Paolo Curto/The Image Bank

Transkei, shark attacks on swimmers and divers occur at a low rate, approximately one per year. Between 1940 and 1978, 29 attacks occurred, of which six (21 per cent) were fatal. For the entire period attacks averaged 0.7 per year and ranged from none to four per year. The decade 1940–49 had three attacks (0.3 per year); 1950–59 had six attacks (0.6 per year); 1960–69 had ten attacks (1.0 per year); and the nine–year period 1970–78 had ten attacks (1.1 per year). The apparent trend is for a noticeable increase in attacks from 1940 to 1960, reminiscent of a similar trend in California, and a possible levelling off from 1960 to the present time. In the past few years three shark attacks have been reported in the eastern cape, two by raggedtooth sharks on bathers, who sustained minor injuries, and one on a surfboard rider by a white shark, without injury to the surfer.

Presumably the phenomenon of increasing shark attack in these waters in postwar years was related to a growth in the popularity of such water sports as surfing, scuba diving and spearfishing, brought on by advances in technology that produced aqualungs, wetsuits and other dive gear, as well as fibreglass surfboards. The fatality rate is low and the principal perpetrator of attacks that produce serious injuries in Cape waters may be the great white shark, though raggedtooth sharks occasionally nip people and dusky and copper sharks are suspected of doing so.

In Natal the warm inshore water and splendid beaches have long enticed bathers into the shallows and exposed them to a relatively high rate of shark attack. Some 69 attacks were reported in Natal waters between 1940 and 1978, of which 25 (36 percent) were fatal. For the entire period attacks ranged from none to six per year and averaged 1.8 per year. The decade 1940–49 had 25 attacks (2.5 per year, with 1.1 fatalities per year); 1950–59 had sixteen attacks (1.6 per year, with 0.8 fatalities per year); 1960–69 had 22 attacks (2.2 per year, with 0.6 fatalities per year); and the nine-year period 1970–78 had five attacks (0.6 per year, with no fatalities). Widespread shark netting off the Natal beaches began in earnest in the mid-1960s and has had a marked effect in virtually eliminating shark attack since the late 1960s.

The higher attack rate in Natal, in comparison with Cape waters, has been attributed mainly to the fact that people there use the water more, particularly for bathing and swimming at popular beaches. A likely additional contributing factor is the greater diversity and abundance of dangerous sharks in warmer waters, particularly certain species of large, powerful and omnivorous requiem sharks such as the Zambezi and tiger sharks. The fatality rate for the decades 1940–49, 1950–59, and even 1960–69, when shark netting was introduced, is strikingly higher than in the eastern Cape or in California. This may reflect differences in the species of sharks responsible for attacks and the greater inclination of at least some of the attackers (presumably certain omnivorous requiem sharks) to attack without provocation and actually to eat people.

ANTI-SHARK MEASURES

Protective measures against shark attack in South Africa were initially centred on the popular bathing beaches of the greater Durban area and the beaches south to Margate and Port Edward, but more recently have been extended to kwaZulu (Zululand) in the north and the Transkei in the south. Durban, with its surrounding beaches, attracts the highest number of holidaymakers in South Africa and each summer has the country's highest concentration of bathers and swimmers.

The 43 or so shark attacks and twenty shark fatalities off Natal beaches between 1940 and 1960 generated much publicity, shark hysteria and public clamour for protection. Records of shark attacks before this period are sketchy, though attacks were recorded before the turn of the century and the Durban city council approved the construction of a semicircular enclosure 200 metres in diameter to protect bathers. This was constructed in 1907 and lasted 21 years, but eventually had to be demolished after corrosion and wave action had rendered it useless.

Although drownings and injuries in the water as well as boat accidents and the inevitable accidents connected with beachside holidays undoubtedly caused more fatalities and injuries in Natal than shark attack during the 1940s and 1950s, none of these more mundane events had the same spine-chilling effect on the holiday public as did

▲ The first sharkproof enclosure in South Africa was constructed by the Durban city council in 1907. It was demolished in 1928.

shark attacks. Shark attacks, fatal or otherwise, ruined holidaymakers' enthusiasm for the southern Natal beaches, and many people cut short their beachside holidays and packed up for home.

Shark fear intensified to a fever pitch in southern Natal during the summer holiday season of 1957–58. In five months there were some seven attacks, five of them fatal. Four of the attacks occurred during the 'black December' of 1957. These attacks, and the publicity generated by radio news broadcasts, resulted in wholesale desertion of beaches and resorts, first during the Christmas holiday and then during Easter. The panic climaxed in April 1958 when two fatal attacks off Uvongo, just north of Margate caused a mass evacuation of the beaches and an enormous traffic jam as thousands of automobiles clogged the roads away from the beaches. One of the results of the shark panic was economic disaster for hotels, resorts, businesses,

◀ Netters of the Natal Sharks Board at work. At present 46 beaches are protected by some 385 nets.

▲ Shark netting in Natal. The Natal Sharks Board is responsible for installing and maintaining shark nets at 46 beaches. The nets are set in two staggered rows beyond the surf line and are serviced daily by meshing teams working from skiboats. (After Wallett 1983)

▶ A net in position at sea. Between 1978 and 1984 some 8333 sharks were caught in Natal Sharks Board nets. About 9.7 per cent were great whites, tigers and Zambezi or bull sharks; 2.8 per cent were hammerheads and Java sharks; 1.2 per cent were shortfin makos. The rest – by far the majority – were relatively harmless to human beings. (After Wallett 1983)

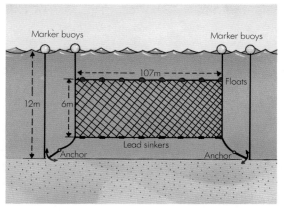

and municipalities dependent on holiday patronage.

To help recoup their losses from the 1957 Christmas disaster, some of the hotels and municipalities built anti-shark barriers in early 1958. These gave absolute protection from shark attack while they remained intact, but they were unsightly and proved extremely expensive and difficult to maintain. After 'black December' and its aftermath, the South African navy dispatched a frigate to drop depth charges off Margate and Uvongo in the hope of killing sharks – with unwanted and unexpected results. While few sharks were killed, many others were attracted by the bony fishes stunned and killed by the blasts. At Margate small boat patrols were organised and local police were authorised to drop hand grenades on sharks when they were sighted!

The City Council of Durban had earlier responded to public concern about shark attacks off Durban and elsewhere in Natal; in 1948 it proposed the construction of a beach enclosure to replace the one built in 1907. This was delayed for a few years due to expenses and problems with materials, but meanwhile the council was evaluating other methods of protecting its beaches. It was greatly impressed by the successes of the shark meshing program at Sydney beaches in New South Wales, Australia, and proposed a similar program for South Africa. This would use offshore wide-mesh gillnets to reduce the numbers of dangerous sharks off Durban's beaches. The program was initiated in 1952 and has so far eliminated shark attacks at beaches where the nets were installed. A new shark enclosure was considered superfluous.

Four municipalities in popular holiday areas copied Durban in the early 1960s by installing anti-shark nets off their beaches. Eventually, in 1964, local anti-shark activities coalesced into a centralised Natal-wide organisation analogous to the military and police and fire departments. This unique organisation, for many years titled the Natal Anti-Shark Measures Board but recently renamed the Natal Sharks Board, is a kind of shark police that maintains a Natal-wide shark-netting program. The Sharks Board's officers wear the same kind of uniform as is issued to conservation bodies in South Africa, and its almost military discipline and esprit de corps combine to make it both efficient and effective in its primary task of protecting beaches by 'shark control'. It also undertakes elaborate, and expanding, public relations activities that make for extensive community recognition and attract widespread support in Natal. Originally the Natal Sharks Board was limited to netting the beaches of all of Natal (except for the Durban beaches, which were netted by the Durban municipality). More recently its activities have expanded to take over the Durban municipal operation and to extend north to Richard's Bay in kwaZulu.

The Durban municipality operated a few large inboard fishing boats that docked at Durban for their netting program, but the Natal Sharks Board currently uses a large fleet of 5.5 metre skiboats with twin outboard motors, towed by four-wheel drive vehicles and launched directly from the beaches or from nearby launch sites, to tend the nets. Six-man shark meshing teams operate these boats and set, retrieve, and repair the nets, which are set in a staggered double row offshore just beyond the surf line. Each shark net is 107 metres long by 6.1 metres deep, except for nets used off Durban, which are 304 metres long by 7.3 metres deep. The nets do not form an absolute barrier for the protected beaches and equal numbers of sharks are caught in the seaward and landward sides of the nets. Except where weather prohibits it, nets are serviced daily throughout the year and are replaced every three weeks for cleaning. They are made of black twine that is barely visible under ordinary lighting conditions, but their effectiveness is reduced by fouling organisms that make the nets more visible to sharks. Bad weather and rough seas can tangle and damage the nets, and bathing may be banned temporarily while they are repaired and repositioned. Every year during the annual sardine run, the nets are removed for a few days to avoid excess catches of migratory shark, game fish, dolphins and rays that follow the run, and to prevent the damage these could cause. The Sharks Board has the authority to close beaches if a shark danger is perceived, and during the sardine run bathing is banned until the nets are replaced.

At present 46 beaches are netted and approximately 385 nets are deployed, the numbers per beach being dependent on local conditions. Large resorts and municipalities pay for the cost of the nets, while the expenses of smaller entities are subsidised by the Natal authorities. Nets are built and repaired and other gear maintained at the headquarters of the Sharks Board at Umhlanga Rocks, in a large, impressive, ultramodern installation that features exhibits on sharks and the operations of the board, and also houses

maintenance and research facilities. Recently the facilities of the board were greatly expanded; they now include a lecture theatre where visitors are shown audiovisual presentations and can watch a shark being dissected. Such educational work is an increasing aspect of the board's activities, quite apart from its primary purpose of protecting beaches and secondary function of collecting data and undertaking research on sharks.

Considerable data are collected by the board on the sharks captured by the shark nets. Field data collected by meshing teams and laboratory data taken by dissecting teams from all over the Natal and kwaZulu coasts are brought to Umhlanga Rocks and entered on a series of specialised forms, which are archived and entered in a special database program on a microcomputer.

The netting activities of the Natal Sharks Board have recently been extended to Transkei and Cape waters. In the Cape area the low shark attack rate, the lower utilisation rate of beaches, the prohibitive cost of protecting these areas, and some opposition to shark netting by anglers, scientists, and other concerned parties make such an extension unlikely. Resort development in Transkei, however, could well generate a demand for the installation of shark nets.

▲ 'No liability accepted', says this warning sign at a Durban beach. Shark meshing has been so effective in reducing the risk of shark attack in South Africa that nearly all attacks since meshing began have occurred either at beaches where nets are not deployed or at times when normally netted beaches are without protection.

▼ The netting of potential killers, such as this 3-metre tiger shark, is seen by many as justification for wholesale meshing programs, though ecologists and fishermen argue that there have been adverse and long-term environmental effects on the populations of other marine animals.

AMANZIMTOTI: THE WORLD'S WORST SHARK ATTACK BEACH

The resort beach of Amanzimtoti, 27 kilometres south of Durban, has had more shark attacks recorded than any other beach in the world. Since 1940 eleven attacks, three of them fatal, have been documented. All took place close to a rocky headland called Inyoni Rocks. There have been six attacks since 1962 when offshore shark nets were laid; five of these occurred between January 1974 and February 1975. The 1974-75 attacks seem to have been linked with the presence close to the beach of larger than usual numbers of fish. It has been sugested that temporary increases in food supply may well stimulate increased predatory activity by sharks and thus explain such an abnormal number of attacks in a short period.

ATTACK ON DAMON KENDRICK, 13 FEBRUARY 1974

Fourteen-year-old Kendrick had been training for the lifesaving championships when he was attacked in water 1.5 metres deep. Swimming had been banned because shark nets had not been serviced for several days and the sea was murky, with visibility less than a metre. Water temperature was 24.5°C. Kendrick and a friend, Joe Kool, reached the Inyoni Rocks after their training session and decided to wash the sand from their bodies in the shorebreak. They moved exuberantly through the shorebreak into the channel and then body surfed to the sand.

"Joe was about five metres away from me when he suddenly shouted. As I turned a shark bit my leg and I heard a growl as its powerful jaws shook me viciously . . . Everything took place so fast that I really didn't know what was happening. The shark shook me for about two seconds and as it let me go I was pushed into the shorebreak, which washed me on to the sand. I pushed myself backwards up the sloping beach holding my injured leg up in front of me. Only then did I know what had happened and my mind did not want to accept what I was seeing. Great strips of skin and muscle hung like old rags from where my calf muscle used to be. Blood spurted and dripped from my leg and formed a river of blood in the sand."

Kendrick's serious injury was caused by three bites: the first severed the fibula above the ankle, the second cut partly through the fibula near the knee, and the third took away the calf muscle and fibula. His calf muscle was so severely damaged that the right leg was amputated below the knee.

ATTACK ON JAMES GURR, 21 MARCH 1974

James Gurr, 21 years old, was attacked 50 metres south of Inyoni Rocks. Water visibility was two metres and the water temperature was 25°C. Swimming had been banned because conditions were thought to be conducive to shark attack. Large waves were breaking over a sand bank 150 metres offshore. They were then reforming and breaking about 50 metres from the shore. A strong current had created a deep channel at the water's edge. Gurr was riding a surfboard when he saw a shark's fin coming straight for him. Murky water obscured its form.

"Sitting on my surfboard I felt helpless, there was nothing I could do. I lifted my legs and the shark hit the board, tumbling me into the water. A feeling of terror took my breath away but I made a conscious effort to remain calm. My surfboard was about two metres away, I swam to it and turned it the right way up. As I was about to pull myself aboard a violent shove pushed me sideways and simultaneously I felt the shark against my chest and under my arm. This was the last straw – panic swept through me – and I began paddling for shore . . . I had unbelievable strength and was surging through the water. Without warning there was a terrific jolt and next thing I was upside down in the sea again . . . In a frenzy I remounted my surfboard and in desperation began paddling shorewards again. The shark zig-zagged in front of me and, if it was possible, my fear increased as a broken wave overtook me and pushed me over the shark. I paddled into the shorebreak, which dumped me on to the sand."

Gurr miraculously escaped the attack without injury. When the shark pushed him sideways, it bit into his surfboard. A clear imprint of its teeth, nineteen centimetres in diameter, was left in the fibreglass.

ATTACK ON ANTHONY BAKER, 4 APRIL 1974

Seventeen-year-old Anthony Baker was attacked while surfing about 50 metres offshore just south of Inyoni Rocks. His brother Raymond was about 10 metres further out. Swimming had been banned because conditions were believed to be similar to those of earlier shark attacks. Waves were breaking on a sandbank 150 metres offshore, then reforming and breaking about 50 metres from the beach. The sea temperature was 24.5°C. Baker had a white sock tied to his right foot, to which a surfboard leash was attached.

"I was facing shore when there was a tug at my foot and it felt warm. Because of the other attacks I knew instantly that a shark had bitten me. I felt no pain but I had heard that shark bites were painless so I turned around to make sure both my legs were still there. There was a lot of blood in the water and the sock tied around my ankle was stained red. Only when I saw the blood did I begin to feel frightened. I shouted a warning to Raymond and began paddling shorewards . . . On the beach I checked my foot and saw a gaping cut on my right heel which was bleeding badly. I remember feeling thankful that it didn't look too serious."

Baker was taken to a local doctor by his brother and two holidaymakers. He received nineteen stitches to a 10-centimetre laceration on the outer side of his right heel. A number of punctures were visible along the outer edge of the foot for another eight centimetres. The shark may have been attracted to the white sock around Baker's ankle; ironically the bite was cushioned by several layers of sock material.

THE FUTURE OF ANTI-SHARK MEASURES

The increasingly wide-ranging activities of the Natal Sharks Board have generated considerable controversy in Natal. There is concern about the ecological effects of long-term shark netting, particularly among anglers, some scientists, and conservationists. Big-game fishermen have been affected as much by the cessation of whaling off Durban as they have by netting, and have either abandoned their sport or have moved further afield to kwaZulu or Transkei in search of large sharks. More generally, anglers and scientists have noticed a marked increase in numbers of juvenile dusky sharks, milk sharks and possibly other small sharks, and attribute this to the shark nets. According to this view, which is opposed by the Sharks Board, the nets have depressed the numbers of larger sharks – including Zambezi, large dusky, great white, tiger, hammerhead, and raggedtooth sharks – that sometimes feed on smaller sharks. There is an apparent decline in bony fishes targeted

Ben Cropp

◀ Copper or bronze whaler sharks *(Carcharhinus brachyurus)* are feared wherever they occur, and rank with the bull or Zambezi shark, the tiger shark, the great hammerhead and the great white shark as proven maneaters. Twelve per cent of sharks netted by the Natal Sharks Board between 1978 and 1984 were copper sharks.

▼ The blacktip reef shark *(Carcharhinus melanopterus)* is common in shallow water near reefs and islands, and will often approach divers out of curiosity. Spearfishing, however, will excite blacktips and cause them to rush in to take wounded fish. This species has been identified in several attacks, mainly on divers' legs and feet.

AF Photographic Library

for sport, which may at least in part be an effect of increased numbers of small sharks as well as of increased angling pressure. The Natal Sharks Board has denied that such an increase in sharks is occurring, though organised anglers in Natal, who generally keep detailed records of their catches, argue otherwise. One scientist, Dr R. van der Elst of the Oceanographic Research Institute (ORI), Durban, published a paper that strongly supports the claims of anglers. The small sharks controversy suggests a broader question of whether or not the

▲ A meshing team aboard a Natal Sharks Board skiboat. The South African meshing program began in Durban in 1952 and has been considerably expanded since the early 1960s.

shark netting program is doing damage to the inshore ecosystem. So far there have been little or no efforts to conduct environmental impact assessments before new areas are netted, though daily monitoring of catches is carried out during netting operations.

Alternatives to the shark netting program have been tested, but so far have not proved practicable, have not attracted interest, or have not been implemented to the same degree as shark netting. The effective, if expensive, use of enclosures and the rather theatrical use of explosives on sharks have already been mentioned. Dr. E.D. Smith of the National Physics Research Laboratory, Council for Scientific and Industrial Research, Pretoria, has developed a pulsed-current cable system that forms an electromagnetic barrier to repel sharks. This has been tested successfully in the ORI shark tank and in the field at St Lucia. This 'eddy current electrode system' has, when it is operating properly, the interesting effect of working in direct proportion to the mass of the animal that enters its field. Large sharks are repelled but small ones are not; individual humans are not affected but five people holding hands would feel the presence of the field. The great advantage of this system is that it

has the potential to rid bathing areas of large dangerous sharks without killing them. A pilot cable installed at Margate has run into problems and has experienced delays in operation, particularly as a result of sea damage and burying with sand. After several years of attempts to solve the problems, the cable is due to become fully operational in 1988.

HYSTERIA AND SHARKS

The Natal Sharks Board has grown steadily over the years and is undeniably expensive to operate. It must be seen in the context of the public demand for some sort of protection from sharks, and like all bureaucracies it defends itself and its work. But it has grown in the fertile soil of shark fear, fed by the irrational attitudes of the public and stimulated by sensational headlines in the media. I find it difficult to believe that Natal's record of no more than 124 recorded shark attacks should cause crowds to desert the beaches and to rush like lemmings back home. If bathers didn't want to risk being bitten by sharks they could have left the water and still enjoyed themselves at the beach, or could have chosen one of the many beaches protected by netting or enclosures. It must be remembered that the sea is an alien environment, that people always enter at risk of life and limb. The hundreds of drownings and near drownings that occur each year do not cause panics and desertions of beaches. In the Port Alfred area in the Christmas holiday of 1983-84, one person was bitten by a raggedtooth shark on one weekend without serious results; on the same weekend fourteen people drowned. But the shark attack attracted the greater attention.

Until there is a qualitative change in the public image of sharks in South Africa, and widespread public education on the nature of sharks and shark attacks, there will be a perceived need for a shark police. At present sharks are considered by many people in South Africa as murderous vermin to be exterminated without regard to their value and conservation. Many anglers, however, now take a less hostile attitude and tag and release sharks after hooking them. If sharks are to be accorded a more reasonable treatment than at present, a shift to a policy analogous to game park management, in which sharks are seen as the oceanic equivalent of dangerous large mammals, will be necessary. People entering large game parks in South Africa are encouraged not to expose themselves to the predators and big herbivores, and their movements are regulated with both their needs and those of the wildlife in mind. Occasional injuries and fatalities occur nevertheless, but are acceptable to the populace at large. Such a policy transferred to the Natal coast would involve initially an exercise in public education through the media – a shark awareness campaign to encourage the public to view sharks in the same realistic way as they regard dangerous land animals, and to

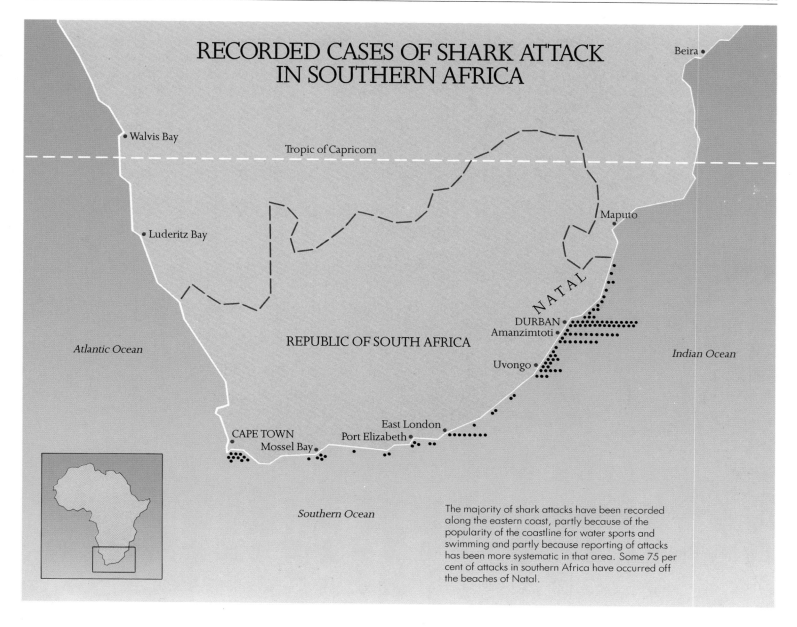

RECORDED CASES OF SHARK ATTACK
IN SOUTHERN AFRICA

Beira

Walvis Bay

Tropic of Capricorn

Maputo

Luderitz Bay

NATAL

DURBAN
Amanzimtoti

REPUBLIC OF SOUTH AFRICA

Atlantic Ocean

Indian Ocean

Uvongo

East London
Port Elizabeth

CAPE TOWN
Mossel Bay

Southern Ocean

The majority of shark attacks have been recorded along the eastern coast, partly because of the popularity of the coastline for water sports and swimming and partly because reporting of attacks has been more systematic in that area. Some 75 per cent of attacks in southern Africa have occurred off the beaches of Natal.

understand their role in the marine ecosystem.

Under such a scheme limitations would be set on the activities of the Sharks Board in its present role, which consists largely of controlling sharks by netting them (though numbers are tagged and released each year). Only 22 kilometres of the Natal coastline are netted on a regular basis; the remaining 296 kilometres could be designated 'unprotected shark reserves', and bathers could be warned realistically of the danger of shark attack in these areas and would use them at their own risk. Increased efforts would be put into devising alternative non-lethal methods of beach protection, of promoting game-park conditions to protect people from sharks and sharks from people. Enclosures have met with mixed success in the past, but with modern materials more durable types may be possible in the future; perhaps electronic shark barriers in appropriate locations.

Whether such a shark-management – rather than a shark-extermination – policy will ever be

adopted in Natal is doubtful. That the current arrangement is the only viable policy for such an area is open to question. In the United States, northern California has between none and seven shark attacks per year; the current average is about 1.9 per year. Florida exactly resembles Natal in its warm waters and huge tourist industry, and has a higher attack rate than California – in 1981 Florida had fourteen attacks, with two fatalities. Despite occasional media-induced spates of shark sensationalism in the United States there are no anti-shark measures in either Florida or California and no plans to introduce them. A more radical alternative for Natal than shark management would be to eliminate anti-shark measures entirely, and to try to educate the public to accept the occasional shark attack as an inevitable result of entering the sea. This may seem utopian at present, but many land predators that are now protected were hunted as vermin not so long ago. Perhaps sharks will win the same sort of protection, too.

SHARK ATTACK IN NEW ZEALAND

LARRY J. PAUL

Summertime. Long, warm days beside, on, or in the sea. New Zealanders flock to their favourite beaches to indulge in a variety of recreational activities: boating, fishing, swimming, surfing, diving. Local radio stations report on weather, beach and traffic conditions, sometimes aided by spotter aircraft. A few shark sightings are reported, nearby beaches are cleared and the media begin running shark stories. Apparent experts are consulted, tragedies are retold and questions and speculation begin. What kind of shark are they, and are they dangerous? Where have they come from? Are water temperatures rising? Have fishermen so depleted the sharks' natural food that they are forced inshore to seek other prey? Is there a detectable pattern to shark attacks? How does one avoid becoming the next shark attack statistic?

◄ More than forty species of sharks have been recorded from New Zealand waters, though most are small, inoffensive and deepwater varieties. There has never been a verified attack by a tiger shark in New Zealand, but its fearsome reputation and its capture off the North Island indicate that the potential exists for a fatal attack on a human.

KINDS OF SHARK

This is one of the easier questions, at least in a general sense. However, the actual species involved in each sighting or attack is less easily determined. There are more than forty species of shark in New Zealand waters. About 25 live in deep water and are encountered only by commercial fishermen and scientists. Most are smallish, about a metre or less in length, dark in colour and, though they are clearly efficient little predators, not dangerous to humans unless handled carelessly when caught. A few of these are at least semi-pelagic, roving into mid or surface waters to feed.

A second group of half a dozen species is found in shallow coastal waters. Four of them – the catshark, smoothhound and two spiny dogfishes – are smallish, bottom-dwelling, and essentially harmless unless provoked. The school shark, though larger, is also harmless. The broad-snouted sevengill, however, is larger again and is powerful and aggressive, particularly when caught.

The third group comprises nine species of large, open-water pelagic sharks. All range widely through the world's oceans, and many have been implicated in shark attacks. The white shark and tiger shark are the most dangerous, while the mako, blue shark, and bronze whaler must also be regarded as dangerous. The thresher and hammerhead are suspected of attacks elsewhere and must be treated with caution, while the porbeagle, though uncommon locally, is a potential danger. The large basking shark, not uncommon seasonally in some localities, is an inoffensive plankton feeder but, because of its sheer size, strength, and abrasive skin, can become dangerous when trapped. Further notes on the identity and New Zealand distribution and abundance of these potential attackers are given in the box on the following page.

RECORDED SHARK ATTACKS IN NEW ZEALAND WATERS

Hauraki Gulf

AUCKLAND

Bay of Plenty

New Plymouth

Napier

40°S

Castlepoint

Wellington

Cape Foulwind

Christchurch

Oamaru

Dunedin

● Fatal attacks
  Non-fatal attacks

▲ The great white shark has been blamed for several attacks in New Zealand waters, but its indictment may often owe more to publicity surrounding this species than to positive identification.

WHERE HAVE THEY COME FROM?

There is undoubtedly a real increase in shark numbers in coastal waters in warmer months. This is due to some extent to the seasonal southward movement of wide-ranging Indo–Pacific, Australasian or Pacific Ocean sharks, either actively migrating or simply moving with the currents, to New Zealand's coastal feeding grounds. Several tuna and marlin species also arrive this way.

These movements continue along the coastline, with northern species becoming more common in southern localities. Some species occur in southern waters only during summer. Then there are inshore movements – generally by pregnant females to give birth in warm, sheltered bays, but probably also by other parts of the population to feed on the summer increase in small fishes and bottom life.

Sharks are more clearly visible during summer and people are, therefore, more aware of them. The higher layers of water warm up more rapidly than those at the bottom and this brings sharks to the surface; and calmer weather makes cruising fins easier to see. And there are simply more people at the beach, in boats, or spotting from the air.

HAVE WATER TEMPERATURES CHANGED?

Although the evidence is rather meagre, New Zealand's seawater temperatures appear to have risen slightly this century. This, presumably, has

DANGEROUS SHARKS OF NEW ZEALAND WATERS

The sharks described below are all widely distributed in other oceans and seas; only their New Zealand distribution is noted here. They all tolerate a wide range of environmental conditions and, though most are typically open-water fishes, they may at times be found close inshore. Most are not strongly limited by the currents around New Zealand, but an understanding of these does help to explain their distribution.

Most of the surface water surrounding New Zealand derives from the Tasman Sea and moves eastwards – around North Cape, through Cook Strait and around southern New Zealand. It moves south and east past the North Island, and northwards up the east coast of the South Island to flow eastwards along the Chatham Rise. Some South Pacific Ocean water appears to come more directly from the north. The entire coastline and much of the

continental shelf are influenced by this subtropical water, with warmest water in the northeast but, particularly in summer, still reasonably warm water in the southwest. Coolest surface temperatures are found in the subantarctic water that moves northeastwards across the Campbell Plateau south of New Zealand. The boundary between these two water masses, the Subtropical Convergence, lies a short distance off the southeast coast and swings eastward across the Chatham Rise; this mixed zone provides some of the country's richest fishing grounds.

Tropical species such as the tiger shark are more or less confined to the northeast, while species that can tolerate cooler water, such as the white shark, are also – and perhaps more commonly – present along southern coasts. Most are warm temperate species and range widely, particularly during summer.

WHITE SHARK (*Carcharodon carcharias*) Heavy but streamlined body; crescentic tail; short conical snout; long gill slits; large triangular serrated teeth; colour greyish, white below, often with a dark blotch at the base of the pectoral fin. Widely distributed around New Zealand but not common. More usually encountered in shallow water than in the open sea, typically around islands and reefs, in bays, and even harbours and estuaries.

TIGER SHARK (*Galeocerdo cuvier*) Large head and short blunt snout; tapering body; broad serrated teeth; colour brownish with the tiger markings most prominent in small fish. Present, but not common, off northern (mainly northeastern) New Zealand in summer, both offshore and in shallow coastal waters.

MAKO SHARK (*Isurus oxyrinchus*) Sturdy but streamlined body; conical head and snout; crescentic tail with prominent lateral keels; large smooth-edged teeth, the anterior few curved; colour grey to bluish above, white below. Present around much of New Zealand but more common in the northeast, usually in open to offshore waters but on occasion may be encountered close inshore.

allowed some increase in numbers and a southward extension of the range of warm-water shark species. Complementing this gradual temperature increase is an irregular cycle, from warmer to cooler and linked to the meteorological southern oscillation, that recurs every few years. There are also shorter-term and more localised coastal temperature variations and current shifts caused by changes in prevailing wind patterns. The difficulty of monitoring these factors means that shark distribution and behaviour remain fairly unpredictable.

HAS THEIR FOOD SUPPLY CHANGED?

The popular theory that overfishing – by foreigners or by New Zealand commercial fishermen – has so altered the sea's food chain that top predators such as sharks are forced to scavenge inshore is, at best, highly dubious. While detailed feeding patterns are not known, most large sharks appear to be opportunistic carnivores, or even omnivores, taking whatever is locally and seasonally most abundant; they seem well adapted to a changing food supply. Throughout the world shark attacks seldom appear motivated by hunger; aggressively feeding sharks could be expected to do far more damage than occurs in most cases. It is more likely that commercial fishermen are reducing some shark populations more rapidly than those of other fish.

BLUE SHARK (*Prionace glauca*) Slender body; long pointed head and snout; long upper tail lobe with small lateral keels; long pectoral fins; finely serrated teeth; colour bright blue above, white below. Present around much of New Zealand but more common in the north. One of the most strongly oceanic sharks but may also occur inshore, particularly as juveniles.

BRONZE WHALER SHARK (*Carcharhinus brachyurus*) Fairly slender body; pointed head and snout; upper tail lobe longer; finely serrated teeth; colour brownish grey, often with a bronze sheen. Present around the North Island, moderately common in some northern areas; a coastal species typically occurring close inshore and entering estuaries, but may also be encountered in the open sea.

THRESHER SHARK (*Alopias vulpinus*) Easily recognised by the tail length. Present around the North Island and northern South Island, both in offshore waters and, particularly as juveniles and small adults, closer inshore.

BROADSNOUTED SEVENGILL SHARK (*Notorynchus cepedianus*) Large head and short blunt snout; tapering body and long upper tail lobe; single dorsal fin; seven gill slits; lower teeth combshaped and serrated; colour brownish with small dark spots. Present around much of New Zealand, usually in shallow coastal waters, including estuaries; quite common in some areas, particularly in the north.

SMOOTH HAMMERHEAD SHARK (*Sphyrna zygaena*) Easily recognised by the head shape. Present around the North Island, particularly in the north. Generally inhabits open coastal to offshore waters, but juveniles are very abundant in some shallow bays.

OTHER SHARKS The porbeagle is not common in New Zealand coastal waters, and elsewhere is regarded as only potentially dangerous. The school shark, *Galeorhinus galeus*, is probably New Zealand's most common moderate-sized shark (it reaches two metres) and because of its schooling behaviour at or near the surface, is probably responsible for many of the shark sightings off beaches; however, it is quite harmless unless directly provoked or mishandled during capture. The 'grey nurse' so often mentioned in newspaper accounts does not occur in New Zealand (though a related species is occasionally caught in deep water): it is an Australian species, and unless provoked is not notably aggressive there:

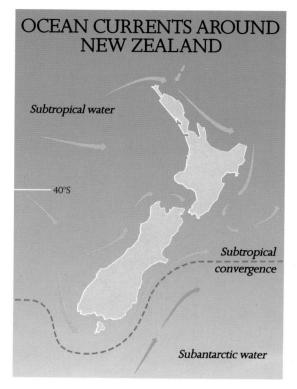

OCEAN CURRENTS AROUND NEW ZEALAND

Subtropical water

40°S

Subtropical convergence

Subantarctic water

▶ The Subtropical Convergence, where subtropical and subantarctic water masses meet, provides rich fishing grounds for sharks and other fish.

▶ The oceanic blue shark has been indicted in attacks in the open ocean and in deep coastal waters. It is regarded as especially dangerous to survivors of plane crashes or ship sinkings, but to date has not been verified as responsible for attacks in New Zealand waters.

1964, 1967 and 1968 might have resulted from a single shark, but most New Zealand attacks appear to have been unlucky encounters with particularly aggressive individual sharks.

Two possible explanations of shark attack (as shown by overseas studies) seem relevant in at least the more recent New Zealand incidents: a defensive retaliation by the shark for inadvertent intrusion into its individual territory; or an investigatory slash at supposed food – either (with people spearfishing) stimulated by the smell and vibration of wounded fish, or (with boardriders and wetsuited divers) prompted by a similarity to seals.

HOW DOES ONE AVOID BECOMING A SHARK STATISTIC?

Only by never going into the water, for sharks are unpredictable and no measures give total security. However, in New Zealand the risks are low, and can be reduced further by using commonsense and some knowledge of what may invite or provoke an attack. In particular, avoid areas where large sharks have been reported, particularly if they show erratic behaviour. If an attack has occurred in an area, there is some chance there may be more. Do not trail wounded fish when spearfishing or remain overlong in an area where many fish have been speared, or where waste and offal have been dumped. Avoid diving near seals; not only may a white shark be waiting for stragglers, but in certain situations the seals themselves may become aggressive. And never provoke a shark; a few sharks that look small and harmless are so, but the majority will defend themselves – using teeth, spines, and abrasive skin – with surprising strength and vigour.

IS THERE A PATTERN OF ATTACKS?

No. Despite the large number of people who use the water and the fact that potentially dangerous shark species are quite regularly in their vicinity, shark attacks in New Zealand are extremely rare. There are too few to detect any common features. They are distributed right around the coastline, with as many in the cooler and less populated south as in the north. Only a few of the sharks involved have been tentatively identified and suspicion generally falls on the white shark, a cool-water species. The three Dunedin fatalities in

FATAL SHARK ATTACKS IN NEW ZEALAND

YEAR	MONTH	LOCALITY	ACTIVITY
1852	Jan	Wellington Harbour	Swimming; a soldier, attacked 300 metres off Te Aro Beach
1886	Dec	Kumara, Westland	Probably swimming near a river mouth but details not known
1886	Dec	Napier	Not known
1907		Moeraki, Otago	Swimming; leg stripped to bone as swimmer came ashore
1911?		Manukau Harbour, Auckland	Not known
1964	Feb	Dunedin	Surfing 250 metres offshore; leg taken and body severely mauled; probably a white shark
1966	Jan	New Plymouth	Swimming and surfing 100 metres offshore; probably a white shark
1967	Mar	Dunedin	A surf lifesaver, swimming out through surf during a competition
1968	Sep	Dunedin	Spearfishing in a wetsuit; identified as a white shark from tooth fragments
1976	Jan	Te Kaha, eastern Bay of Plenty	Spearfishing in a wetsuit

IS THERE A 'HUMAN ATTACK' PROBLEM?

Yes. In New Zealand, as in most parts of the world, the conflict between humans and sharks is very one-sided. There have been only ten fatal shark attacks in more than 130 years; the number of sharks killed during the same period is enormous. Several thousand tonnes of school shark and smoothhound, amounting to more than one million fish, are caught annually by commercial fishermen. Thousands of large sharks (mako, blue, tiger, whaler, and others) are caught on tuna longlines in the vicinity of New Zealand, and hundreds more by big-game fishermen. Recreational fishermen catch, and usually kill, thousands of sharks each year – though they seldom eat them – in the mistaken belief that 'the only good shark is a dead one'.

Most shark species are slow-growing and long-lived, with a low reproductive rate, and are hence susceptible to overfishing. Although none are yet endangered, population sizes of some are falling. While it is perhaps inappropriate to balance these considerations against the individual horror and tragedy of a fatal shark attack, it must be recognised that, in terms of aggression, humans clearly have the upper hand.

Kevin Deacon/Auscape

▲ The basking shark (*Cetorhinus maximus*) is an inoffensive filter feeder seasonally common in the colder waters of New Zealand. It does not attack humans but its size (up to ten metres in length), great strength and abrasive skin have caused injury and damage to people trying to harpoon or trap it for its flesh and oil-rich liver.

▶ Despite the number of potentially dangerous species found around its coastline and the popularity of swimming and surfing, shark attacks are rare in New Zealand. Nevertheless, too many recreational fishermen believe that 'the only good shark is a dead shark' and kill virtually every specimen they catch — regardless of its size or species.

NON-FATAL SHARK ATTACKS IN NEW ZEALAND

YEAR	MONTH	LOCALITY	ACTIVITY
1868?		Auckland Harbour	Not known
1880		Auckland Harbour	Not known
1914		Oamaru	Not known
1920		Auckland Harbour	Not known
1927	Feb	Banks Peninsula	Not known
1928		Firth of Thames	Two women involved
1956	Dec	Not known	Provoked attack on a fisherman
1960	Feb	Mangawhai, Hauraki Gulf	Not known
1962	Jan	Westport, Westland	Not known
1962	Jan	Oreti Beach, Southland	Not known
1962	Jan	Slipper Island, Bay of Plenty	Spearfishing, holding speared fish
1962	Mar	Aldermen Islands, Bay of Plenty	Provoked attack
1962	Feb	Longbeach, Canterbury	Provoked attack
1964	Feb	Pukerua Bay	Spearfishing, holding speared fish
1968	Dec	Dunedin	Surfing
1971	Mar	Dunedin	Surfing
1973	Mar	Moeraki, Otago	Swimming
1977	Jan	Castlepoint, Wairarapa	Underwater diving in wetsuit

The list is almost certainly incomplete; there must have been many more close but non-fatal encounters not reported to authorities or mentioned in the newspapers. Most of the activities listed here as 'not known' would probably have been swimming.

SHARK ATTACK IN THE

▲ The indigenous peoples of Oceania have an intimate relationship with the sea and interact with sharks on a daily basis. They have therefore come to regard the danger of shark attack in a far more realistic way than the continental inhabitants of Australia, the United States or South Africa, to whom the sea is inherently alien and frightening.

Any review of shark attack in the Pacific Ocean is burdened by at least three factors: the huge geographic expanse of the area; the remoteness and isolation of many islands; and the lack or incompleteness of written records. In remote areas many shark attacks go entirely unrecorded. Others are noted only in the files of small medical clinics or dispensaries. At best, attacks may be documented in small, unindexed regional magazines or newspapers of very limited circulation. The shark attacks accounted for in the scientific literature probably represent only a small fraction of those that occur. However, as marine scientists travel widely in the Pacific area and have excellent communication networks, the proportion of attacks reported is probably higher than one might expect.

In researching this chapter I spoke to marine scientists, fisheries officers and residents of many Pacific areas, carefully reviewed the scientific literature and, where possible, reviewed local newspapers. I am convinced, however, that the number of cases I have been able to document is much smaller than the actual total.

Students of shark behaviour owe a large debt to the Shark Research Panel of the American Institute of Biological Sciences (AIBS), formed in 1958 and ably chaired by Dr Perry Gilbert. The panel established the Shark Attack File, which maintained worldwide records of shark accidents for a number of years. Subsequently, the file was maintained by Mote Marine Laboratory (Sarasota, Florida) and later by the National Underwater Accident Data Center (University of Rhode Island). Auxiliary files are now kept by the American Elasmobranch Society (University of Miami, Florida), the

TROPICAL PACIFIC OCEAN

LEIGHTON R. TAYLOR JR

California Department of Fish and Game and the Waikiki Aquarium, Honolulu, Hawaii.
Because of the vastness of the Pacific area it has been possible to cover only part of it in this chapter. The survey is limited to selected major island groups in the tropical Pacific between 140°E and 130°W and between the tropics. Island groups included are Hawaii (including Johnston Island), the Line Islands, French Polynesia, Western Samoa, American Samoa, Fiji, the Phoenix Islands, the Marshall Islands, the eastern and western Carolines, the Cook Islands, the Solomon Islands, Tonga and New Caledonia. The Philippines, Papua New Guinea and southern Japan are excluded.

▼ A shark in shallow water will cause panic among swimmers in most countries, even if it is an inoffensive species such as this zebra shark (*Stegostoma fasciatum*), recognisable by its long caudal fin and unaggressive behaviour. It is common off reefs and atolls of the western Pacific and grows to three and a half metres in length.

The indigenous people of these areas have a long cultural history that has been strongly influenced by the ocean and its living creatures. In most Pacific cultures, sharks are viewed from a variety of perspectives. They play central roles in religion, culture, fishing techniques, folklore, and may provide important resources for tools and weapons. Most Pacific Islanders literally grow up with sharks and, while recognising their danger, have attitudes toward them quite different from those of their fellows from Western, continental cultures.

Ron & Valerie Taylor

157

A SUMMARY OF SHARK ATTACK RECORDS
FROM SELECTED AREAS OF THE TROPICAL PACIFIC OCEAN

Some cases are recorded by more than one author; therefore a total of cases reported for a given area cannot be calculated by summing all reported cases. Where detailed reports have been published in books, scientific journals or periodicals I have merely listed the reference. More detailed information is included here if the reporting source is ephemeral - such as a personal interview or local newspaper. The bibliographic sources referred to in the table are cited in the bibliography at the end of this publication.

NUMBER OF CASES AND/OR DATE	SPECIES	LOCALE AND RESULT (F = fatal)	SOURCE
HAWAII			
52; 1886–1980	various	various	Balazs & Kam (1981)
9; 1981–1983	various	various	Lipman, V. (1983)
35; 1941–1968	various	various, including Midway Island	Baldridge, H.D. (1973)
25; 1886–1960	various	various	Schultz & Malin (1963)
13 June 1982	Carcharhinus sp.(?)	Ho'okipa, Maui. Windsurfer; 120 stitches in upper thigh	Schweitzer, D. (1982)
5 June 1984	Sphyrna lewini (?)	Kaneohe Bay, Oahu. 13-year-old girl swimmer bitten on right foot	Personal communication with victim's mother
24 May 1985	Galeocerdo cuvier (?)	Makaweli, Kauai. Board surfer severely bumped	Cook, C. (1985)
13 October 1985	Carcharhinus sp.	Barber's Point, Oahu. Lobster diver's arm gashed	Anonymous (1985)
18 October 1985	Galeocerdo cuvier	Solitary adult male boogie-boarder lost right hand; board bitten in two	Personal communication with victim; and Taylor and Thompson (in prep.)
22 April 1986	Galeocerdo cuvier (?)	Only fragments of shoreside drowning victim recovered	Personal communication with George Balazs
JOHNSTON ISLAND			
19 December 1965	Carcharhinus amblyrhynchos	Lagoon	Fellows & Murchison (1967)
1; October 1960	unnamed	Lagoon	Schultz & Malin (1963)
FRENCH POLYNESIA			
16	various	Tahiti, Tuamotus (some F)	Fouques et al (1972)
10; August 1962–June 1966	Carcharhinus amblyrhynchos and others	Tahiti, Tuamotus	Bagnis (1968)
14; 1942–February 1972	Carcharhinus amblyrhynchos in 10 cases	(some F)	Lagraulet et al (1972)
3; 1975	Triaenodon obesus	various	Randall (1977)
2; 1951	unnamed	Tuamotus	Schultz & Malin (1963)
MARSHALL ISLANDS			
3; September 1957–Sept 1960	Carcharhinus amblyrhynchos	Enewetak	Schultz & Malin (1963)
1; March 1976	Triaenodon obesus	Enewetak	Randall (1977)
–	unnamed	Enewetak	Baldridge (1973)
1; April 1978	Carcharhinus amblyrhynchos	Enewetak	DeGruy, pers. comm.
2; August 1968–January 1972	Carcharhinus melanopterus	Enewetak	Randall & Helfman (1973)
TRUK (eastern Caroline Islands)			
2; July–September 1910	Carcharhinus albimarginatus	Truk, Namonuito	Jones (1972)
PALAU (western Caroline Islands)			
15 September 1970	Carcharhinus sp.	Western Babelthuap	Read (1971)
April–May 1970	Carcharhinus melanopterus	Babelthuap, Ngerobelobang	Randall & Helfman (1973)
PHOENIX ISLANDS			
6 February 1972	Carcharhinus melanopterus	Canton	Randall & Helfman (1973)
LINE ISLANDS			
2; November 1959–June 1965	Carcharhinus melanopterus	Palmyra	Randall & Helfman (1973) and Baldridge (1973)
AMERICAN SAMOA			
2; August 1955–Dec 1963	unnamed	Tutuila (F)	Schultz & Malin (1963)
WESTERN SAMOA			
1; February 1972	Galeocerdo cuvier	Nu'u'lua	Balazs, pers. comm.
TONGA			
1; 1930	unnamed	Niua Fo'oa Island (F)	Schultz & Malin (1963)
FIJI			
5; 1925–61	unnamed	various (1F)	Schultz & Malin (1963)
SOLOMON ISLANDS			
11; 1880–1957	unnamed	various (some F)	Schultz & Malin (1963)
NEW CALEDONIA			
2; 1950–196?	unnamed	various	Schultz & Malin (1963)

Such late arrivals to the Pacific as the European-derived peoples tend to look on sharks very negatively; they will react significantly to the mere sighting of a shark. It is not surprising, therefore, that an attack or incident in an area such as Hawaii will be more widely reported than one that occurs in an outlying island of the eastern Carolines.

One observer, Dr Charles Jones, MD, chief surgeon at Truk Hospital, estimated that on average there was at least one attack reported every three months. He suspected that many more attacks go unreported and that the 'inherent toughness of island people and their frequent isolation both contribute to the failure of more shark attack victims to seek medical aid'.

Even in areas where shark attacks are likely to be well reported and widely publicised there are ambiguities. For example, occasionally shore fishermen will be washed offshore or fishermen will fall from boats; their remains are seldom recovered. Although these are reported as accidental drownings by medical authorities, the deaths could equally be the result of fatal shark attack.

The nature and result of shark attacks and the circumstances surrounding each incident vary widely. Captain David Baldridge has made a

detailed review and statistical analysis of 1165 shark attacks that occurred worldwide between 1941 and 1968 and were carefully recorded in the AIBS Shark Attack File. Of these, 127 were in the tropical Pacific area. While Baldridge reported some interesting and suggestive correlations, he was unable to state any definite principles of cause and effect. This is of course due to the accidental nature of shark attack. Certainly no careful experiments have been conducted in which variables have been scientifically controlled. Such experiments are (let us hope) unlikely ever to be performed and, therefore, any suggested patterns, beyond very general ones, are impossible to verify.

▲ The Pacific may be an attractive recreational destination, but it has several records of shark attacks on boardriders and windsurfers. Most of these attacks are blamed on tiger and great white sharks, both aggressive species that hunt large marine animals which could be confused from below with surfboards or sailboards.

▼ Great whites are among the very few species of sharks that appear actually to eat humans, perhaps mistaking divers and surfers for seals and sea lions. The only seal populations in the Pacific are found in the northwestern islands of Hawaii; the only great white attacks on humans in this vast ocean are also recorded from Hawaii.

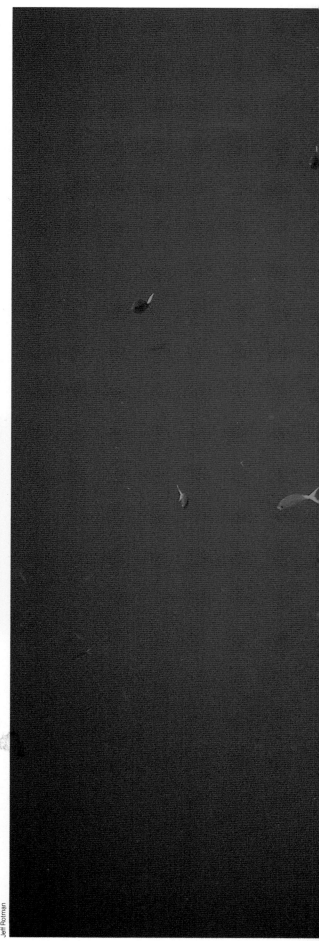

► Most attacks on divers in the Pacific have apparently been motivated by confusion with turtles or by spearfishing, when blood in the water has excited reef sharks. On some occasions, however, a diver's accidental intrusion into a particular shark's hunting grounds will stimulate a sudden attack that can result in severe injury.

Baldridge's analysis includes the following cases from the Pacific Islands. (The number of documented attacks is in parentheses.)
Admiralty Islands (4)
Bismarck Archipelago (28)
Caroline Islands (4)
Fiji Islands (22)
Galapagos Islands, Ecuador (2)
Guam (1)
Hawaii, United States (including Midway) (33)
Johnston Island (2)
Line Islands (2)
Marshall Islands (5)
New Caledonia (3)
Samoa (3)
Society Islands (3)
Solomon Islands (19)
Tonga Islands (2)
Wake Island (3)

Until fairly recently, scientists believed shark attack was motivated by stimuli relating to food and feeding. Starkly stated, this hypothesis held that sharks attacked humans because they wanted to eat them. A booklet prepared by the United States Navy in 1944 for the information of naval personnel

▲ Spearfishing is a popular and relatively efficient way of catching fish for the table, but one that increases the possibility of shark attack through the struggles and bleeding of a speared fish. Like all predators, sharks are sensitive to signs of a potential meal and have been known to injure divers while stealing speared fish.

who might encounter sharks in tropical waters stated that 'The truth about sharks biting people seems to be this: like most fish the shark is a carnivorous or meat-eating animal ...' Since the publication of that booklet there has been substantial research on the behaviour of sharks, much of it supported by the same Office of Naval Research that prepared the original edition.

Feeding has certainly been an important motivation in some attacks in the Pacific, particularly in those involving large species such as tiger sharks and great white sharks and in incidents where bleeding, either by an injured victim or speared fish, had occurred. However, it is now widely believed that behaviour relating to a 'territorial imperative' is important in shark attack. This 'aggression' of certain perhaps territorial species may be responsible for most non-fatal

160

▲ The tawny nurse or sleepy shark (*Nebrius ferrugineus*) is common throughout the Pacific and Indian oceans. It is normally docile and will usually react to harassment by grunting and spitting water at its tormentor; however, there are records of tawny nurse sharks biting divers and holding them underwater for extended periods.

from his board. The two bites to his right thigh resulted in little tissue loss and were probably caused by a frightened and threatened shark rather than a hungry maneater.

In simple terms most shark attacks can be classified as either 'feed stimulated' or 'aggression stimulated'. Attacks on humans by large species such as tiger sharks, which commonly feed on large prey such as sea turtles, and great white sharks, which commonly feed on seals, are almost certainly related to feeding. Attacks by most other species are probably due to responses other than feeding. Exceptions occur where other stimuli relating to feeding – such as speared and bleeding fish, injured victims or an abundance of the shark's normal prey – are in the water.

Some attacks in the Pacific, such as open-ocean attacks following accidents, have clearly been the result of feeding behaviour. The 1945 tragedy of the USS *Indianapolis* is an example. Four hundred sailors went under when the heavy cruiser was torpedoed; nearly 800 jumped clear and were adrift in the equatorial Pacific, 300 kilometres from the Philippines. During the next four days and five nights nearly 500 perished. It has been estimated between 60 and 80 of them were killed by sharks, many fewer than the 600 that were counted by the fictional Captain Quint in Peter Benchley's *Jaws*.

shark attacks. Simply put, some sharks bite some people for the same reasons that dogs bite mail deliverers. A well-fed spaniel will sink its teeth into the calf of an intruder into its yard with no thought of eating the poor visitor; the dog is simply defending its territory against an interloper.

A similar explanation probably holds for many Pacific shark attacks. For example, in 1982 a windsurfer was attacked off Ho'okipa Beach, Maui, after rapidly sailing into a turbulent area and falling

SHARK ATTACK: ANOTHER PERIL OF WAR

CARSON CREAGH

Prior to World War II, shark attack was an accepted hazard of life in Pacific waters: sharks were certainly treated with caution by native fishermen and European settlers, but they were regarded as an everyday risk. Fatal traffic accidents – barely reported today – were given front-page attention. An objective view of the risks of shark attack in the Pacific was provided by George Llano in *Sharks and Survival* in 1963: 'Concern about the shark menace was noted in a study of some 2500 aviation survival accounts from World War II archives, particularly from men who flew over tropical waters . . . Analysis of these records revealed only 38 shark sightings, of which only 12 resulted in casualties or injuries.'

Those statistics translate as a 1.5 per cent chance of seeing a shark, and a risk of around 0.5 per cent – one in 200 – of attack. Given the number of servicemen in the Pacific theatre, and the chance of shipwreck or aeroplane crash, the risk could hardly be called a major one.

Llano's interviews reveal a surprising number of wartime shark 'contacts' that were no more than sightings. From one interview, we learn that: '. . . I saw a large fin come toward the life raft . . . It rolled over and reappeared on the other side . . .

The shark repeated the behaviour several times at varied intervals but at no time seemed concerned with us or touched the raft . . .' From another, 'The raft was followed for a great part of the time [ten days] by sharks . . . each time, the shark sounded and did not bother us again. Aside from the nuisance, they did not bother the raft'.

Many personnel found that the fish that sheltered beneath their rafts, and not themselves, were the focus of attention: 'From practically the first day,' said one pilot, 'sharks were continually hitting up against the boat trying to get the small fish under it. I was quite scared at first, but soon got accustomed to it when I learned what they were after'. That this was a common attitude is borne out by remarks such as 'Sharks around all the time – no bother', and 'He never came very close and did not constitute a problem'. Even aggressive behaviour was regarded as normal; one pilot laconically recalled dealing with a shark that, excited by its companions feeding on fish, repeatedly attacked the pilot's life raft: 'One large one . . . came to the surface and started to bump the boat with his nose. This had become a rather commonplace procedure with me by this time and I put the .45 about six inches [fifteen centimetres] from

Feeding was also the most likely motivation in at least three other documented shark attacks in the Pacific. In February 1972 Alan Banner, a marine biologist studying sea turtle biology in Western Samoa, was taken by a large tiger shark while snorkeling off a beach known to be a turtle hatchery. Sea turtles are a common prey for large tigers. Banner's snorkeling partner looked on in shock as the large tiger dragged him away; no remains were recovered.

On 18 October 1985, boogie-boarder Joe Thomson was attacked off Princeville, Kauai, by a tiger shark, also presumably motivated by turtle feeding. The yellow-contoured bottom of Thomson's boogie-board closely resembled the plastron (the underside of the shell) of a large green sea turtle. Thomson had sighted several turtles in the area, where on the day of the attack the normally clear water was very murky. Thomson survived the attack with the loss of his right hand and a severely injured left wrist.

Attacks involving great white sharks are almost always related to feeding behaviour. In the tropical Pacific records of attack by this species are limited to Hawaii. John McCosker of the California Academy of Sciences has suggested that a growing number of attacks by great white sharks on surfers off the west coast of the United States may be due to

Yves Lanceau/Auscape

▲ Tawny nurses are usually found resting on the bottoms of reefs or in coral caves, where they also search for their prey of crabs, lobsters, squid and sea urchins. This species employs its muscular pharynx to inhale prey from crevices, and may respond to being disturbed by using its powerful jaws on a diver's arm or leg.

similarities both in appearance and behaviour between surfers and seals, sea lions, and elephant seals – the normal prey of coastal white sharks. With the exception of the northwest Hawaiian islands, seals are not found in the tropical Pacific. However, there seems little doubt that the fatal attack by a white shark on William J. Goins while he was swimming near Haleiwa, Oahu, Hawaii on 18 May 1926 was due to feeding behaviour. According to a report Goins gave a sudden shriek and then

his head . . . to give him his iron for the day . . .'

Even where survivors were harassed or attacked, few succumbed to the sort of panic that would today be regarded as almost mandatory. Eleven survivors of a 1944 plane ditching were approached and occasionally harassed by sharks. The men drove the sharks away by shooting and kicking: one man was 'bitten slightly', became frightened and died during the second night of the 42-hour ordeal.

At five o'clock on the third morning, the remaining six men were rescued. Their rescuers were 'greatly agitated' by the presence of sharks and one survivor remarked that, 'We got a kick out of it'.

A US Navy officer named Kabat, whose ship had been sunk and who was floating in the water, felt a 'scratching, tickling sensation' in his left foot. 'Slightly startled, I held it up. It was gushing blood . . . not ten feet away was the glistening, brown back of a great fish . . . swimming away. The real fear did not hit me until I saw him turn and head back toward me. I thrashed out . . . brought my fist down on his nose again and again. I discovered that he had torn off a piece of my left hand . . .' Kabat's matter-of-fact account continues with details of further attacks: 'The big toe on my left foot was dangling. A piece of my right heel was gone. My left elbow, hand and calf were torn . . .' In the excitement of trying to attract the attention of a passing ship Kabat forgot the shark, which struck again and bit him on the thigh, exposing the bone. Several sailors began

firing at the shark: 'A terrible fear of being shot to death in the water . . . swept over me. I screamed and pleaded and cried for them to stop . . .'

An impression of calmness and resignation, due no doubt to shock, is common to many of the reports. A US Navy pilot reported the death of his radio operator: 'A. said he felt something strike his right foot and that it hurt. I told him to get on my back and keep his right foot out of the water, but before he could the sharks struck again and we were both jerked underwater . . . I knew that we were in for it as there were more than five sharks around. He showed me his leg . . . not only did he have bites all over his right leg, but his left thigh was badly mauled. He wasn't in any particular pain except every time they struck I knew it and felt the jerk.'

Although interviews and research revealed a surprisingly low incidence of shark sightings, much less attacks, the fact remains that a great number of servicemen were injured or lost their lives from shark attacks in Pacific waters during World War II. The presence of hundreds of thousands of people in the area, the obviously increased risk of shipwreck or aeroplane crash and the likelihood of blood in the water meant that investigation by predatory and aggressive sharks was inevitable. The final total of attacks will never be known. Allied war records did not list shark attacks as such, referring merely to 'unspecified animal bites'; and as Llano himself notes, 'When sharks are successful they leave no evidence'.

► Marine turtles are important in the diet of tiger sharks and serious attacks have been reported from areas where turtles are common. In one case, a surfer whose board resembled the plastron (the ventral part of a turtle's shell) of a green turtle was attacked and injured by a positively identified tiger shark.

▼ At least twelve species of requiem sharks (family Carcharhinidae) have been identified or implicated in attacks in the Pacific region. Several species are especially active at night or around dawn and dusk on tropical reefs, when divers' visibility is more than usually limited and the risk of an attack unconnected with feeding is greatest.

disappeared; his remains were found in a 3.5 metre great white shark that was caught nearby two days later.

Attacks by smaller species such as the blacktip reef shark and the whitetip reef shark are undoubtedly motivated by factors other than feeding, except in those cases where dead or injured fish were present before the incident.

Although many shark incidents are now attributed to territorial defence, there is little formal experimental evidence that this is the cause. Johnson and Nelson (1972) first described agonistic display in the grey reef shark and suggested in subsequent writings that this was warning behaviour that preceded attack. Although this hypothesis has been questioned by other biologists, no rigorous testing has disproved it. Indeed the attack on Michael deGruy by a grey reef shark in Enewetak Atoll, Marshall Islands, in April 1978, provides empirical evidence that supports the hypothesis.

SPECIES IMPLICATED IN ATTACK

At least eighteen species in four families and nine genera have been implicated in attacks on humans in the tropical Pacific Ocean. Only in a minority of cases have attacking sharks been confidently identified. Such cases include those in which the shark was captured and contained the remains of the victim, or in which the shark species was very distinctive (eg tiger, hammerhead) and the victim or a witness was a trained observer. In many cases, the specific identity of the shark has been guessed at. The following list includes shark species known to occur in the areas frequented by humans and whose size and ecology suggest that they are potentially dangerous to human beings.

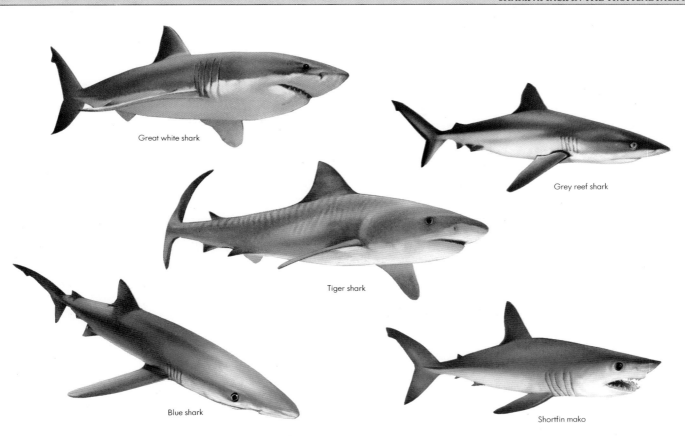

Great white shark

Grey reef shark

Tiger shark

Blue shark

Shortfin mako

POTENTIALLY DANGEROUS SHARKS IN THE TROPICAL PACIFIC OCEAN

FAMILY	SCIENTIFIC NAME	COMMON NAME
Lamnidae	*Carcharodon carcharias*	great white shark
	Isurus oxyrinchus	shortfin mako
	I. paucus	longfin mako
Carcharhinidae	*Carcharhinus amblyrhynchos (menissorah)*	grey reef shark
	C. albimarginatus	silvertip shark
	C. falciformis	silky shark
	C. galapagensis	Galapagos shark
	C. limbatus	blacktip shark
	C. longimanus	oceanic whitetip shark
	C. melanopterus	blacktip reef shark
	C. plumbeus (milberti)	sandbar shark
	Galeocerdo cuvier	tiger shark
	Negaprion brevirostris	lemon shark
	Prionace glauca	blue shark
	Triaenodon obesus	whitetip reef shark
Sphyrnidae	*Sphyrna lewini*	scalloped hammerhead
	S. mokarran	great hammerhead
Ginglymostomatidae	*Nebrius ferrugineus*	tawny nurse shark

SHARK ATTACK IN OTHER
PARTS OF THE WORLD

CARSON CREAGH

While Dr David Baldridge's research for the Shark Attack File indicates that fewer than 2000 humans have been attacked, fatally or otherwise, by sharks in the past two hundred years, his conclusions carry three warning notes: there is no accurate information available on the numbers of people killed by sharks during World War II; more than 90 per cent of attacks were recorded from English-speaking nations; and information-gathering for the file ended in 1967.

The real total may be closer to 4000 attacks – an average of twenty to thirty per year. In contrast, *at least* 4.5 million sharks were killed by humans in 1976 alone, making the shark fatality rate from human 'attack' about 225 000 times higher than for shark attacks on humans. It may seem a specious distinction, but it is important to remember that we run a far greater risk of death by drowning than of even seeing a shark. A significant number of so-called 'attacks' occur when fishermen (most of them professional fishermen) are bitten, hit or scratched by one of those millions of sharks caught each year.

In fact, the most northerly shark attack on a human occurred when fisherman Hans Joachim Schapper was bitten on the arm by a small shark near Wick, Scotland, (58°26′N) on 27 June 1960. Similar incidents, misleadingly termed 'provoked attacks', have taken place around the world and a number have occurred off both Ireland and Scotland, where basking sharks harpooned for their oil-rich livers have retaliated by smashing boats and occasionally injuring their hunters.

The world's highest risk areas are Australia, where 50 people drown each year for every person attacked by a shark; South Africa, where the ratio is 600 to one; and the United States (1000 to one). Although statistics for the rest of the world are sketchy (due, in part, to language differences and a decreased likelihood of extensive media attention), the Shark Attack File lists the most dangerous areas as: eastern Asia, from Singapore to the China Sea and Japan (19 attacks); the Mediterranean (18 attacks); the east coast of India, especially the Ganges delta and the mouth of the Hooghly in Bengal (17 attacks); and the Arabian Gulf and the Red Sea (15 attacks).

Apart from the Schapper 'attack' in 1960, the only other attacks in European waters took place in 1937, when two sailing boats were attacked (possibly by the same shark) off Scotland; and on 4 August 1960, when William Capel was injured by an unidentified shark off the coast of Devon, England.

Three rather doubtful attacks are recorded from Canada: the first allegedly took place in 1848, when an Indian family crossing the Gulf of St Lawrence by canoe escaped attack by throwing a baby overboard; a warden was 'menaced' by a shark as he crossed ice floes near Basque Island in 1940; and a 4-metre dory was capsized by a shark off Cape Breton Island, Nova Scotia, in 1953.

▲ In a melodramatic illustration, Tunisian boatmen watch in horror as a sponge diver is attacked and his leg bitten off by a shark. *Le Petit Parisien*, 1909.

In eastern Asia most attacks have, unsurprisingly, been recorded from densely populated areas such as Singapore (where six unprovoked attacks, all but one fatal, have occurred), Hong Kong (five fatal attacks), China (four fatal attacks) and Japan (four fatal attacks). The most northerly fatal attack in the eastern Pacific took place in 1938 at Tsingtao, in northern China (36°3′N).

The east coast of the Indian subcontinent, in particular Bengal and Bangladesh, has a bad record for fatal attacks. The Ganges shark (*Glyphis gangeticus*) was once regarded as a ferocious maneater responsible for innumerable attacks, mainly in the Hooghly River at Calcutta: a sixteenth century traveller claimed that, 'They which are weary of this world, and desire . . . a quick passage to Paradise, cast in themselves here to be devoured of these Fishes'.

Recent research, however, indicates that the widely distributed and aggressive bull shark (*Carcharhinus leucas*), a confirmed maneater that has been identified in fatal attacks as far from the sea as Lake Nicaragua, is responsible for attacks in India – not on those 'weary of this world', but on pilgrims performing ritual ablutions at the numerous bathing ghats on the banks of the Hooghly. Partially cremated bodies dumped into the Hooghly at Calcutta are also a source of food for sharks, and may have predisposed them to attack living humans.

◄ Convicts escaping from Devil's Island are surrounded by sharks off the coast of Guyana; the outcome is unknown. *Le Petit Parisien*, 1906.

Mary Evans Picture Library

Although there are few confirmed attacks from the warm waters of Sri Lanka, western India and Pakistan, the Arabian Gulf and Red Sea feature heavily. The Shark Attack File lists one mass attack in 1949, where 27 people were attacked (fourteen fatally) near Ahwaz in the Persian Gulf. Fishermen, pearl divers and boatmen are in greatest danger of attack, though the file mentions non-fatal attacks on a British constable near Tel Aviv (1945) and a Gurkha soldier at the junction of the Tigris and Euphrates (1941).

Given the long history of civilisation on its shores, its dense population, heavy water traffic and the recorded presence of many dangerous species, it is surprising that the Mediterranean does not have a worse shark attack record.

It was from the Mediterranean that sharks – and shark attacks – were first described. Herodotus wrote of the destruction of a Persian war fleet in 492 BC when thousands of soldiers and sailors were 'seized and devoured' by 'monsters'. Caius Plinius Secundus (Pliny the Elder) told in 77 AD of divers involved in 'fierce fights with the dog-fish; these attack their loins and heels and all the white parts of the body'. Our understanding of sharks made little progress from those times until the nineteenth century, when oceanographic research institutes in France and Italy began scientific investigations of sharks and their behaviour.

The Shark Attack File lists eighteen attacks in the Mediterranean, from 1863 to the death of Sabit Plana at Opatija, Yugoslavia, in 1961 (no attacks since that date have been reported in scientific journals). Italy has the highest number of attacks (five),

followed by Greece (four), Egypt and Yugoslavia (three each) and one each from Malta, France, an unspecified location and one off the African coast. The northernmost attack in the Mediterranean occurred on 4 September 1934, when Agnes Novak lost her life at Susak, Yugoslavia (45°19′N).

All three Egyptian attacks took place at Port Said on 8 August 1899; none was fatal. The pattern of attacks throughout the Mediterranean shows a predictable bias toward the northern hemisphere summer months: three attacks on unknown dates, four in July, five in August, five in September and one in December (the December attack occurred in warmer waters off the coast of Africa), reflecting the usual increase during warm holiday months when more people are in the water.

The most interesting features of shark attack in the Mediterranean are the unusually high proportion of fatal attacks – two thirds of the attacks listed were fatal, which is twice the world average – and the absence of both the bull (*Carcharhinus leucas*) and tiger (*Galeocerdo cuvier*) sharks from Mediterranean waters.

Although the Shark Attack File does not seek to identify species responsible for attacks in the Mediterranean, the great white (*Carcharodon carcharias*), shortfin mako (*Isurus oxyrinchus*), copper shark (*Carcharhinus brachyurus*), blue shark (*Prionace glauca*), scalloped hammerhead (*Sphyrna lewini*), great hammerhead (*Sphyrna mokarran*) and smooth hammerhead (*Sphyrna zygaena*) have all been collected from the region; all have been confirmed or implicated in attacks on humans.

Mary Evans Picture Library

▲ The hammerhead's alien shape has inspired many people to see it as an incarnation of evil rather than a superb predator.

MYTH

AND REALITY

THE LEGENDARY SHARK

RICHARD ELLIS

The Polynesians told of the shark-god Kauhuhu who lived inside a great cavern from which no one who entered ever emerged. In Australian Aboriginal mythology, the tiger shark Bangudja attacked a dolphin-man in the Gulf of Carpentaria, leaving a large red stain that can still be seen today on the rocks of Chasm Island. The Solomon Islanders, whose religious life consists of ghosts, spirits and other manifestations of the supernatural, believed that the bodies of sharks were inhabited by the ghosts of the departed. In the art of the Northwest Coast Indians of North America, the dogfish was often used decoratively as a reminder of the woman who was carried off by a shark and then became one.

But, except by the peoples of the Pacific, the shark was generally ignored as a symbol. European legends contain few references to the shark – there are no sharks in Aesop's fables, for instance. Sharks generally appear only in natural histories or seafarers' journals, where it was common to write about and occasionally identify these often large, always mysterious, creatures. It was not until fairly recently that the shark insinuated itself, figuratively and literally, into our collective consciousness.

▶ A shark-god from the Pacific, depicted in human form. Carved in wood, the statue is 39 centimetres high.

▶ Olaus Magnus gave the world the first illustration of a man being attacked by sharks in *Historia de Gentibus Septentrionalibus*, published in Rome in 1555. Australian shark researcher Gilbert Whitley felt the bather was about to be rescued by the 'benevolent' ray on the right, but its teeth and fierce expression may mean it is about to join the feast.

Icones Animalium

We 'advanced' folk of the late twentieth century probably think of ourselves as being beyond pagan mysticism; in fact we are in the grip of an even stronger mythology. We have elevated the shark to a position in our pantheon that transcends that of any other animal. Only the whale has achieved a comparable mythification; but there we have fabricated a benevolent spirit, a spirit contrasted with the shark as the embodiment of evil, the representative of the underworld. Perhaps it is the mysterious nature of the shark that has been responsible for its enthronement. After all, we know very little about this animal and we tend to fear that which we do not understand. Elsewhere in this volume, the reader will encounter discussions of shark biology, the shark's senses and shark behaviour but, even in these relatively well-researched areas, our knowledge is sadly deficient. When it comes to discussions of shark attacks around the world, writers can do little more than inventory the attacks and hypothesise on their causes.

There are many creatures in the oceans that we know little about, but none fascinates us or holds us in thrall as does the shark. From the 30-centimetre dogfishes to the 12-metre whale shark (the largest fish in the world), all the 350-odd species have succeeded in withholding some of their secrets from the prying eyes of the scientists. Consider the great white shark, surely the most fearsome of all. We know almost nothing about its breeding habits (no one has ever examined a gravid female white shark), its swimming speed in the wild, its food preferences, its abundance, range or ancestry. For all our ignorance about this fish, perhaps the most disturbing aspect of its behaviour is its predilection for attacking people and occasionally devouring them. This inclination might prove to be nothing more complex than the attempt of a big, carnivorous fish to eat what appear to be edible

▼ Although many Polynesian societies regarded sharks as gods or demigods, the Australian Aboriginal perspective was principally economic. This Yirrkala bark painting of a shark from eastern Arnhem Land, in the Northern Territory, uses the Aboriginal 'x-ray' technique to illustrate the shark's large and nutritionally important liver.

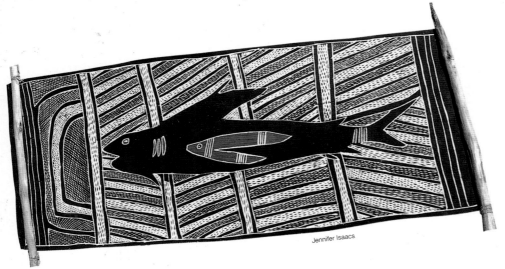

Jennifer Isaacs

Detail of a wooden carving of Menalo, one of the chief shark-gods of the Pacific.

Brian Brake/Otago Museum

A shark spirit, carved into a cuttlefish shell, c 1930.

SHARKS ARE HUMAN

About three years ago I was fishing for barracuda, I was catching them in the night, and a shark took my line. I drew in the line close to the canoe and tied it round my waist and paddled ashore pulling the shark behind me. I pulled the shark onto the beach and took the hook out, I did not cut the line. I cut the hook away at the mouth. Then I helped the shark back into the sea. He was not biting me.

Frightened. What was there to be frightened of?

I wanted to save the shark, yes. But I wanted to save my line too. I saved the line and the hook.

All the fish that are in the sea here we can eat – sailor fish and boar fish and sea slugs and bonito and trevally and barracuda. Dolphins too. But not shark. Sharks are human. To us a dolphin is just like another fish. A dolphin is not a shark.

If an outside man comes here and catches a shark we do not harm the man but we keep away from him. We do not have anything to do with him. We never fish for sharks. He is a person with us. We are related. The other ones we do not eat are rays and crocodiles because they are related to us too.

Oh sharks can save people, yes. I know of two cases. In one case a cutter boat broke in two and was smashed out there in the open sea. There were four people in the boat, two were salt water people like us and two were bush people. The two bush people were lost. The other two people were taken – guided, yes – by the sharks to Florida Island and were safe. The sharks did not touch them, only guided them. They helped them swim to the island. The sharks do not help the bush people because the bush people don't believe in the spirit. They are not related.

Is it safe for you to swim in the sea? Yes it is safe. Of course there are sharks, but it is not dangerous. On the other side, on Guadalcanal, the sharks attack people, but not here. Here you are protected. What happened was that a long time ago a shark, the one that my tribe follows, came out of a woman. The woman gave birth to that shark, yes. We say 'came out of'. Ever since then my people worship the shark, and the sharks stop attacking people in the lagoon. The spirit of that woman entered into the shark, therefore when we worship the shark we are worshipping the old people. It is a belief that was in us before. We can talk to the sharks. We can call them. We don't call them by name, we talk to the spirit as a human on land and transfer the spirit to the shark. We talk to them when there is a sacrifice.

The priest makes the sacrifice, he sacrifices a pig. The shark priest, yes. He is the one who controls the area. The sharks can come in but they can't attack anybody. The priest makes it safe.

He strangles the pig. No, not strangle. He ties a string round the snout and the pig cannot breathe. He says a prayer as the pig is dying. On the island there is a channel where the sharks come and a stone where he makes the sacrifice over the channel. First he kills the pig, then he cooks it, then he cuts it up and divides it for eating. There are no women there. We eat the meat and the priest calls the sharks with an offering of the same meat – so we share the same spirit.

Oh, the sharks come in! They come right in, almost onto the beach. The last time we called the sharks – my brother was there, everyone was there, women, children, everybody, we were all in the water with the sharks, talking to them and patting them on the back. Nobody was harmed.

Nobody has ever been harmed by a shark in this lagoon. I never heard of a case of injury except one – a man came down who was not from here and he went fishing and got lost. He was a man from the bush.

Yes, the priest still makes the sacrifice. He sacrifices to all the sharks. To us, the shark is known as *the* shark. We call to all the sharks that come here. The white shark, the black-tip shark, the grey reef shark, the shark-like-the-whale, the hammerhead shark, the tiger shark, the shark-with-no-proper teeth. They are familiar to us, we never eat them. We adore them.

Moses,
Malaita, Solomon Islands

objects, but the simplicity of this interpretation does not diminish the terror – it may even intensify it.

Similar gaps exist in our knowledge of other species. We can only guess about the function of the whip-like tail of the thresher or the pattern of spots, stripes and ridges that decorate the whale shark. Since I have accepted the intimidating task of describing 'the legendary shark', I will leave the natural history of the sharks to others; but I wish to emphasise that it is our paucity of hard knowledge that has contributed substantially to our mythification of the shark. Here let me acknowledge that there is no such thing as 'the shark', any more than there is one bird that fulfils all avian criteria. Just as all birds have feathers and lay eggs, so do all sharks have multiple gill slits, cartilaginous skeletons and denticular skin. But there are as many differences between a mako and a nurse shark as there are between an eagle and a sparrow. Nevertheless, legends do not differentiate on specific grounds, so unless I want to make a point about a particular species, I will continue to refer to 'the shark'.

Since the cartilaginous skeletons of sharks lend themselves poorly to fossilisation, we have only fragmented evidence regarding their evolution. (Only the teeth and the vertebral centra have been preserved and, as we shall see, these often cause more problems than they resolve.) There is no question that sharks are among the oldest of the vertebrates, and we can trace their lineage back some 300 million years. (*Homo sapiens* can claim at best a 3 million-year-old forbear.) If the origins of the sharks themselves are lost in the mists of elapsed time, so too are the origins of the legends. We can easily identify some of the early folktales, but I wish to address the position that the shark currently holds in our culture.

THE SHARK IN LITERATURE AND ART
From the time people first put to sea in dugouts, canoes, dhows or coracles, they were probably aware of the sharks around them. Pliny the Elder, who lived from 23 to 79 AD, wrote of sharks in his *Historia Naturalis,* and authors have been vilifying them ever since. Sharks appear in many whaling journals, since they appeared to many whalers, especially when the bloody whale carcases were brought alongside the ships for the flensing. In

Ben Cropp

◄ Carved from a single piece of wood and using genuine sharks' teeth, this sculpture from Wuvulu Island in the Bismarck Sea celebrates the beauty, power and grace of the shark and expresses an attitude of respect and understanding that is far from the fear and hatred common to Western societies.

▲ ▼ Western attitudes to sharks are so coloured by emotion that it is sometimes difficult to reconcile the docility and unaggressive filter feeding of the gigantic whale shark with the images conjured by the word 'shark' – an alien and mindless ferocity that apparently relishes the taste of human flesh.

Neville Coleman

THE LITERARY SHARK

From the witches' curse in *Macbeth* to the graphic descriptions of *Jaws*, the shark has featured in literature in the English language.

> *Scale of dragon, tooth of wolf,*
> *Witches' mummy, maw and gulf*
> *Of the ravined salt-sea shark,*
> *Root of hemlock digged i' th' dark . . .*

Macbeth, Act four, Scene one

At the height of the slave trade, dead and dying slaves were thrown overboard to the sharks:

> *. . . here dwells the direful Shark, lured by the scent*
> *Of reeking crowds, of rank disease and death.*
> *Behold! he rushing cuts the briny flood,*
> *Swift as the gale can bear the ship along;*
> *And from the partners of that cruel trade*
> *Which spoils unhappy Guinea of her sons,*
> *Demands his share of prey . . .*

The Book of Fishes, 1835

In 1952 Ernest Hemingway wrote brilliantly about the mako:

> He was built as a sword fish, except for his huge jaws which were tight shut now as he swam fast, just under the surface with his high dorsal fin knifing through the water without wavering. Inside the closed double lip of his jaws all of his eight rows of teeth were slanted inwards. They were not like the ordinary pyramid-shaped teeth of most sharks. They were shaped like a man's fingers when they are crisped like claws.

The Old Man and the Sea, 1952

And then, in 1974, came Peter Benchley's *Jaws:*

The fish slid backward out of the cage and turned sharply to the right in a tight circle. Hooper reached behind his head, found the regulator tube, and followed it with his hand until he located the mouthpiece. He put it in his mouth and, forgetting to exhale first, sucked for air. He got water, and he gagged and choked until at last the mouthpiece cleared and he drew an agonized breath. It was then that he saw the wide gap in the bars and saw the giant head lunging through it. He raised his hands above his head, grasping at the escape hatch.

The fish rammed through the space between the bars, spreading them still farther with each thrust of its tail. Hooper, flattened against the back of the cage, saw the mouth reaching, straining for him. He remembered the power head, and he tried to lower his right arm and grab it. The fish thrust again, and Hooper saw with the terror of doom that the mouth was going to reach him.

The jaws closed around his torso. Hooper felt a terrible pressure as if his guts were compacted. He jabbed his fist into the black eye. The fish bit down, and the last thing Hooper saw before he died was the eye gazing at him through a cloud of his own blood.

RICHARD ELLIS - 1974

'The mako has more deadly beauty and fighting spirit than any other shark'. *Peter Goadby*

Moby Dick, Melville wrote about the sharks around the *Pequod* this way:

They viciously snapped, not only at each other's disembowelments, but like flexible bows, bent round, and bit their own; till those entrails seemed swallowed over and over by the same mouth, to be oppositely voided by the same wound . . . It was unsafe to meddle with the corpses and ghosts of these creatures.

A sort of generic or Pantheistic vitality seemed to lurk in their very joints and bones, after what might be called their individual vitality had departed.

There have been many books written about sharks. Probably the first that dealt exclusively with these creatures was Horace Mazet's *Shark! Shark!* This 1934 chronicle told of Captain William Young's obsessive hunt for sharks that began in Honolulu and took him around the world, killing sharks for sport, for the safety of swimmers and for sharkskin leather. At one point, Young refers to the sharks as 'savage, armoured sea tigers which had become my totem, my fetish'. Then there were books about shark fishing (including *Tigers of the Sea*, written by C. Hugh Wise in 1937, and Zane Grey's numerous accounts of his big-game fishing exploits in California and New Zealand) and also about shark attacks: Victor Coppleson, an

Australian surgeon, wrote *Shark Attack* in 1958; David Davies, a South African scientist, wrote *About Sharks and Shark Attack* in 1964; and other, less rational, discussions of the 'shark menace' followed.

Nor has the shark been a particularly popular subject for artists. In almost all pictorial representations of sharks the shark is depicted as a menace to swimmers or sailors. Think of Copley's *Watson and the Shark*, where a host of boatmen try to save Brook Watson, who seems to have been swimming naked in Havana harbour. One of Watson's would-be rescuers is poised on the bow of the skiff with a boathook raised, about to drive it into the head of a huge but unrecognisable species of shark with a Moorish arch for an upper lip. (Watson, who commissioned the painting, actually lost a foot to the shark, but survived to become the Lord Mayor of London.)

The other celebrated appearance of the shark in art is Winslow Homer's *The Gulf Stream*, where a sailor gazes listlessly over the stern of his dismasted sloop as several sharks circle hungrily, waiting for whatever happens next in this permanently arrested drama. There is a waterspout visible on the horizon, and also a fully rigged ship. Does the hurricane come and dump the hapless sailor, or is this the very hurricane that wrecked his boat in the first place? There seems to be plenty of blood in the

▼ Winslow Homer's famous 1899 oil *The Gulf Stream* brings together drama, fear and improbable hope of salvation in the first 'modern' interpretation of human versus shark.

The Gulf Stream; Winslow Homer; Metropolitan Museum of Art, New York; Wolfe Fund, 1906; Catherine Lorillard Wolfe Collection

▲ John Singleton Copley's *Watson and the Shark,* first exhibited in 1778, is one of the most famous of all shark paintings. At a time when few people believed that sharks would attack humans, Copley's painting and questionable claims of its hero, Brook Watson (later Lord Mayor of London), were advanced as graphic evidence.

water, so I think the sharks have already eaten the other crew members and are awaiting their next meal.

When the painting was first exhibited in 1900, so many people found the subject depressing that Homer wrote a letter to his gallery in which he explained, probably facetiously: 'You can tell these ladies that the unfortunate negro, who is now so dazed and parboiled, will be rescued & returned to his friends and home, & ever after live happily.' Neither Copley's nor Homer's painting glorified the shark; rather they embellished its already nefarious character.

THE SHARK'S MODERN STATUS

It was not until 1974 that the reputation of the shark took a quantum leap forward – or backward, if you will. In that year, Peter Benchley wrote *Jaws,* a novel that has as its main character not a man, but a fish – and not just any fish, but a great white shark.

Benchley was not the first person to contribute

to the white shark's elevation to totemic status. As early as 1916, reports of a series of shark attacks in New Jersey vied for newspaper space with the Battle of the Somme in France. Four people died in the New Jersey surf within a period of three weeks and another lost a leg. Although these attacks were attributed to the great white, the identity of the attacking shark (or more likely, *sharks*) was never proven. Later interpretations favour the bull shark as the culprit, but the white shark got the credit at the time. In the development of *Jaws,* Benchley incorporated the 'rogue shark' theory, where a single hungry shark cruised the beaches of a particular area, seeking to satisfy its craving for human flesh. This was Victor Coppleson's explanation for many shark attacks in Australian waters, but I do not believe it is correct. Nor do I think that sharks develop a taste for people. If they did, there would be no beach on earth that was safe for swimming.

Later in the century, shark attacks became

▶ The manufacture of a legend. Valerie Taylor poses beside one of the three 7.3-metre mechanical sharks, collectively named Bruce, that movie special effects expert Bob Mattey created for *Jaws*. Weighing about 1.5 tonnes and costing $150 000 apiece, the three Bruces were operated by thirteen technicians.

▶ Bruce is 90 centimetres longer than the maximum recorded real great white, though there are probably individuals eight metres long. It is unlikely that even an 8-metre great white would sport teeth as large as Bruce's, which were deliberately oversized to add to the impact of the shark's appearance on screen.

▼ Australian underwater filmmakers Ron and Valerie Taylor spent weeks training live great white sharks near Port Lincoln, in South Australia, to attack on cue for action sequences in *Jaws*. The local talent, said Valerie Taylor, responded superbly, though a 1.5-metre stuntman was hired to make a 4.8-metre great white's attacks on a diving cage look more like those of the movie's 7.3-metre star.

front-page news all over the world, especially in South Africa and Australia. In 1959, the American Institute of Biological Sciences convened the Shark Research Panel which collected data on shark attacks around the world. The Shark Attack File, maintained at the Mote Marine Laboratory in Sarasota, Florida, was reviewed by H. David Baldridge, who first compiled a report on the data contained in the file and then wrote a popular book called *Shark Attack*. Published in 1975, it contained this message on the jacket: 'True tales of shark attacks on man – facts more terrifying than the fiction of *Jaws*.' Other books were written, but the sharks did not have to rely on published material to get themselves noticed. They were doing very nicely on their own.

In South Australia, three divers were attacked by white sharks: in 1961, Brian Rodger was bitten; the next year Geoff Corner was killed; and in 1963, Rodney Fox was savagely attacked by a white pointer. It took 462 stitches to sew Fox together again. In 1967 Rodney Fox went to Spencer Gulf to look for the fish that nearly killed him. With him were Henri Bource, another victim, who had lost a leg to a white shark in 1964, Ron Taylor and Alf Dean, the fisherman who holds the record for the largest fish ever caught on rod and reel – a 1200-kilogram white shark. The photographs that Ron Taylor took on this expedition are still among the best ever taken and they have probably been used more often than any other pictures of the shark the Australians call 'white death'. One of Taylor's photographs of a shark approaching the camera with its jaws agape is used on the poster advertising Peter Gimbel's 1968 film of his search for the great white shark, *Blue Water, White Death*. It was the first time the white shark had been filmed underwater, but it was not going to be the last.

The novel *Jaws* was a smashing success, selling hundreds of thousands of copies around the world, and the movie made from the book was a blockbuster; for a while it was the highest grossing film in Hollywood history. *Jaws II* followed with less box-office and critical success, and then *Jaws III* limped into the theatres, an ineffectual shadow of its predecessors.

In a 1979 article in *Skin Diver* magazine, underwater cameraman Stan Waterman wrote: 'Something there is about the shark that continues to tickle the macabre fancy of man. And it is, of course, both simple and profitable to exploit.' There were now shark movies, shark novels, shark television specials. On the cover of its 23 June 1975 issue, *Time* magazine featured a shark bursting out of the water accompanied by the headline 'The Summer of the Shark'. In the past decade, we have indeed elevated the shark to mythic proportions; it has now become one of our own culture's legends. Like the Hawaiians, we too have a shark-god.

GREAT WHITES, MODERN AND ANCIENT

Much of the shark's status is based on misinformation, but it is nowhere written that legends must have a foundation in fact. (Was the Hawaiian shark-god *really* a man with a set of shark jaws in his back?) In this new mythology, there is an emphasis on one species, *Carcharodon carcharias*, the great white shark. Forget that there are another 350 species of sharks, most of which are harmless to humans. Forget also that there are no authenticated reports of white sharks over six and a half metres in length. (The shark in *Jaws* was never measured, but the ichthyologist suggests that it might be more than seven and half metres long.) There continue to be reports of monster sharks, ranging from nine to 35 metres in length. In a 1963 edition of *Sharks and Rays of Australian Seas*, David G. Stead recounts a tale of a monster shark, which fishermen knew 'was not a whale', seen in 1918 off Broughton Island off the coast of Queensland. Stead writes that 'in this occurrence we had one of those very rare occasions when humans have been vouchsafed a glimpse of one of those enormous sharks of the White Death type, which we know to exist, or to have existed in the recent past, in the depths of the sea'.

In 1982, I went to the Azores to track down reports of a 9-metre shark that was supposed to have been harpooned by sperm whalers. I spent the better part of two weeks in these islands, interviewing scientists, fishermen, newspapermen and administrators. I found no evidence at all that a white shark of such a size had ever been seen in the Azores. Of course, that does not conclusively prove that such a fish does not exist, but it does mean that

75 CENTS   **JUNE 23, 1975**

TIME

SUPER SHARK

'Jaws' on Film and Other Summer Thrillers

▲ *Time* magazine's edition of 23 June 1975 capitalised on the popular image of the great white as 'one of nature's most efficient killing machines', to quote the edition's story on the making of *Jaws*. The movie's box-office success also sparked a wave of shark attack hysteria in Australian, American and South African newspapers.

a dedicated investigator was unable to document its existence.

A similar situation exists with *Carcharodon megalodon*, an extinct relative of the white shark. With teeth that measured fifteen centimetres or more along their serrated edges, these monsters probably reached lengths of between twelve and fifteen metres – large enough to swallow a horse. The only evidence for the existence of these terrifying creatures is their huge fossil teeth, but quite often in the popular literature these teeth mysteriously lose their fossil character and are used to prove that *megalodon* still exists. In Peter Matthiessen's otherwise excellent book, *Blue Meridian,* the chronicle of the *Blue Water, White Death* expedition, the author incorrectly assumes that *C. carcharias* and *C. megalodon* are the same species and that, therefore, there could be 15-metre white sharks cruising the seas today. Then there is Robin Brown's novel *Megalodon,* which concerns

itself with 60-metre, barnacle-encrusted sharks that lie on the bottom, waiting to gobble up nuclear submarines like so many peanuts. Like *Jaws*, *Megalodon* is fiction, but in our search for symbols, we are often willing to allow novelists to contribute to our fears and thus to our legends.

The white shark has come to represent all sharks because in a sense, it *is* all sharks. It is big, powerful, extremely dangerous and frightening to behold. It has all the equipment that characterises the voracious shark: razor-sharp, serrated teeth; a soulless black eye (Matthiessen wrote that it was 'impenetrable and empty as the eye of God'); and of course, that all-important triangular dorsal fin, always 'knifing' through the water.

Of all large, predatory animals, the white shark is probably the most dangerous to humans. Cobras in India kill many more people than sharks around the world, but as they don't eat their victims, they do not, at least in Western countries, have the same reputation. Lions, tigers, polar bears and grizzlies also attack people on occasion, but their attacks are rare, probably because the carnivores themselves are rare. We don't often hear about big cats or bears as a threat to our existence or even our safety; in fact, we tend nowadays to regard these animals as relatively harmless inhabitants of zoos and circuses.

While some species of large sharks, such as nurses, lemons and sand tigers, are successfully kept in aquariums, all attempts to keep whites or their relatives, the makos and the porbeagles, have met with unqualified failure. Therefore, we can see the shark only as an offshore menace, unreachable even by those who only want to learn a little more about it.

The shark occupies a habitat that is not of our terrestrial understanding. Despite the technological advances that have enabled us to enter the water, we do so as trespassers in an alien and decidedly hostile world. Even the *medium* is hostile – unlike the fishes, we cannot breathe it without a face-mask; we can barely see through it. In its thick, liquid environment, the shark evidently reigns supreme. Are we jealous of the ease with which sharks move, breathe, feed and reproduce in the water? What are the elements that make up this love–hate relationship? Is it that these big fish with the small brains have circumvented our every effort to control or even understand them? Do we admire these hunter–killers because we have lost these natural abilities ourselves? Or do we admire their lethal graceful form, their spare economy of line and motion, their smooth, sleek and overwhelmingly ancient efficiency? Is it something that goes even deeper into our collective psyche? Perhaps it is our atavistic fear of being eaten that simultaneously lends distance and a disturbing proximity to our relationship with the shark. It is, after all, the only animal on earth that we fear can – or worse, *will* – eat us, and that is the stuff of which legends are made.

◀ 'The most terrible monster that the seas of Mother Earth have produced,' wrote David Stead in *Sharks and Rays of Australian Seas,* referring to the shark he preferred to call 'white death'. Richard Ellis's painting seeks to illustrate the predatory grace and undeniable power of the animal behind the image.

Richard Ellis

© RICHARD ELLIS-1975

RICHARD ELLIS - 1974 ©

Richard Ellis

◄ In South Africa it is the raggedtooth shark; in the United States it is the sand tiger; Australians know it as the grey nurse. Despite its ominous appearance, it is not considered dangerous to humans.

USING SHARKS

A.M. OLSEN

To many people, inspired by hysterical newspaper headlines or sensational movies, sharks symbolise terror: they are portrayed as sinister, silent killing machines, ceaselessly patrolling the oceans in search of human prey. The reality is very different. Sharks are far less dangerous than humans or their inventions and, in fact, provide a host of benefits. Their meat is eaten or used for fertiliser and their fins are made into soup. Oils rich in vitamin A are extracted from their livers, and anticoagulants from their blood. Their eyes provide corneas for transplants; their cartilage is used in the treatment of burns. Chances are a shark has provided meat for your table, lubricants for your machines, oil for your plants – even squalene for your cosmetics.

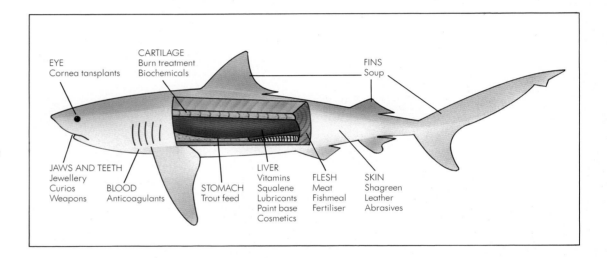

► The usable shark. Although they generally inspire only fear, sharks provide a remarkably wide range of products useful to humans. *(After Moss 1984)*

SHARK FISHING: AN AUSTRALIAN CASE STUDY

When the first white settlers arrived at Sydney Cove in New South Wales in 1788 they depended, at least in the short term, on food they had brought with them. They supplemented these scanty resources by fishing. It is known that sharks were caught and eaten and the oil extracted from their livers for lighting, and other purposes. Liver oil from the grey nurse shark (*Eugomphodus taurus*) was available in 1794 for one shilling a quart. As late as 1857 the oil from this same shark was still being used for lighting the tower at the government station on the northern entrance to Botany Bay and in the homes of the nearby villages. At that time imported candles were too costly for general use.

The fins of sharks were also used for the sharkfin soup trade. Samuel Lord, merchant of Sydney Cove, advertised in 1804 'for a contractor to supply a quantity of shark fins, properly dried and preserved', presumably for the Chinese market.

With the discovery of gold in 1851, gold fever gripped the colony and men deserted the coastal settlements in droves to try their luck as gold-diggers. Thus there was a dearth of maritime fishing activity and the industry languished for some time. Furthermore the discovery of mineral oil reserves in Western Pennsylvania, USA, in 1859 and aggressive merchandising of this new lighting oil slackened the demand for shark liver oil.

Hence in 1875, when the Reverend Tenison Woods visited the fishing establishment at Recherche Bay, southern Tasmania, he found a depressed situation with the men of the ten families catching school sharks (*Galeorhinus galeus*) for their fins and drying abalone or mutton fish for the Chinese market. (Vessels trading between England and China called regularly at both Hobart and Sydney and could pick up consignments of abalone and sharkfins for the Chinese market.)

There are few records of the use of elasmobranch resources in Australia between 1875 and the early 1920s. Some fishermen in Tasmania, however, found they could use burley to attract school sharks around their vessels. The sharks were gaffed and hauled aboard. This operation took place during the October–December run of gravid

Coo-ee Historical Picture Library

◄ Until World War II sharks were never a significant part of popular mythology. They were known to attack and eat humans but were seen as 'chinless cowards', in the words of one naturalist, and their major importance was as competitors for food or as food themselves. This 1881 etching shows a shark being harpooned off the Australian coast.

▼ Netting, harpooning and shore-based fishing for sharks were of fluctuating economic importance in the nineteenth century. Shark meat was used for human consumption, skin — or shagreen — for sandpaper, liver oil for lighting and lubrication and undressed carcases were sold to farmers as fertiliser for orchards.

Coo-ee Historical Picture Library

▲ The discovery of squalene in 1916 gave fresh impetus to shark hunting, as industry became aware of its value for lubrication and cosmetics. Liver oil (also sold as cod liver oil) from this tiger shark was worth 2s 9d a gallon in Australia in 1932.

▼ Near Santa Rosalia, on the Baja Peninsula in western Mexico, hammerheads are captured by hook and line and by netting, forming a major element in the area's subsistence economy. As well as providing food, sharks caught in this area are utilised for their skins, which are tanned for the manufacture of wallets, belts and other leathergoods.

females toward the pupping grounds in protected and sheltered bays and inlets around the southern coasts of Tasmania. As much as three or four tonnes of school shark could be landed by this arduous method in a single day. The undressed carcases were sold to farmers as fertiliser for their apple orchards and buried in the loamy soils around the bases of the trees.

In 1927 a school shark fishery to provide flesh for human consumption was established in Victoria in the east Gippsland port of Port Albert. A small shipment of two tonnes of shark fillets was sent to Melbourne to test market reaction. The response was cautious and further small orders were forthcoming to encourage the fishermen. Within two years other Victorian ports were forwarding small consignments of school shark to Melbourne markets. Twenty-six tonnes passed through the

market in 1929 but the demand was reduced in the Depression years. However in 1934, 115 tonnes were marketed and by 1939 this had risen to 514 tonnes.

The demand for livers, rich in Vitamin A, gave impetus to the fishery. This demand intensified during World War II when the Vitamin A-rich oil was used to fortify rations for Australian troops. In July 1942 the fishery was put under manpower control, fuel rationing was introduced and prices were controlled. The catch comprised about 80 per cent school shark and 20 per cent gummies (*Mustelus antarcticus*), whiskery sharks (*Furgaleus macki*) and sawsharks (*Pristiophorus* spp).

Within a decade, however, the demand for livers had disappeared. In 1946 Japanese interests flooded the world's markets with high potency Vitamin A fish liver oil, and in 1950 the marketing of synthetic Vitamin A by Dutch manufacturers made shark livers redundant. The fishery continued to operate only for the flesh it supplied.

The total catch for southeastern Australia peaked at 2215 tonnes in 1969–70, but declined the following year. The introduction of legislation banning the landing of school sharks with mercury concentrations greater than 0.5 parts per million had a disastrous effect on the shark industry. It recovered somewhat after a few years and now yields between 1600 and 1800 tonnes annually. The composition of the catch has altered, too, with school shark comprising 40–50 per cent of the catch.

Methods have also changed; longline fishing has now been replaced by the use of mesh nets. Because of concern about the stocks of school and gummy sharks, fishery authorities have introduced a limited entry regime to manage the resources.

USING THE SKIN
The most characteristic feature of the skin of sharks is its roughness, due to the placoid scales embedded in the skin itself. The scales are variously called 'skin teeth' or dermal denticles. Each scale

has a flat base and one or more backward-pointing spines – cored with dentine and tipped with ivory or enamel – rising from its upper surface. These scales or denticles are arranged in various patterns over the whole or parts of the body surface; some rays are entirely lacking in placoid scales. The dried skin is called 'shagreen' because it is thought to resemble the granular, untanned leather of the same name made from the backs and rumps of horses. The distribution, shape and height of the spines of the denticle determine the purpose for which a particular shagreen is used.

Shagreen was once used for polishing wood; glasspaper or carborundum sheets have now supplanted it as a smoothing agent. In Sumatra the stretched and dried skin of the cowtail skate (*Dasyatis sephen*) is used for the tympanums of drums and tambourines; in certain Pacific islands shagreen from another skate species (*Himantura*) is said to be preferred for this purpose. Shagreen from the cowtail skate was used also by sword makers in Japan for binding on the hilts of their swords – the surface provided a non-slip grip for the hand!

Certain Moroccan sharks provide shagreen for 'Boroso leather', which is in great demand in the specialties market; the denticles are not removed but are lightly polished to make an extremely tough and beautiful covering. In the seventeenth century shagreen-covered articles from the Orient created immense interest and were in great demand. European artisans soon learned the art of using this treated shagreen to cover such personal articles as jewellery boxes, spectacle cases and cases for silver ware as well as for book bindings. Despite the beauty and durability of the shagreen covering the fashion for such articles waned and now the 'galuchat' – polished shagreen – covered articles are in demand only as antique collectors' items.

LEATHER

People have known for centuries how to tan the hides of mammals but it was not until after World War I that two teams of research chemists working independently in the United States achieved a successful method for tanning the skins of large sharks without denticles. The breakthrough was made by the discovery of a chemical process that would remove the denticles without adversely affecting the tanning properties of the shark hides.

Shark leather has a higher tensile strength than leather made from cattle hides. The intermeshing connective fibres within the skin of sharks are much longer than the fibres in mammal hides. The high collagen content of sharks' connective fibres also facilitates the tanning process.

CORNEAS

In the United States elasmobranch corneas have been used as successful substitutes for human corneas. It is a peculiar characteristic of corneas from eyes of elasmobranch fishes that they do not swell when placed in varying concentrations of salt solutions. On the other hand, the corneas of

◄ Sharkskin with its denticles intact is still used as fine sandpaper by craftspeople. With the denticles removed by a special chemical process, sharkskin leather is in demand for applications where, paradoxically, both great tensile strength and flexibility are needed. Sharkskin leather is still used in the manufacture of fine quality handmade shoes.

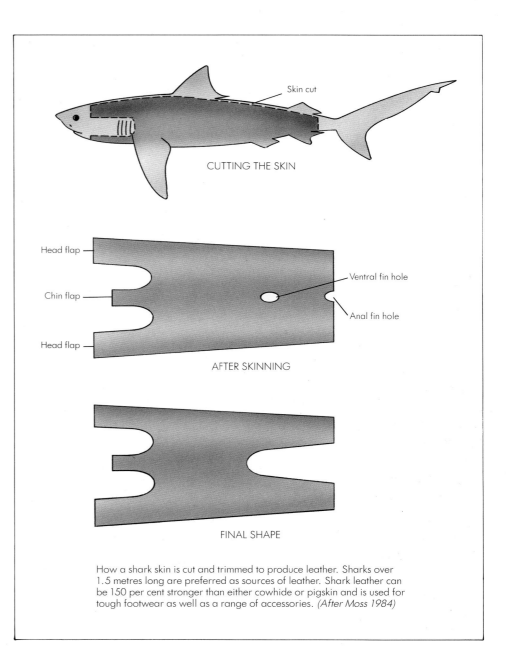

CUTTING THE SKIN

Head flap
Chin flap
Head flap
Ventral fin hole
Anal fin hole

AFTER SKINNING

FINAL SHAPE

How a shark skin is cut and trimmed to produce leather. Sharks over 1.5 metres long are preferred as sources of leather. Shark leather can be 150 per cent stronger than either cowhide or pigskin and is used for tough footwear as well as a range of accessories. *(After Moss 1984)*

Not all parts of a shark are used for practical purposes: shark teeth have traditionally been used for weapons, decoration or ritual, though today they are more likely to be employed in the design of jewellery or curios. A selection of large and expensive 'fossil', modern and gold-plated great white shark pendants *(right)*; a fanciful shell shark manufactured in Taiwan and sold in Cairns in northern Queensland *(above)*; and a carved wooden shark with genuine teeth from Pitcairn Island *(below)*.

teleosts (bony fish) do swell when placed in salt solutions and hence have no value as transplants.

In Australia corneas for transplant operations are supplied from banks of stored human corneas that have been built up in the capital cities of the different states.

SHARKS' TEETH

The use of sharks' teeth as ornaments has a long history. Even today, mounted whole jaws are popular adornments for the walls of game fishermen's homes and as decorations in places sponsoring marine interests. Mounted jaws of sharks are good conversation pieces. In Hawaii a

pair of jaws of a large shark costs about US$200, while in Australia large jaws are more costly; those of a 5–6 metre white shark – when they can be obtained – fetch up to a thousand Australian dollars.

In the watch-chain and waistcoat era, mounted sharks' teeth were fashionable as attachments to watch-chains. Wristwatches do not lend themselves to such adornments!

Among South Sea islanders, teeth have been used for both ceremonial and warlike purposes. Swords made from teeth fitted into slots of a wooden strip are fearsome weapons because the serrated edges of the many teeth inflict painful jagged wounds. A shortened version of the same basic design is the double-edged knife. The teeth of whaler sharks (*Carcharhinus* spp.) are in demand for weapons, particularly in Kiribati.

The Maoris of New Zealand use the teeth of the spotted sevengill shark (*Notorhynchus cepedianus*) to make their war weapons and the teeth of the mako (*Isurus oxyrinchus*) are greatly prized as ear ornaments (ngutukao). Eskimos make knives from teeth of the Greenland sleeper shark (*Somniosus microcephalus*).

SHARK FINS

The shark fin market is dependent on the demands of Chinese ethnic groups who use fins in the preparation of their classic and traditional dishes. Hong Kong is probably the best world market for shark fins, with 60 or more countries exporting fins to it. Several tonnes of fins from western ports of Mexico are exported annually into the western United States, then re-exported to Hong Kong and other Eastern markets. In 1982 more than 2700 tonnes of dried shark fins, valued at HK$245.4 million, were imported.

Only the single dorsal, the pectoral fins and the lower lobe of the caudal (tail) fin are acceptable for making soup. The price paid in Hong Kong depends on size, colour, species, cut, trim and moisture content of the fins. Fins of almost all species except mako, nurse and thresher sharks are marketable in the United States.

In the preparation of shark fins for soup, the skin from both sides is removed and any muscle tissue scraped off to leave clean the inner cartilaginous fin rays and outer horny fibres (ceratotrichia). Only the horny fibres are used; they are compressed into fibrous mats and added to the stock. The fibres are composed of one of the scleroproteins, elastoidine, which differs from collagen in that it contains sulphur and does not yield gelatin when it is boiled in water.

LIVER OILS AND VITAMIN A

The liver oils of many sharks have proved a valuable source of Vitamin A. Vitamin A is essential for the formation of visual purple in the retina of the eye; people whose diet lacks or is deficient in this vitamin are likely to suffer night blindness.

When liver lipids (oils) of bony fishes are treated with alkalis (saponification) a chemical soap and a free alcohol are formed and only traces of unsaponifiable matter remain. The lipids from elastobranches are more complex and on saponification not only are soaps and alcohols formed but a high concentration of unsaponifiable matter remains as residue. This residue contains

the concentrations of long-chain carbon saturated and unsaturated fatty acids and other hydrocarbons present in the lipid. Vitamin A ($C_{20}H_{29}OH$) occurs in the unsaponifiable fraction of liver lipids of fish.

Because of its commercial and therapeutic importance, Vitamin A has been studied intensively to establish its occurrence in the liver lipids (oils) of different species of teleosts and elasmobranchs and to investigate the effects of its potency on such factors as sex, age, length, maturity, seasonality and geographical distribution.

As they do not need Vitamin D for bone growth, elasmobranchs have very low concentrations of this vitamin in their liver lipids and correspondingly high levels of Vitamin A. The Vitamin A potencies and percentages of oil in the livers of a number of Australian and New Zealand elasmobranchs are given in the table on the following page.

SQUALENE

The unsaturated terpenic hydrocarbon, squalene ($C_{30}H_{50}$), is the other major component of the unsaponifiable residue of liver lipids. Its presence in liver lipids was first recognised in Mediterranean sharks. In 1916, a Japanese chemist isolated this unsaturated hydrocarbon from the livers of sharks and named it 'squalene'. Two years later an English chemist, working independently on liver oils from eastern Atlantic Ocean sharks, also isolated the same hydrocarbon and, not being aware of its previous discovery, named it 'spinacene'. This important constituent of shark livers is now known by its earlier name.

In general squalene is present in high

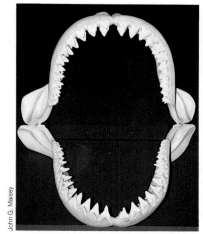

▲ *Carcharodon megalodon*, ancestor of today's great white shark, appeared 60 to 65 million years ago and grew to more than twelve metres long. The first reconstructions of its jaws were inaccurate and oversized by two or three times; this more realistic version is based on more extensive fossil material and serves as a tourist attraction in its own right.

▲ Game fishermen are proud of their victories over 'fighting' sharks such as great whites, makos and threshers, and often preserve their catches' jaws to commemorate a struggle that may last several hours. Divers also obtain trophies by less honourable means, killing inoffensive species with powerheads.

◄ Simple butchery, with no justification other than to satisfy the masculine ego, has seen thousands of harmless sharks killed by powerheads. This sand tiger or grey nurse (*Eugomphodus taurus*) was killed by trophy hunters, its jaws removed and its valuable flesh and liver (shown here after the carcase was senselessly disembowelled) abandoned.

▲ One of the most popular uses of sharks is for recreational fishing and the oceanic blue, mako, thresher and great white are highly regarded as fighting fish by game fishermen. Alf Dean *(centre)*, an Australian game fisherman shown here with a 4-metre great white caught off South Australia, holds several world records for shark catches.

concentrations in liver lipids in those sharks that have low levels of Vitamin A. It is synthesised by the shark, not ingested, and is the precursor of cholesterol. It is also a component of vegetable oils. The concentration of squalene in the liver lipids of sharks ranges from 63 to 96 per cent in some species, particularly in some deep-sea dogfishes. One deepwater dogfish, a kitefin shark (*Dalatias licha*), 126 centimetres long and caught at a depth of 450 metres, had a lipid content of 83 per cent of which 40 per cent was squalene. Basking sharks have a squalene content of about 50 per cent.

Squalene has many commercial applications. It is used in high-technology industries, in cosmetics as a skin rejuvenator and also in pharmaceuticals that require a non-oily base.

ANTICOAGULANTS

In recent years attention has been directed to the benefits of controlled diets in combating fatal cardiac arrest. In some way the incidence of this cardiac condition is associated with increased consumption of dietary fats.

Polyunsaturated fatty acids from certain vegetable or marine sources are thought to be beneficial in controlling this disease. The liver oils of certain teleost fish, particularly deep-sea dogfish, have been found not only to have high concentrations of squalene but also to be rich in the polyunsaturated fatty acids, docosahexaenoic acid (DHA) and eicosapentaenoic acid (EPA), and low in cholesterol.

Both these polyunsaturated long-chain fatty acids are undergoing rigid animal experimentation and results to date show a desirable effect in prolonging blood coagulation time and in lowering cholesterol levels in heart tissues.

Eskimos have been found to have a longer blood clotting time than Europeans and the reason is believed to be the high level of these polyunsaturated fatty acids in their diet.

RECREATIONAL USES OF SHARKS

The annual total catches of various shark species by recreational fishermen have been poorly documented in the past. Only catches of single extremely large or heavy sharks taken on fine gear appear to have been documented by game fishing clubs. Through better communication and participation by recreational fishing clubs, surveys are now yielding much more valuable data on annual total shark catches. More than 30 000 pelagic sharks have been tagged and released to date in a fifteen-year program by game fishermen operating in eastern United States waters.

The fighting qualities of mako, porbeagle, white, thresher and tiger sharks are respected by game fishermen and the International Game Fish Association has included these five shark species in its list of 50 species of game fish.

VITAMIN A POTENCIES AND LIVER OIL CONCENTRATIONS OF SELECTED SHARKS

Common name	Scientific name	Vitamin A International units/g oil	Percentage oil in liver
broadnose sevengill shark	*Notorynchus cepedianus*	1700–7500	71.5
smallnose gulper shark	*Centrophorus moluccensis*	nil	68.7–73.5
plunket shark	*Centroscymnus plunketi*	370–500	84–93
longsnout dogfish	*Deania quadrispinosum*	nil	78–90
piked dogfish	*Squalus acanthias*	300–21 200	8.9–70
shortnose spurdog	*S. megalops*	1500–18 600	8.3–70.4
longnose sawshark	*Pristiophorus cirratus*	500	NA
shortnose sawshark	*P. nudipinnis*	13 400	42.5
spotted wobbegong	*Orectolobus maculatus*	2000	NA
grey nurse shark	*Eugomphodus taurus*	600–2000	NA
shortfin mako	*Isurus ocyrinchus*	100–2000	NA
porbeagle shark	*Lamna nasus*	18 000	42.5
tiger shark	*Galeocerdo cuvier*	500–5000	NA
Australian swellshark	*Cephaloscyllium laticeps*	670	53.6
gummy shark	*Mustelus antarcticus*	50–15 000	4.1–56
school shark	*Galeorhinus galeus: embryo*	0–300	29–75
school shark	*G. galeus: juvenile*	0–10 000	2.2–62
school shark	*G. galeus: adult*	6000–156 000	16.4–84

Neville Coleman

Neville Coleman

▲ Although far less impressive than the sharks caught by game fishermen and, in fact, each less than a metre in length, these dogfishes (*Squalus blainvillei,* top, and *S. megalops*) are economically of much greater importance. *Squalus acanthias,* the piked dogfish, is possibly the world's most abundant shark and supports an industry of global significance; an estimated 27 000 000 piked dogfish have been caught in one year in only one location for use as food, oil and fertiliser, and other members of the genus provide many communities with the bulk of their income.

SHARKS AS FOOD: A TRADITIONAL DELICACY

KEVIN SINCLAIR

Shufunotomo

The fins of shark, tough, grisly protuberances with little if any nutritional value, play a unique role in Chinese cuisine. For centuries, they have been eagerly sought by gourmets along the coastal provinces as the basis for dishes destined for the table of emperor and mandarin. These days, in such citadels of Chinese gastronomy as Hong Kong and Singapore, wealthy merchants will pay a fortune for specialist dishes the basis of which is shark fin.

The reason anyone would consume with gusto anything as unlikely as the fin of a shark is a secret whose origin is lost to history. But scholars hold that the expensive, exotic custom began more than 2000 years ago for the very best of reasons: they suspect that during one of the many famines that through the course of history has clamped disconsolate hunger on the land, some starving peasant boiled the fin of a shark and ate it. It was a diet of desperation, eaten simply because there was nothing else.

But the fins give to the soup in which it is cooked an elusive quality much sought by gourmets who delve into the more esoteric realms of Chinese cuisine. Dishes are supposed to have four attributes. Taste, smell and appearance are the three most obvious and the trio on which gastronomes lay most stress. But the fourth is often of equal importance, and a quality that is more elusive. It is texture. As dish after dish is carried to the banquet table, one should be crunchy, the next bland.

Shark fin, after many hours of treatment, results in a smooth, glutinous dish. The texture as well as the taste is vital. One of the other major dishes of Chinese cooking that gives a similar texture is sea cucumber; Western gourmets may claim it results in a dish that is something akin to chewing a well-cooked and well-used truck tyre, but to Oriental epicures it is a taste sensation that is difficult to equal.

It is also an expensive addiction to aficionados of the fin. A dish of shark fin soup in a top speciality restaurant in Hong Kong could almost pay for a fishing boat in some of the lands fringing the South China Sea where sharks are caught. Although ancient Chinese recipes of more than 2000 years ago are quite specific about the lengthy and complex process which sees a raw fin prepared for the gourmet table, there is a surprising lack of emphasis on the source of the raw material. The fin can come from any shark. Hammerhead or Blue or Great White or Grey Nurse – in Chinese cuisine a shark is a shark is a shark and as long as the fin is the right circular shape, it matters not from what variety it came. Indeed, when the dish arrives at the table an unsuspecting diner would never know that the basis of the mixture in the traditional deeply-moulded silver tureen was the fin of a shark.

Although used in other dishes, and prepared as a medicinal draught by traditional herbalists, the most famed preparation of shark in any cuisine is the Chinese shark fin soup. Cooking this delicacy is an exacting, demanding process aimed at preserving the gelatinous texture of the raw material. But to achieve this, great care is needed.

Making shark fin is left to the energies of skilled professional chefs: the process is not one that could fit into the schedule of a busy housewife because from raw fin to soup bowl is a series of precise procedures that take more than a week. Recipes handed down from the time of the Southern Song Dynasty 800 years ago call for the raw fin to be scraped clean of meat, then boiled for two hours. The stock is then thrown away, the fin put into fresh water and boiled another two hours. This is repeated for five days. After many hours of soaking, simmering, boiling, standing in water then being drained and boiled again, the fin is skinned and what little remains is ready for the attention of the chef. His job is to build on the basis of the transparent threads of gelatinous matter a tasty and tempting dish.

He achieves this by making a rich, thick stock of chicken, mushroom, ham, ginger, scallions, soy sauce, sweet yellow rice wine, vinegar, salt and sugar. In this mixture, almost anything would taste good and it is submerged in the hearty soup that the gourmet gets his shark fin. It lies in the bottom of the bowl, a heavy layer of thin thread-like noodles, a delight to the Cantonese gourmets and a matter of some bemusement to many western tourists to such places as Hong Kong. To the horror of restaurant staff, many visitors to Asia order shark fin, sip the soup with great appreciation, then leave the expensive shark fin in the bowl.

The niceties of preparation are lost on all but the most discerning of adventurers. The most excellent of shark fin comes from a fish whose fin is cut off neatly when it is hauled aboard a fishing boat. During the long boiling process, the fin is skinned and the contents become transparent. To keep the correct shape, classical cook books call for the fin to be wrapped in a bamboo net which preserves the shape of the fin. The raw material of costly cuisine in Hong Kong is likely to have originated far away. Although fishing fleets in the South China Sea are keenly aware of the value of a fin, many are imported from other parts of the world. Some are netted off Ireland, others in Norway, Mexico, Venezuela and the Indian Ocean. The fins are exported to the great gourmet cities of the Far East.

No matter where shark is caught, the fins are but part of the commercial catch. The rest of the fish is consigned to local markets where it often has a considerable economic and epicurean value.

Shark has traditionally, although in some secrecy, been a staple food in European, American and Australian food. Disguised under such names as dogfish, sharkflesh has for centuries been sold in fish markets. And why not? The flesh is firm, tasty, nutritious. In the Mediterranean, it is much prized as a delicacy and forms the basis for many a hearty stew, simmered with onion and garlic and tomato. In South America, shark of all varieties are eaten in cuisines from the Yucatan Peninsula of Mexico to the icy shores of the Straits of Magellan. Early explorers wrote in their logs of the wild Indians of frigid Terra del Fuego roasting shark over fires on the shore.

When John Farley wrote *The London Art of Cookery* in 1787 he included instructions on how to fricassee skate. The method, using mace, nutmeg, white wine and cream, applies equally to other sharks.

Greek and Roman gourmets ate shark with enthusiasm and throughout the Mediterranean today it is a delicacy in many a kitchen. Few places appreciate shark more than Sicily and the island's cooks have a multitude of ways of cooking the fish. Many of these call for large portions of fish to be casseroled with sharp goat cheese, a preparation which adds a characteristic piquancy to shark.

Just as sharks cruise in every ocean of the world, so are they a truly international food. Humans have been eating shark for as

Weldon Trannies

long, if not longer, than the fish have been attacking swimmers. In cuisines as different as Serbian and Vietnamese, Jamaican and Javanese, shark has appeared on the menu for centuries. In different cultures, varying preparations give the ubiquitous shark specific local flavour. A favoured Vietnamese preparation calls for lime juice, coriander and red-hot chillies, giving the dish a distinctive character. In Italian recipes, parsley and Parmesan cheese predominate. But the housewife in Lebanon may use olive oil and capers to give the fish a familiar flavour. The French monks of Chartreuse, famed for their cooking, in medieval times invented a preparation for porbeagle shark which called for the fish to be wrapped in leaves with onions and carrots, then braised. Turkish chefs baked porbeagles with green olives for the edification of the Caliphs. In Melanesia, shark is roasted on hot rocks on the beaches, then eaten with coconut sauce.

Why has a fish so universal, so plentiful, been regarded for so long by Western diners as distasteful? Presumably because of the fearsome reputation of the shark. No such hesitation exists in most cultures and shark of all descriptions is rapidly gaining in stature in classical French cooking. Such authorities as George Lasalle, author of *The Adventurous Fish Cook Book*, hold that such species as monkfish, dogfish, tope and porbeagle all deserve the best culinary treatment and the respect of chef and gourmet. Monkfish tail, he declares, is food fit for angels.

Such attitudes have led in recent years to the redemption of the gastronomic reputation of the shark family. In some trendy restaurants, menu writers are now less coy and label shark dishes by their correct name instead of trying to disguise the dish under a pseudonym.

SHARKS AT CLOSE QUARTERS

VALERIE TAYLOR

For more than twenty years my husband, Ron, and I have mingled at close quarters with a great variety of sharks in our quest for ever more spectacular footage. The vast majority of our experiences have been exciting and often exhilarating, and only occasionally have we felt threatened.

► Most close encounters with sharks are accidental and in the majority of cases the shark, more startled than the diver (and with more to fear), will flee. All sharks, however, should be treated with caution and respect; even this angelshark could deliver a nasty, if non-fatal, bite with its small but sharp teeth.

Marty Snyderman

SHARKS FIERCE AND TAME

Because underwater visibility is poor, divers are generally unaware of sharks until they are fairly close. In the case of wobbegongs, grey nurse and the like, this never causes any alarm but the sudden appearance of tigers, bronze whalers and great whites can give the heart a nasty jolt. In fact, I know of divers who have given the sport away after such a frightening encounter.

Fortunately people are now far better educated about sharks than they were when I started diving, thirty-two years ago. Then almost every shark was a potential killer and the 'get it before it gets me' syndrome prevailed. Thousands of innocent sharks were blasted into eternity before experience replaced ignorant fear. Take the dear old grey nurse. Once killed indiscriminately as so-called attackers of man, these gentle fish have been proven innocent and are, I am delighted to say, now totally protected in New South Wales. I can see a day in the very near future where the reefs populated by these sharks will become great tourist attractions.

► Even experienced divers and scientists must approach sharks with caution. At right, Herwarth Voigtmann feeds grey reef sharks from his mouth on a reef in the Maldives. At far right, Dr Samuel Gruber and colleagues inject a lemon shark during a growth study experiment at Bimini in the Bahamas.

Ron & Valerie Taylor

Ron & Valerie Taylor

Ron & Valerie Taylor

▲ Filmmakers have come from many countries to work with Australian great whites, setting out from Port Lincoln in South Australia to obtain spectacular footage of great whites for box-office successes such as *Blue Water, White Death, Jaws, Jaws II* and *Orca*. According to Valerie Taylor, Australian great whites are 'the best performers'.

Already in areas such as the Maldives and Caribbean, divers pay to go down and see reef sharks being fed by the dive master. Herwarth Voigtmann from Bandos Island in the Maldives actually feeds his group of grey reef sharks from his mouth. They are all nicely trained to come in one at a time for a fish – not a bad effort considering the mad frenzies usually associated with large numbers of feeding grey reefs.

In Australia, a diving charter boat, the *Reef Explorer*, working from Cairns, organises an incredible shark feed at Osprey Reef in the northern Coral Sea. For American tourists it is the high spot of their visit. The baits are taken down twenty metres by the vessel's dive master and fastened to the bottom. Because the area is adjacent to deep water and some really huge sharks, the guest divers stay back near the coral wall. Anything can happen and usually does: grey reefs, silvertips, whitetips, tiger sharks and the odd hammerhead, can appear.

On the southern end of the Barrier Reef, Heron Island resort has recently purchased an underwater viewing vessel called *Subsea*. Capable of taking up to thirty non-divers, it is a superior version of the glass-bottom boat. In the Heron Wistari channel live a group of amazing predators we call the garbage sharks. They do exactly as their name implies: feed on garbage from the dining room. The idea is to take guests out when the garbage is being dumped, enabling them to observe without danger large silky sharks and tiger sharks feeding.

Wearing our mesh suits, Ron and I have swum with these sharks and although they treated us with caution, they were all very large and could easily become a threat. The *Subsea* is a perfect way to observe dangerous sharks from dry safety. In fact it is a great way for non-divers to see other marine dwellers as well.

MEETING THE BIGGEST OF THEM ALL

The drama of meeting a shark at close quarters is enhanced by the potential danger presented by some species. Of them all there is no doubt the great white shark, or white pointer as it is sometimes called, tops the danger list. It is not that these sharks are responsible for most attacks on humans, because in my opinion they are not; but ever since the feature films *Blue Water, White Death* and *Jaws*, great whites have been not only the world's best-known sharks, but also the most feared.

Since 1965, when Ron became the first person to film a white shark in its natural element, these awesome fish have been held in a special place in the public consciousness. Unlike most sharks, whites do not survive in captivity, no matter how large the aquarium. Because of this it remains very much a mystery – the big danger out there controlling the world's liquid surface.

Seeing white sharks at close quarters is either accidental and terrifying (if not fatal), or contrived and expensive. With only two exceptions all our meetings have been planned and executed utilising experience and expense. First, huge quantities of meat, minced tuna and blood are needed to attract the marauder. It is impossible to go out and simply

◄ Jeremiah Sullivan, co-developer of the Neptunic anti-shark suit, seems to be sharing a good joke with a juvenile mako (*Isurus oxyrinchus*).

find a white; we must lure him to us. Next we need steel cages and a boat capable of supporting us and our equipment for weeks at a time. Once the expedition is organised, we move to offshore locations, preferably near a sea lion colony, and wait for the food slick to work.

Sometimes it takes days, and occasionally weeks, for the shark to come. Seeing a live great white underwater swimming toward you smiling his saw-tooth smile – beautiful, deadly, the epitome of grace – has to be one of life's greatest

▼ Meeting a great white underwater is a thrill divers from around the world will pay to experience, though it is one most of us would gladly leave to others. Their power and silent grace are certainly impressive, but the possibility of being killed and eaten by even a relatively small great white makes any encounter a matter for extreme caution.

Nowadays, thrill-seeking divers come from all over the world to experience visual contact with a great white shark. It is considered to be the ultimate diving trip. They pay, not only in money but in mental and physical endurance, to hang in a cage waiting for a glimpse. It may not be a fun experience, but it is one of the greatest.

Most white shark trips leave from Port Lincoln, South Australia. *Blue Water White Death, Jaws, Jaws II, Orca:* all used live shark footage shot out from Port Lincoln. Filmmakers come from all over the world to work with Australian sharks. It is not that they don't have white pointers elsewhere; they do. The northwest coast of America, if the reports are to be believed, is practically swarming with them. It is just that ours are the best performers and also, I guess, the most famous.

WORKING WITH SHARKS

While great whites may not be the easiest sharks to find and work with, there are several species that, with a little tasty encouragement and once they know you, will, like Herwarth Voigtmann's trained sharks, give guaranteed performances year after year on cue. We call our group the Marion Reef sharks. They have appeared in countless films and picture stories, are generally well behaved and, best of all, there are dozens of them all willing to work for us.

However, it wasn't always so easy, as this abbreviated extract from my diary tells. The location is Marion Reef; the date 28 December 1975:

Well, John and I nearly cashed in our chips this morning. I can still hardly believe it. This afternoon we had the worst shark experience imaginable without actually being bitten. It was terrifying. Ron, John, Alex and myself decided to stir up some sharks for filming. I planned to use the 35mm Eymo movie camera because we had been having such good shark action, so fast that I could not take still photographs quickly enough. I thought using the 35mm movie film would be like having a motor drive on a still camera containing a 30-metre load of film.

Wally, our skipper, pointed out an area near the main entrance into Marion Lagoon. Wally reckoned it would be a real hairy place to work. His exact words were, 'I think a lot of big tough sharks live down there.' Well! I considered myself to be a big tough shark photographer; fighting off sharks was a daily occurrence. After lunch, Alex, John, myself and Ron loaded our dinghy with fish skeletons and diving gear. We anchored our aluminium dinghy over a big sandy hole on the edge of the pass about nine metres in from the drop-off. I took my fish carcasses down. It was a very unusual looking area. The sand patch was around 45 metres across and curved in a big half-circle back into the coral reef. The front of the half-circle opened into deep purple nothingness. It

Ron & Valerie Taylor

▲ Diver Mark Heighes has trained this whitetip reef shark *(Triaenodon obesus)* to take food from his hand, demonstrating not only the shark's intelligence and learning ability but its essentially unaggressive nature. On reefs where spearfishing is common, whitetips will gather around divers and take food offered to them.

experiences. Game fishermen boast of the thrill they get sitting safely on the deck of a game boat watching some wretched creature fighting hopelessly for survival on the end of a line. Personally I find that type of thrill rather distasteful; it certainly cannot compare with confronting the same marauder free, at home in his natural element. Down there he is king; you the alien.

In 1965, when Ron had his first encounter with a white, he was working from a tuna boat. On board was Alf Dean, probably the greatest shark fisherman in the world. Alf had attracted the sharks near Dangerous Reef, South Australia. Here is what Ron wrote about seeing his first white pointer:

Embedded in my mind is the 'grin of death' as a twelve-foot [3.7-metre] great white came toward me. Hair prickled my neck, my heart pounded. At a distance of two feet [60 centimetres] the mouth started to open. White triangular teeth filled the viewing frame. With a violent lunge, I heaved my body from the water. No one had ever filmed a white shark in its natural element before. I could well understand why. It was dangerous to the point of stupidity.

was a very strange and eerie, like a marine colosseum. Beautiful but unfriendly.

Alex vanished behind some yellow coral. He is an enthusiastic spearfisherman, full of energy and a great help to us. All was still in my warm pale blue world. I stuffed my baits into the coral where I planned to work. Blood and gore drifted gently up from the hard yellow coral, staining green trails in the water.

We had been down around ten minutes when I heard or perhaps felt a thump. I was told later that Alex had hit a fish. My eyes strained toward the distant purple. I thought if monsters could live anywhere, they could live out there, and from out there they came – a squadron in ragged formation, eight or nine sharks swimming high, their smiling maws black semicircles against their white undercarriages. I felt a twinge of fear. These were different sharks from the usual: bigger, fatter, less nervous, in fact not nervous at all. They cruised around in midwater sniffing the current, oozing confidence, eyeing us with cold yellow eyes. This was their world and it showed. Alex, however, had (luckily for him) lost the fish. The current must have told the marauders this, for one by one they slipped away, vanishing like wraiths into the deeps until the great purple void hung empty over the white edge of sand.

Ron & Valerie Taylor

▲ A grey reef shark trails behind a spearfisherman.

A coral trout appeared. John followed the fish, trying to get in a good shot. I heard a thump, then a flapping. John rose from the obscuring coral with the trout struggling on his spear and began to swim toward me. What I saw behind John chilled me to the bone. I surfaced and yelled at Ron, who was sitting half asleep in the dinghy, 'Get Alex out of the water quick.' I descended fast. John had not looked behind. He waved his fish at me, appearing very pleased with himself. I pointed frantically behind him. One over-the-shoulder look and John picked up considerable speed. The lead sharks swimming

▼ Feeding frenzies are well documented in grey reef sharks and are not – despite popular belief – directed at divers. They are, however, terrifying experiences and there is a real danger of a diver or underwater photographer being bitten by sharks that are apparently totally unaware of their surroundings.

Ron & Valerie Taylor

midwater were only metres away. He began trying to shake the fish off the spear, sending up tantalising puffs of blood. As he drew alongside he gave me a very worried look. The fish had dropped on to the sand, where it struggled feebly. No sharks approached it. I was somewhat amazed by this unusual attitude so I left my camera on the coral, swam down and cut the trout's throat. Green blood drifted up. 'Now for some action,' I thought.

Back on the coral ledge, John was waiting, his spear gun loaded, eyes round and worried inside his face mask. The sharks were big and fast, bigger and faster than any we had seen on the trip. I sensed trouble in those moving torpedo shapes.

One of the larger sharks circled only a few metres away. I noticed it was a female – fat, arrogant and without fear. I was puzzled that these sharks showed no interest in the baits. John and I, by now sitting back to back high on the coral, were the sole recipients of their attention. It was very nerve-racking. 'Why don't they eat the baits? Why don't they behave normally?' was all I could think.

The female shark circling closest dropped to the bottom of our coral patch. Almost out of sight behind the outcrop, she began to swim back and forth, back and forth, gathering speed with each pass, the turns lightning quick, yellow eyes watching. I stared, horrified. I knew what was coming, but felt helpless to alter the situation.

Suddenly she shot away some ten metres, spun in her own length, then sped like a bullet, jaws distended, straight for me. As she hit I rammed the

BLUE SHARKS ARE REAL SHARKS, TOO

MARTY SNYDERMAN

Ninety kilometres out to sea, in water several thousand metres deep, and everywhere I looked I saw sharks. There were at least 35, perhaps as many as 50, and all were at least two metres long. I had seen two makos earlier in the day, but at that moment all the sharks within my field of vision were blue sharks, the most common of the open-ocean sharks in southern California.

Although I had been in similar situations on literally dozens of dives, there was something noticeably different about the sharks this day. Usually blue sharks will swim away quite readily if you hit or push them. Although they will turn and come right back towards you after they have been struck, especially if you are filming from a position that is downstream from a bait, they will almost always retreat when a diver tries to fend them off. Not so this day.

I was working as a safety diver behind cameraman Howard Hall, who was filming a sequence for the television show *Animals, Animals*. My job was to keep Howard from getting bitten while his eye was glued to the viewfinder of his camera. Howard and I were filming some sequences of the blue sharks; later in the day we were going to make another dive with Ron and Valerie Taylor from Australia. Ron and Val are world-renowned shark experts and filmmakers, and they have worked with many species of sharks in a diversity of settings. For this particular episode, Val was to be the on-camera talent, a job for which she is well qualified.

During my dive with Howard it was all I could do to keep the sharks away from us. I have no idea how many times I hit, poked, pushed and shoved the sharks. Exactly why they were so excited I don't know, but the action never slowed down. By the end of our dive I was both physically exhausted and emotionally drained. The prospect of making a second dive gave me a knot in the pit of my stomach, especially considering the fact that Valerie

C.S. Johnson

big 35mm movie camera housing into her maw. The impact pushed the housing up into my face and I went rolling over backwards into the coral. She turned and struck at my legs. Again the camera housing held her off. John came in between my legs and poked hard with his gun to her belly. Mouth still open, teeth showing, she struck once more. I landed a futile unfelt blow to the top of her head, but it was John who really saved me as he beat her with his gun in a fury of fear and desperation. The water foamed. I couldn't get enough air from my tank, my lungs strained to suck more than the regulator would allow. Never leaving our immediate vicinity, she flicked around to John. He kicked with his flippers, hit with his gun. 'Shoot it, shoot it, shoot it!' I screamed over and over, but

though John heard his hands were stilled by horror. 'Shoot, Shoot!' I screamed, and became furious that he hesitated. I thought John was mad not to try and save himself.

Together we twisted in a foamy, sharky mess, hacking, kicking, punching. I was becoming exhausted. I hardly knew what I was doing any more. I felt breathless, faint. Then, like a blessed miracle, John fired, the headless shaft ramming deep into the shark's gills. It shot away, John swam to the surface and yelled to Ron, 'Bring the boat quick!'

We have now worked with those Marion Reef 26 grey reef and seven whitetips. When we arrive they are waiting, coming up to the dinghy hoping

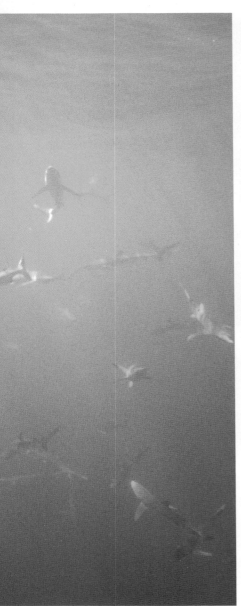

Marty Snyderman

Ron & Valerie Taylor

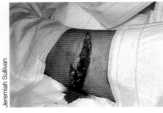

Jeremiah Sullivan

▲ After being bitten on the leg by an oceanic blue shark (*Prionace glauca*), apparently frustrated in its attempts to take fish from her hand, Valerie Taylor is winched aboard the helicopter that will take her to hospital. The wound was serious and required extensive cosmetic surgery to repair the damage caused by the blue shark's teeth.

was going to be working without the benefit of having a safety diver behind her.

Sitting on the boat between dives we discussed the plan for the coming dive. I strongly suggested that Valerie have a safety diver, but Ron, Val and the show's producer thought it unnecessary. Having worked with blue sharks before, they were convinced that Valerie could handle the situation. Having worked with Valerie and Ron on several previous occasions, I was also convinced that on most days Valerie could have protected herself. In fact, on the previous dive I had believed that I would have no trouble fending the sharks away from Howard and me. But now I had the advantage of having made one dive on the particular day in question and I knew it was an unusual day. That day we all made a mistake. The sharks were unusually aggressive, but from a vantage point aboard the boat it was impossible to detect their mood.

I insisted that Fred Fischer join me and that we work in tandem to protect Howard. Rarely before in my work with sharks had I suggested the need for two safety divers to protect one cameraman. Valerie entered the water with a string of fish, with which she could attract the sharks, attached to her weight belt. The fish were not necessary. Within a matter of minutes she was badly bitten on the shin and calf by a blue shark. It had her leg in its mouth for only a few seconds but the damage was done.

I got a real education in documentary film-making that day. Immediately after being hit, Val surfaced and yelled out to the topside cameraman, 'Roll the cameras. I have been hit. I think it is bad.' Then she descended, placed her regulator in her mouth and allowed herself to be towed back to the boat. The topside crew was able to film the action from that point on.

Valerie's wound was severe enough that we called a coastguard helicopter to fly her to a hospital. The doctors did a remarkable job and she was back in the water filming sharks only a few weeks later.

I know that many experts consider blue sharks to be pussy cats, more closely related to housepets than to maneaters such as white sharks and tiger sharks. But the lesson learned from Valerie's misfortune is never to take blue sharks – or any sharks for that matter – for granted.

for a pre-dinner snack. We have trained them to understand that a certain pattern of behaviour brings rich rewards, bad behaviour a sharp whack on the nose. We still work the colosseum, but now it is familiar, no longer unfriendly.

Recently, we were there with filmmaker Dick Dennison shooting a segment for a TV special, when our usual reef marauders were joined by a beautiful female tiger. I know tiger sharks supposedly eat people, but in our experience they have always been slow, gentle and obliging. This tiger took her first piece of fish from my hand. For the rest of the dive she swam around us – pure magic for the film. Several times she actually bumped me, so close did she come. The other, smaller sharks gave her space. Big means a great deal in the marine world, but she accepted us and in return we respected her. I was sorry when the film ran out and can remember seeing her circling around as I climbed into the dinghy.

All the tiger sharks we have met have behaved in a similar fashion. To achieve the same compatibility with a wild and dangerous land animal would be impossible.

A FRIENDLY GREAT WHITE

Perhaps the most amazing example of working with a shark at close quarters took place during a white shark filming expedition on the charter boat *Tradewind*. There were two whites around, but one was more willing to perform. We were throwing out small baits tied to a rope. As the shark reached for the fish we would pull it away, drawing the predator closer. Eventually the shark, realising he would only receive his reward close to the stern, started popping up next to the little swim platform, almost like a dog begging for food. The great white has one trait not found in other fish: he will lift his head above the surface to get a better view of what is happening – a rather disconcerting habit until you become used to it.

This shark was doing just that – lifting his head out of the water and looking at us. Ron suggested I try hand-feeding him from the swim platform.

White pointers have the ability to rise above the surface and take a bait or a seal lying near the water's edge, so the idea was not without danger. The shark watched as I climbed down, my weight causing the plaform to submerge a little. I offered a fish by leaning down and dangling it under the surface. Whitey cruised over. He seemed a rather clumsy eater, raising his pointy head up next to the fish rather than under it. I had to put the fish into his mouth. He took it nicely – no snapping about, just one big splashy bite. It was exciting, it was easy, it was fun. I gave him five more fish with a little pat on the nose each time while Ron filmed.

There was no doubt the shark knew how the game was being played. I was totally vulnerable; he could have taken me at any time, but he didn't. He took only the fish. In about twenty minutes this giant marine predator had learnt a little trick; no punishment was needed, just a small reward.

Ron and I know that one day we will swim with a white. We expect him to behave like his cousin the tiger, slow and polite, but we are going to have to choose the conditions, place and shark very carefully.

A NOTE OF CAUTION

The excitement of mixing at close quarters with sharks in their own environment is something that can only be enjoyed after years of experience in dealing with these fascinating but often dangerous creatures of the deep. Ron and I, after more than twenty years of working professionally with sharks, still don't profess to be experts, though we can claim to know and understand the species we have worked with a little better than do most people.

What we do may seem crazy, and perhaps it is. But patting great whites and handfeeding tigers are skills that have been acquired only after years of patient observation and discipline. To try and copy us would very likely mean becoming another statistic in the shark attack files. Sharks can be very dangerous and are far smarter than 'experts' often give them credit for. They should always be treated with caution and respect.

▲ The great white is the only shark – indeed, the only fish – that lifts its head out of the water. This behaviour is believed to be analogous to the 'spy-hopping' of orcas (killer whales); both species include seals and sea lions in their diets and may lift their heads to look for prey on rocks or to scare potential prey into the water.

◄ The tiger shark (*Galeocerdo cuvier*) has a justly infamous reputation as a maneater and indiscriminate feeder. However, as Valerie Taylor found at Marion Reef in Queensland, even these fearsome creatures can be 'slow, gentle and obliging'.

▼ A mature and potentially lethal male great white shark demonstrates his intelligence and apparent willingness to cooperate by taking fish from Valerie Taylor's hand and, notwithstanding her vulnerable position, makes no move to attack her. The great white has no nictitating membrane (or 'third eyelid') and usually rolls the eye back to protect it during an attacking rush; this shark is so relaxed and confident that he does not attempt to protect his eye, apparently aware that he is in no danger.

Marty Snyderman

HOLD YOUR BREATH OR YOU'LL SCARE THE SHARKS

MARTY SNYDERMAN

The sight before me was enough to make my knees shake and my mouth go dry. I was looking up at a minimum of 200 hammerhead sharks between two and three metres long. I was approximately eighteen metres deep at the now famous El Bajo seamount in Mexico's Sea of Cortez, and there was no shark cage in the water. The seamount is well known among the diving community that visits the Sea of Cortez for frequent encounters with manta rays, whale sharks and large gatherings of scalloped hammerheads (*Sphyrna lewini*).

The hammerheads were swimming in a large circle as they cruised around the seamount. The scene above me was truly spectacular and I felt fortunate to have the chance to film it. My pounding heart seemed to be in my throat. Although I had heard about the large gatherings of hammerhead sharks at the seamount, this was my first encounter of the kind. I watched for a moment and then tried to approach the sharks so that I could photograph the scene. I was on scuba, and as soon as I began to approach I exhaled – and the sharks bolted away. The noise from my exhaust bubbles scared every one of the 200 or more sharks; they simply vanished beyond the 30-metre range of visibility. When I first broke into the business of underwater filming I never thought I would have to worry about scaring the sharks.

Over time I have learned that the only way successfully to film these large groups of scalloped hammerheads is while free diving, without the use of scuba. Skilled free divers have acquired some awesome photographs by breath-hold diving into the schools at depths of 25 metres or more, but the sharks almost always bolt as soon as they hear the noise from scuba systems.

The most interesting question as far as the scientific community is concerned is why these sharks gather in large groups or schools. (In strict scientific terms these gatherings are not true schools because there is no one leader, the swimming is not synchronised and the sharks mill about instead of all swimming in the same direction.) Schooling is a rare behaviour for apex predators – animals at the top of a food chain. Scalloped hammerheads have few, if any natural predators. So what advantage can they possibly gain by schooling? Surely it takes a lot more small fish to feed 200 hammerheads than to feed one. After years of study, no one in the scientific community is prepared to make the definitive statement. Perhaps migration or mating is the heart of the issue, but no one is sure.

One thing is certain, however. Anyone who wants to study or film scalloped hammerheads must be a good free diver. The schools are almost impossible to get close to on scuba.

IN THE SHARK CAGE

HUGH EDWARDS

▲ An angered shark prepares to attack the steel cage.

T he day I first came face to face with *Carcharodon carcharias*, the great white shark – sometimes called white pointer, or white death – remains sharp and clear in my memory.

It was a bright morning in July 1976, off the Albany whaling station on the granite bastion south coast of Western Australia. Nature had done her best to provide a beautiful day. The sun glinted golden on the granite of the wet rock slopes of the hill above the whaling station, reflecting on the silver oil storage tanks and making a pretty rainbow through the steam that rose from the factory.

But from the flensing deck of the whaling station a river of red blood ran down to the sea, turning it crimson for hundreds of metres around. A bunch of dead sperm whales – giants sixteen metres long – lay with their rippled bellies blown and distended with compressed air, tethered to a pontoon. A floating mountain of dead flesh a kilometre from the factory. My fibreglass boat *Beachcomber* was tied alongside the dead whales, and the shark cage was already in position in the blood-murked water.

Peter Newstead, the other diver, and I hesitated a moment in our hooded black rubber suits, taking in the scene around us. Though there were no sharks in sight, we knew they were there. On the flanks and jaws of the dead whales were monstrous scooped bites, some half a metre across. We had heard all the stories about the sharks at the whaling station, and had received our warnings. Now was the first time to step into the cage and find out at first hand.

◀ A diver watches in fascination as one of the world's great predators moves in effortlessly to take a chunk of horse meat.

▼ With a thick spindle-shaped body and stiff swimming style, the great white is superbly evolved for extended cruising in the open ocean.

► There is no doubt that this is one of the most intelligent fishes, combining great visual acuity, hearing and smell with the capacity to learn and the cunning needed to capture seals and dolphins. Although not as curious as the grey reef sharks, a great white will investigate anything unusual in its domain, especially if lured by bait or blood in the water.

Hugh Edwards

▼ 'The pattern of their approach was often the same,' writes Hugh Edwards. 'The sharks would swim past, doing figure of eight patterns to assess us. Then, often quite suddenly, one would come straight at us . . . It would have been easy to reach out and touch a white on the nose at those moments.'

I had known about great white sharks for more than twenty years. I had spoken with fishermen who caught them – Ted 'Sharkey' Nelson, who became a legend fishing sharks professionally out of Fremantle; and Peter Goadby, the Sydney and Brisbane game fisherman who hooked several record-breaking whites and made a special study of them. Peter wrote of the species:

The feature most noticed and remarked on by those who have seen big white sharks in action, is the great dark eye which forces itself into the human mind by its apparent intelligence, ferocity, and constant watchfulness . . . When attacking it resembles a silent giant bomber with its graceful pectoral fins and effortless lithe manoeuvering. The silence ends when it attacks [the berley baits over the side of the gamefishing boat]. Then, if its head is out of the water the growls and ripping sounds are never forgotten. These sharks are inquisitive and at times fearless in their attacks on boats.

I met Goadby when we spent a day and a night in 1967 on a fishing boat off Jurien Bay, Western Australia, vainly trying to catch a white shark that had killed and eaten a friend of mine. Robert Bartle, a top competition spearfisherman, had been bitten in half and devoured a few days earlier.

I had also spoken to other divers who had survived white shark attacks. Brian Rodger and Rodney Fox both cheated death by the barest margin when they survived massive injuries from great whites at Aldinga Beach in 1961 and 1963 during the South Australian spearfishing championships. Henri Bource lost his left leg to a white off Lady Julia Percy Island in Victoria in 1964. Like the others he survived only through massive blood transfusions: by the time Henri was carried into hospital he had lost three and a half of the normal four and a half litres held in the human system.

Ron & Valerie Taylor

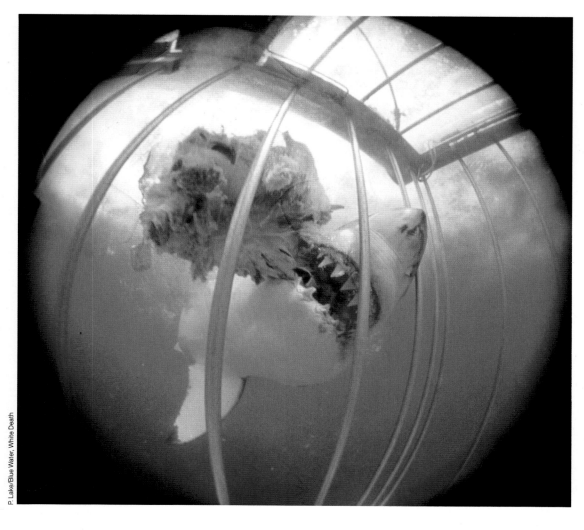

P. Lake/Blue Water, White Death

◄ A fish-eye view — literally — of a great white's attacking rush. The speed of its attack often took photographers by surprise, sending them sprawling in a corner as the impact caused the cage to spin and buck. So powerful is the great white's momentum that it has been seen to leap right out of the water.

I had seen dead great whites. As long ago as 1956 I had looked at one caught by Sharkey Nelson, hanging up by the tail on a tackle under the Fremantle railway bridge. It was huge, and even in death the power of the muscular body was evident. It seemed different from the other sharks I had seen, and I said so.

'Different?' Sharkey said. 'Now there's a bloody understatement! There's no other shark in the sea can compare with these buggers. You see that big dark eye there, big as the palm of your hand? When you bring them up on the line they watch you every minute, waiting for you to make a mistake. Sets the hairs up on the back of your neck, sometimes it does, when you're out fishing on your own.'

He gave me a tooth, which I kept as a talisman. It was five centimetres long, triangular, serrated on the cutting edge like a steak knife, and so sharp it would shave the hairs off your arm.

My preliminary education on *Carcharodon carcharias* – jagged teeth according to its scientific name – had lasted more than twenty years. Now I was going to meet the creature face to face. I would not have been human if my stomach had not knotted as I stepped off the stern board of the boat, and when I looked down into the shark cage it seemed as inviting, at that moment, as a gallows drop.

Once in the cage the nerves vanished and I was in a completely new environment. The cheerful sunlight of the surface was gone. The world beyond the bars was now grey and spectral, and tinged with the blood of the whales, forms only dimly seen in the murk.

The surface formed a steel-glinting ceiling just above our heads. The underside of the boat was a vague shape, similar to, but less than half the length of the whales. The rest of the panoramic view from the cage was a bottomless void, a valley filled with fog. Though the sea floor was only twelve metres below it was invisible in the darkness of the water. We could not see the bent harpoons that had fallen out of countless whales, the broken wire strops, or the white gleam of sharks' teeth that had broken off during their attacks on the whales, and drifted down like sinister flower petals.

The loss of the teeth was of no account to the sharks. They grew new ones. At any one time they had several rows of teeth in their jaws. As one of the front row was broken or torn out with the impact of a strike, a new one would move forward to take its place.

Efficient. That was one of the words you could

Hugh Edwards

► The shark cage's high-tensile steel bars gave divers and photographers a reassuring amount of protection while filming, but the 50-centimetre gap left for the bulky movie camera to manoeuvre allowed enough room for some nasty surprises.

Hugh Edwards

▲ The photographers' support crew aboard the *Beachcomber* checks the shark cages before a day's filming off Albany, close to the southern tip of Western Australia. 'Sometimes sharks put their heads right out of the water,' recalls Hugh Edwards, 'regarding those in the boat with a great dark eye.'

use to describe a white shark. Everything about it was streamlined, designed for its function of killing, attacking, surviving. Nature perfected its torpedo design about 30 million years ago, long before upstart humans began to move on the earth.

Tinges of blood seeped through the cage, globules of whale fat coating bars, scuba tanks, wetsuits, our hands and faces. We could smell and taste whale blood through our air-giving regulators. Blood is disturbing to humans and many animals; it excites predators. It was the main reason we were there. The blood-scent made a trail out of the bay – a wide slick, drifting past Limestone Head and away over the undulating swells of the Southern Ocean to the continental shelf, where the whales had been harpooned. An invitation to dinner to the deepwater sharks.

The whales themselves were both an attraction and a frustration for the sharks. Nothing brings sharks like a dead whale; they cluster around one, finning and tailing in excitement, as thick, on occasions, as a school of herring. But sperm whales, hunters of the giant squid, have armour-plated hides. Their blubber is so thick and tough that sharks, even great whites, have trouble getting through it. What they want, of course, is the red meat below the blubber. They tended to attack the mouth and tail regions where the blubber is thinner, but they still find difficulty even there. The frustration makes them wild and unpredictable – crazy at times.

This was the world we had entered in our cage.

It was suggested to us that it was foolhardy to go underwater with the Albany sharks because of their size, and their blood-crazed condition with the dead whales. All the warnings recycled themselves in my mind as we waited on that first morning.

The cage lifted, jerked, and twisted on the end of its line. It was a disconcerting motion. I checked the light meter readings again and with cold, shivering fingers readjusted the lens aperture on the 120 metre load 16mm camera in its big red housing. Peter Newstead looked at the still camera he was holding, and at the two bangsticks – spears with explosive heads – we fervently hoped we would never need. Checking the gear filled in time and took our minds off the waiting.

Suddenly I sensed, rather than felt, Peter stiffen. Looking out through the camera gap I saw what I had been waiting for all those years. Only a metre or two from the cage a great white shark was hanging poised on its pectoral fins, regarding us with a big black glistening eye.

Its mouth was half open, showing an irregular row of bottom teeth like daggers. The body was muscular and powerful – grey-green on top and creamy white on the underparts, where trailing claspers showed the shark to be a male. He was magnificent and quite unafraid. He stayed for what seemed minutes but could only have been a few seconds. Then he worked his jaws slightly and rolled away to one side of the cage with a motion of powerful fins. For a moment he glided, then a quick movement of the tail sent him skimming away out of sight.

Peter looked at me inquiringly and pointed at the camera. I shook my head and tapped the light meter, indicating there was not yet enough light in the water for shooting. The sun was still too low for its angled rays to penetrate. But even if there had been light in the water I doubt that I would have shot a single frame of film on that first meeting with *Carcharodon carcharias*.

In all our lives there are milestones, important moments we remember long after. This was one of them. For the brief time of his appearance I drank in every detail of the shark – his eyes, black as night; the magnificent body; the long gill slits slightly flaring; the wicked white teeth; the pectoral fins like the wings of a large aeroplane; and above all the poise and balance in the water and the feeling conveyed of strength, power and intelligence. To see the shark alive was a revelation. He was strong, he was beautiful. No dead shark or second-hand account could convey the vitality and presence of the live creature. A few seconds face to face were worth more than all the years of hearsay, pictures, and slack-jawed corpses.

When we were building the cage I had been secretly afraid we might be disappointed in the white sharks, that we might have built in our minds the myth of a supershark that was larger than the reality. But there was no disappointment. The great white was all the things I had heard about, and more. Magnificent.

We waited, braced now, for his return, and this time I had my finger on the trigger of the underwater movie housing. The water brightened perceptively as sunlight fell on the surface above. F2.8 said the light meter, then the needle rose to F4. Acceptable light for filming.

A moment later the shark was back, and once again he made us jump, catching us unawares. The whites seemed to have this power to materialise. We seldom saw them coming. We would strain our eyes through the blood-stained, murky water, looking for shadows and seeing none. A momentary glance down at the cameras, and then when we looked up again a shark would be there in the camera gap, breathing down our lenses.

I pressed the trigger and heard the reassuring whirr of the camera, then cursed as a curtain of green-tinged blood obscured the view. Near the surface the blood resumed its proper colour. The shark came through it like the Devil from behind a crimson curtain. From side on, the black eye was wicked and bright as it surveyed us and in the jaw I could see the glint of white spears of teeth. There was a strange sound, like a diesel motor far off, and for a moment I could not recognise it. Then I realised it was the thud of my own heartbeat.

The shark heard it too and cocked his grim head inquiringly. *Carcharodon carcharias* feeds on mammals, seals, dolphins and whales, and to him that noise meant we were edible. The nostrils in the pointed nose contracted delicately, inhaling our scent in the water, separating it from the all-pervading odour of whale, trying to work out what manner of creature we were. In the shark's world there were really only two aspects to consider: were we prey, or predators likely to eat him?

He wasn't in much doubt about our category as he swam backwards and forwards making up his mind whether to attack. He was a young male, as we could tell by his trailing claspers. He was about

Ron & Valerie Taylor

four metres long and weighed maybe half a tonne; not big in comparison with great whites we would see later, but on that first day he looked enormous. At the same time he was beautiful, moving with a fluid grace that took my breath away. But there was no doubt he was a killer, ruthless and competent. And all the time he watched us with those huge, intelligent dark eyes.

A crack of the tail and he was gone again to be replaced by another, much larger shark – a female with mating scars on her back and gills and a sullen expression that brooked no nonsense. This was an older, more experienced and more frightening shark.

'Christ!' The expression, an explosion of bubbles inside my mouthpiece, was involuntary. I had seen what she was going to do. The female rolled sluggishly, almost in slow motion, in a figure eight at the end of her pass at us, then came straight back at the camera gap.

'To hell with this!' I thought as I pressed the button on the camera. There was a crash and a sound like sandpapering as the shark's head hit the cage and her nose came through the gap on cue. Teeth tinkled metallically against steel and I kept filming, hoping that if the shark got us at least the camera would be salvaged and the supreme human

▼ The divers' confidence was not helped by the compromises that had to be made in the design and strength of their supposedly sharkproof cages. They had to be light enough to swing on and off an 8-metre boat, which meant an essentially flimsy construction that might not withstand a charge from a shark weighing two or more tonnes.

▶ An angry or frustrated great white may lash out at anything in its path – a possibility not to be taken lightly with such a large and dangerous animal. There are cases of great whites attacking and severely damaging boats, though Hugh Edwards and crew escaped with no more than bitten-through nylon ropes and a scratched propeller.

Hugh Edwards

Terry Kerby/Ocean Images

sacrifice wouldn't have been entirely wasted.

The cage lurched and I fell over backwards, putting out an arm blindly and instinctively to save myself. It missed the cage and went out through the half-metre-wide camera gap. The bar caught me on the short ribs, knocking all the breath out of me. Sucking in hard with pain, I tried to regain my feet while still watching the dreaded shape that gnawed at the opposite side of the cage, where Peter crouched like a boxer evading punches.

'Peter!' I was caught. Somehow part of my tank or its harness had hooked in the cage mesh. Unable to drop the camera or reach my harness quick-release buckles, I was jammed with an arm, shoulder, head – maybe a third of my body – sticking out through the cage gap for any interested shark. While clear speech is impossible underwater, you can make certain sounds if the need is great. And, in this case, it certainly was.

'Peter!' An explosion of panic bubbles. Peter understandably was concerned with the shark, which was trying methodically to get in through his side of the cage. He heard the noise but thought I was trying to film and ducked his head to be out of shot.

'Peter, for Christ's sake!' The shark was starting to circle the cage now. It passed out of sight on my blind side. I tensed, waiting for the clamp of jaws, the agony of teeth. What would life be like without an arm? What would life be like . . . terminated?

'Peter!' A final desperate trumpet. He turned as if seeing me for the first time and, realising at last what was wrong, slowly and carefully unhooked the tank from the wire mesh. I straightened, to see the shark disappearing in the distance with a capricious flick of its tail.

Peter watched the shark go, then turned to me and pointed upwards. I looked down at the film counter on the camera and saw I had shot the lot. I nodded, gave the diver's okay signal, finger and thumb in a circle, and we rose slowly through the metal hatch of the cage to emerge blinking into the sunlight, back into the human world.

It was the same on that first day as it always was when we came out. A circle of eager faces on the boat. What was it like down there? What happened? We saw that big one hit the cage. Did he give you a hard time? Did you get it all on film, mate? A barrage

of questions. But we could only shake our heads.

It was all right, we said, and remained silent for those first minutes out of the cage. We were too cold for one thing, blue and numbed. But also our minds had to adjust from dealing with the darkness and the primeval. It took a while. Later in the day, warm and dry, we were conversational and by evening we were making jokes about it all.

Next morning, all too soon after dawn, climbing into clammy wetsuits and facing the moment of truth at the hatch of the cage, the seriousness started again.

Looking back on it all, I realise now how much we pushed our luck. The cages were always a

▲ A diver checks out his sharkproof cage, unaware that a 4-metre great white has decided to taste-test the dive platform of his boat. Though most of the sharks Hugh Edwards filmed made a leisurely approach to the boat and cage, divers are always aware that their vision is more limited than that of a sophisticated ocean-ranging predator.

problem. They had to be light enough to swing on and off my 8-metre diving boat. This meant an essentially flimsy construction, which would not withstand a direct charge from a shark that might weigh twice as much as a VW Kombi van. We suspended the cages on lines out from the boat so that they could not be crushed against the boat. Sometimes, isolated as we were in our self-imposed prison, the few metres' distance to safety seemed a million kilometres.

There was an emergency hatch in the bottom in case a shark came through the top. We did not wear fins in the cage but balanced with mini-lead belts around each ankle as well as one around the waist and, after the fright with the tank hooking up, we lashed the tanks in the corners. Anyone abandoning the cage would have had an interesting time. Swimming among sharks in twelve metres of water, with no fins and seven and a half kilos of lead on waist and ankles would have been, as Peter put it, 'like running across a ploughed field in lead boots with a tiger after you'. Theoretically it was impossible to swim with so much lead and no fins. But later we proved it could be done.

One day, when sharks were scarce, we weighted the cage and went down to the bottom to look for those teeth. Gingerly we opened our emergency door and climbed out like moon

Hugh Edwards

► Even from above the water the strength, grace and menace of the great white is obvious. 'Looking into that eye one became hypnotised,' Hugh Edwards says. 'It made the hairs prickle on the back of your neck, the surface crew said, to know that it was a primeval creature that would eat you if it could.'

astronauts with our tanks and began to stroll around looking for teeth. We had become a little blasé by this time and if a shark had shown we figured we could dive back into the cage in time.

Suddenly I saw a peculiar expression on Peter's face and he pointed up. The cage, delicately balanced and now relieved of our weight, had sailed merrily back up to the surface twelve metres above, like a lift going up to the top storey. We suddenly found we could, after all, swim the distance without fins.

The cages had a half-metre gap around them so the camera could be operated outside without getting bars in the shot. Onlookers were always quick to point out that a shark could comfortably get its head in through the gap. 'We know,' we would reply.

The sharks did put their heads in, and it made good film. But the really big ones couldn't open their jaws. They simply flared their nostrils and had a good smell of these funny human creatures that looked so much like the sea lions they loved to eat. It wasn't until we saw other divers in the cage that we realised how visible, vulnerable and exposed we were – 'like a supermarket shopping trolley with a free meal', as someone said.

Day after day we went down in the cages. No two days were ever the same. Some days there were no whites, other days single sharks, and on some never-to-be-forgotten occasions a whole pack. The pack days were the most exciting and probably the most dangerous.

The sharks strike at the whales (and sometimes the cage) with their knife-like grip and spin with the enormously powerful leverage of the great forked tail.

The pattern of their approach to the cage was often the same. The sharks – the biggest and most dangerous were females – would swim past the cage, doing figure of eight patterns to assess us. Then, often quite suddenly, one would come straight at us. Sometimes it would mouth the cage, sometimes ram its conical nose in on us while we retreated as far as the 120-centimetre interior would allow, and the cameras whirred.

Sometimes the attack would be delivered with true ferocity. The cage would spin and buck and we would be thrown in a heap in a corner. When that happened we would signal to the boat, and when

HOW THE GREAT WHITE GOT ITS NAME

Although reflections give an impression of light colouring when great whites swim near the surface, the colour on their backs varies from deep blue, almost indigo, to brown, grey and even green. It is the belly that is white as snow, and this is what shows as the shark bites and rolls.

There has always been some controversy about whether sharks feed on their backs. I have seen both tigers and whalers tearing at prey in the normal position. Whites have attacked humans – on at least two occasions they have bitten divers completely in half – without rolling. I think they only roll when attacking tough prey such as whales in order to get a particular purchase.

Significantly, the name 'great white' was originally used by whalemen.

Ron & Valerie Taylor

the flurry ceased we would be drawn back on the boom to bail out on the duckboard. Several times sharks came up below the duckboard at this moment, within centimetres of divers' toes. Knowing that they sometimes take sea lions off rocks made everyone move a bit more briskly between boat and cage.

Whites are certainly more intelligent than other sharks. Where I have seen whalers and tigers keep on doing the same old things, getting nowhere, the whites would back off and think when their first attacks had failed to reach us in the cage.

One huge ragged-finned female – we called 'Grandma' – was always bad news. She usually attacked in concert with a friend, and having two of them hit the cage from different directions was definitely too much. She actually put her head out one day, saw the two nylon ropes supporting the cage and seizing one in her enormous jaws – which could easily have swallowed a diver whole – methodically began to chew through it.

One of our great fears was that a shark would flick its tail and tangle in the cage support lines. This happened once in South Australia where a cage – fortunately empty – was smashed. The risk was that the cage would be carried away in tow (what fun for divers inside!) or crushed. A steel mesh overcoat would also have been a nasty way to go. The alternative would have been to bail out.

While we were filming underwater, Vic Martin, the producer-director, would shoot from the boat with a surface camera. He got some excellent shots of great whites on the surface. We had an agreement that if anyone got injured, or badly hurt – or worse – the filming was to continue in order to capture the mishap as part of the action. That may sound callous, but film crews would understand.

The sharks were cooperative subjects, quite unafraid of the boat. Sometimes sharks put their heads right out of the water, regarding those in the boat with a great dark eye. 'Counting heads', we called it. Looking into that eye on the surface one became hypnotised, as a small bird is by a snake.

It would have been easy to reach out and touch a white on the nose at those moments. Nobody did, though they often patted fins and tails as they rubbed by along the hull. In routine fashion the sharks touched and bit at everything, including the propeller, keel and bow line.

By the end of July we had shot 1000 metres of underwater film of *Carcharodon carcharias*. This represented one and a half hours of continuous viewing. Since I only pressed the button on 'good' shots, we spent many more hours than that with great whites actually in view. Few people have been so lucky.

Though we had some bad moments, more by good luck than good management we didn't get eaten and survived the experience to put it all in a film, *Quest for the Shark* which, as documentaries

Ron & Valerie Taylor

go, rated well. I guess the film will be forgotten soon enough, but the image of that red world through the cage bars will always remain branded on my soul as one of the most significant experiences of my diving life. To my mind the experience of seeing one of the world's great creatures in a truly wild and free state was well worth the risks involved.

Now the chance has gone. Australian whaling has finished and the station at Limestone Head has closed down. The red waters have reverted to clear green and the great sperm whales off Albany swim unmolested – until they reach the zones hunted by the Russians and Japanese, who know neither moratorium nor mercy.

The sharks we saw and swam with are back in their deep water off the continental shelf. I have some battered cages, a lot of film and a host of indelible memories.

▲ The great white shark has few rivals, in the sea or on land. It is a true superpredator, giving way to nothing – except, perhaps, the orca or killer whale – and embodies the beauty and intelligence of the world's truly great creatures. Humans may fear the great white shark, but it is the undisputed master of its own element.

REPELLING SHARKS

C. SCOTT JOHNSON

The first recorded shark attack was reported by Herodotus in 492 BC. Jonah, of course, was swallowed by a 'big fish' that may have been a shark, but he survived uninjured. Since their earliest encounters with sharks people have been trying to devise ways of protecting themselves from them: Hawaiian women tattooed their ankles as a means of protection; Hawaiians also paid homage to shark-gods who protected them from 'bad' sharks with 'good' sharks; Solomon Islanders offered human sacrifices to shark-gods.

In keeping sharks at bay there are times when almost anything works and there are times when nothing seems to. Fortunately, shark attacks on humans are not common. Human attacks on sharks are much more frequent, for well over half a billion kilograms of sharks are caught each year by fishermen throughout the world. Sharks would have to eat well over four million people a year to equal this amount. In fact, other people are by far the most dangerous animal humans have to encounter. Of the more than 200 million people in the United States about 24 000 are murdered each year and another four million are wounded in acts of violence. Another 50 000 die in automobile crashes. In the United States each year a million people are bitten by pet dogs and several die as a result. In an average year sharks injure only a dozen or so people and only a handful of the attacks are fatal. Despite this we have a morbid foreboding about shark attack; even though we know the problem is more psychological than actual, it is none the less real to us.

▲ One of the oldest and least effective ways of protecting people from sharks is capture of individual animals, such as this great white shark. Capture with rod and line provides more gratification for fishermen than protection for bathers, though often larger and more potentially dangerous specimens are caught this way.

▲ The best method of keeping sharks away from people is to provide a sharkproof barrier like a steel-fenced swimming enclosure. Unfortunately, even this is inefficient as enclosures are difficult to construct and expensive to maintain, and protect only very small portions of shoreline such as this harbour beach in Sydney, Australia.

PROTECTING BEACHES

Most shark attacks occur at bathing beaches. This is simply because of the large number of people there. The chances of being attacked are, however, greater offshore, in deep water where there are likely to be more sharks.

The most effective way to protect beaches is to fence or wall in the bathing area and so physically prevent sharks from entering. This technique has been used effectively in Australia, South Africa,

South America and many other parts of the world. The reason this method is not used more is because it is expensive. Initial construction costs are high and, because the sea is a relentless destroyer, so are maintenance costs. As we review the various methods of keeping sharks at bay we will find that economic factors are almost always the limiting factor in their use.

Since the possibility of attack depends on there being a person and a shark in the same place at the same time, an effective method of lowering the chances of attack is simply to reduce the number of sharks present by catching them. The most common method of shark fishing for this purpose is called meshing and has been used quite successfully in both Australia and South Africa.

Meshing consists of setting large mesh gill nets at distances of between 400 and 500 metres from beaches. The nets are not continuous; usually there are two parallel rows of nets between 100 and 150 metres long with one being 50 to 75 metres closer to shore than the other. While swimming to and from the beach sharks become entangled in the nets and suffocate. Most of the sharks are caught at night when they swim closer to shore in search of food. The nets are checked around every other day to make repairs and remove dead sharks. In areas not on shark migration routes the population of sharks, and hence the chance of shark attack, in a given area can

Ben Cropp

◄ Nothing short of keeping people out of the water will totally eliminate the risk of shark attack, but the most successful practicable method seems to be offshore meshing of swimming beaches. Popular in Australia and South Africa, the method's limitations are cost, maintenance and the impossibility of netting the entire length of every beach.

▼ An Australian invention, the bubble curtain was developed in 1960 and sold to several resort owners in the United States before testing revealed that it was ineffective in preventing sharks from approaching beaches. Of twelve large tiger sharks tested at the Lerner Marine Laboratory in the Bahamas, only one was repelled by the bubble curtain.

be greatly reduced. At certain times of the year large numbers of migrating sharks invade South Africa's beaches. When this happens the nets quickly fill with sharks and are rendered useless. During these periods the nets are not set and bathers are warned not to swim. Because meshing is expensive it can be used to protect only a limited number of beaches. An unfortunate side effect of meshing is that many harmless species of shark, along with large fish and marine mammals, are caught and killed.

THE BUBBLE CURTAIN

New methods of protection are continually being devised and tested. Unfortunately, some inventors, in their quest for the quick buck, begin selling their 'brainchild' before it has been thoroughly tested. One example of inadequate testing was the bubble curtain or bubble fence. This idea, which originated in Australia in 1960, consisted of an

Perry W. Gilbert

▲ Diver Bela Csidei with a 3-metre tiger shark that was killed by a 'bangstick' or powerhead, a hand-held spear whose head is fitted with a 12-gauge shotgun cartridge.

▲ The carbon dioxide anti-shark dart is relatively effective, if brutal, in repelling an attacking shark. It works by injecting CO_2 gas into the shark's body cavity, inflating it so that it loses neutral buoyancy and floats to the surface.

▼ The Shark Shield has shown promising results in laboratory and field tests. Consisting of two electrodes with a pulsed electric current flowing between them, it is ignored by a 2.75-metre lemon shark (below) when the current is turned off, but when the current is on (right) the shark will turn abruptly and retreat from the invisible barrier.

ordinary garden hose in which many holes had been drilled. The hose was laid on the sea floor and when attached to an air compressor a 'fence' of bubbles was created. Sharks, it was advertised, would not cross the bubble fence. Several of the devices were sold to US hotel owners for the protection of their beaches. The bubble curtain wasn't actually tested until the spring of 1961, when Dr Perry Gilbert, working at the Lerner Marine Laboratory in the Bahamas, tested it against twelve large tiger sharks (*Galeocerdo cuvier*). Of the twelve only one shark was repelled by the bubbles; the other eleven swam back and forth at will through the curtain.

The importance of adequate testing cannot be overemphasised. Not only should many different species of dangerous sharks be used; until it has been tested on many members of each of the species, no shark deterrent should be adopted.

ELECTRIC FIELDS

The fact that sharks, and all other species of fish, are affected by electric fields has been exploited in South Africa to develop a beach protection system. When an electric field above a certain minimum value is produced between two wires a shark located between the wires will feel a shock and

swim away rapidly. This is called a 'startle' response. If the voltage between the two wires is raised high enough, the shark will involuntarily turn and swim toward the wire that is positive. This is called an 'electrotaxis' reaction. If the voltage is raised high enough the shark will be paralysed and in several minutes will suffocate because it cannot swim or move its gills to take in oxygen from the water. This state is called 'electronarcosis'. Many years of research and testing have gone into the development of this South African system. The basic idea is to anchor a pattern of electrical cables around bathing beaches, outside the surf zone. By producing voltages large enough to produce electrotaxis sharks swimming toward the beach are forced to turn around and swim away.

There were many problems to be solved in developing this system. Because sea water is a very good conductor of electric current, continuous or direct current generators could not be used. The scientists had to produce a pulsed voltage of just the right character; otherwise too much current would be needed, operating costs would rise and the electrical cables would be destroyed through electrolysis. A successful system was eventually developed but the costs of construction and operation were still too high. The system is not being used, but research is continuing and it is hoped the economic problems will finally be overcome.

PROTECTION FOR DIVERS

Skin and scuba divers run the greatest risk of being attacked. This is because their activities increase the possibility of encounters with sharks. Several weapons have been developed for divers to use against sharks. Many divers carry knives, but most divers' knives are made of stainless steel to prevent saltwater corrosion and neither their edges nor their points are sharp enough. Most sharks have very tough hides that only the sharpest knives can penetrate and then only with effort. Sharks are also very difficult to kill outright. A shark whose spinal cord has been severed near the brain can continue to swim. Neural signals to the swimming muscles are not controlled by the brain; only signals to speed up or slow down come from the brain. Even spear guns with enough power to penetrate the shark's skin are not very effective unless a hit to the brain is scored. A spear gun can be made into a very effective weapon with the addition to the spear top of a 'powerhead'. Powerheads, sometimes called 'bangsticks', are in reality nothing more than short-barrelled single shotguns, designed to discharge on contact with the shark. These can be obtained in almost any calibre from .22 to 12 bore. One very potent version of the powerhead has a small explosive charge in the barrel instead of a cartridge case. However, considerable skill is needed to use such weapons effectively.

Another weapon that has been widely used is

the CO_2 anti-shark dart. This device consists of a small CO_2 cylinder attached to a large hollow needle. When shot into the side of the shark the cylinder is punctured and CO_2 gas flows through the needle into the shark's body cavity, causing a large bubble to form. The shark, which is almost weightless in water, is made buoyant and is forced to the surface. If large amounts of gas are injected the internal pressure caused by the gas can paralyse the shark or force its internal organs out of its mouth. A limitation of CO_2 darts is that they can only be used from the side or bottom; these are the only directions from which the needle can effectively penetrate the body cavity. As a precaution, US Navy frogmen carried CO_2 darts when they aided in the recovery of the astronauts following the splashdowns of Apollo missions 15 and 16.

All these devices are dangerous weapons both in and out of water and must be treated with great care and respect. At least one careless diver has been severely injured in his own garage by the accidental discharge of a powerhead. Many divers are more afraid of these weapons than of the sharks themselves. A cardinal rule for all anti-shark measures is that they present a negligible danger to the user.

An electric anti-shark harpoon was developed several years ago. This device had two electrodes supplied with a large current from a power supply. One of the electrodes had a sharp, thick point and, when it was thrust into the shark, a current was turned on between the inside and outside of the shark. As long as the current was on the shark was paralysed and unable to move or breathe. Because of the high cost of manufacture this weapon has never been produced commercially. However, because it only kills the shark if left on long enough for the fish to suffocate – usually more than thirty minutes – it could be a useful aid to researchers who want to capture sharks.

US Navy scientists have developed a non-lethal device that interferes with the shark's ability to swim. It is called a 'drogue dart' and consists simply of a sharp, barbed point to which is attached a small parachute. When the barbed point is shot into the shark the parachute opens, causing an unbalanced drag force that the shark fights against much as it would it if were hooked by a fisherman. The shark is then distracted from harming the diver. Drogue darts are not presently being manufactured.

Another way of fending off sharks is through the use of a 'shark billy'. Jacques-Yves Cousteau, co-inventor of the aqualung, and his divers developed the shark billy. It is nothing more than a stout wooden club, about two metres long, that is used to push away curious sharks. The 'shark' end of the club has nails driven into it to help prevent sharks from slipping off. Recently an electrified version of the shark billy has found its way on to the market. Called a Shark Tazer, it is nothing more

than an underwater cattle prod. It is held near or against the shark and when a switch is pressed the shark is given a jolt of electric current.

Weapons, no matter how effective they are or how skilfully they are used, are of no value if the shark cannot be seen. This restricts their use to relatively clear water – and records show that only half the divers attacked saw the shark beforehand.

Several efforts have been made to protect divers from sharks that cannot be sighted. One of these is an electric repeller that pulses electric current in the water around the diver about once a second. Several similar designs have been patented and it is not clear who was the first to develop the idea. One version that has been successfully tested

▼ Although the belief that 'the only good shark is a dead shark' saw many harmless animals, such as sand tigers or grey nurses (*Eugomphodus taurus*) killed, powerheads are capable of removing a potential threat from dangerous species such as these copper sharks or bronze whalers (*Carcharhinus brachyurus*).

Ron & Valerie Taylor

▶ In the belief that sharks do not eat their attendant pilot fish because the pilot fish have black and white stripes, striped 'shark repellent' wetsuits have been marketed despite the fact that they have no repellent effect at all — and that sharks do not eat pilot fish because, if they are strong and healthy, they are simply too difficult to catch!

Ron & Valerie Taylor

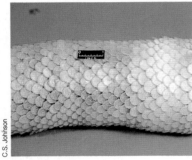

C.S. Johnson

▲ A wetsuit covered with overlapping scales made of very tough plastic and designed to imitate the protection offered by a fish's scales was tested by United States Navy scientists. It was resistant to shark bites but restricted divers' movements too much.

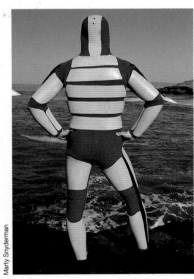

Marty Snyderman

▲ The first practicable sharkproof suit is the Neptunic, which consists of approximately 400 000 small stainless steel rings interlocked to form chain mail. The stainless steel suit is worn over this specially reinforced wetsuit that provides further protection from bruising or injury by the steel suit itself.

Ron & Valerie Taylor

is the Shark Shield. The Shark Shield was originally built to protect the cod ends of shrimp fishermen's trawl nets from damage by sharks. A smaller version was designed to be worn by divers. A rechargeable power supply, attached to the diver's belt, delivers 120-volt pulses to electrodes on the arms and legs of the diver's wetsuit. It is designed to work for twelve hours without recharging. While Shark Shield has been shown to repel several species of dangerous sharks, some divers complain that the large electric pulses generated make their teeth fillings ache. If the power is on and the electrodes are touched while out of water a nasty but non-lethal shock is administered to the careless person. Unfortunately an electrical measuring instrument of some kind is necessary to verify that the device is on and working properly – that is, unless you don't mind getting shocked in order to test its operation. Shark Shields are currently being used only by shrimp fishermen; a market has not developed for the divers' version.

In Japan women divers, called amas, have collected abalone and seaweed for centuries. Some of them wear a *fundoshi* as shark protection. This abbreviated garment is all they wear and consists of a G-string-sized loincloth with a piece of red cloth, fifteen centimetres wide and two metres long, attached. While diving the red tail flutters behind the ama. The idea here is twofold: first the fluttering tail may frighten the shark away; or, failing that, if the shark attacks, it is much more likely to bite the cloth tail than the ama. Finding the tail not good to eat, the shark will leave. The validity of the *fundoshi* as a protection from attack has never been tested

scientifically, but there is no record of an ama being attacked while wearing one. In fact, amas not wearing *fundoshi* have never been attacked either, which may only mean that dangerous sharks are not found where the amas swim.

PROTECTIVE SUITS

Some open-sea, or pelagic, sharks are frequently seen swimming with small, black and white striped fish. These are called pilot fish because they usually swim in front of the sharks. Some think that the pilot fish are not eaten by the sharks because of their black and white stripes. In actuality the pilot fish would be safe no matter what their colour just as long as they were strong and healthy. Sharks, like all predators, seek out the weak and sick; the strong and healthy are too difficult to catch.

Nevertheless, a black and white striped suit has been advertised as having a repelling

effect on sharks. In tests conducted by US Navy scientists with several species of known dangerous sharks, no such repelling effect was found. In fact, in one test with blue sharks (*Prionace glauca*), two man-sized dummies, one in a black wetsuit and one in a black and white striped wetsuit, were placed in the sea with the sharks. Only the striped suited dummy was bitten. Ron and Valerie Taylor, the well-known underwater filmmakers, also tested the striped suit design. They found the suits to have no effect on sharks at all. *Caveat emptor* – let the buyer beware – the ancient Roman caution, is especially appropriate when it comes to shark deterrents.

Developing a suit that is proof against shark bite is probably the most logical way of protecting divers against shark attack. While providing adequate protection, the suit must allow the user complete mobility and must not be too heavy. In order to accomplish this compromises must be made. The worst injuries inflicted during attacks consist of cuts caused by the shark's sharp teeth. A bad bruise or even a broken limb can more easily be survived. For this reason the designer's main aim must be to produce a sharkproof suit that will reduce as far as possible the cutting effect of the shark's teeth. US Navy scientists tested two designs. The first model was basically a neoprene wetsuit covered with overlapping plastic scales much like the scales of a fish. A very tough plastic was used in the scales. The idea was to distribute the force of the bites over an area of a square centimetre or so and negate the cutting action of the teeth. Tests indicated that the suit was resistant to shark bites, but that it restricted the movement of the diver too much. The second design was simply a pair of coveralls made of several layers of a new, very strong material called Kevlar. Kevlar caught the

Ron & Valerie Taylor

▶ A graphic demonstration of how the Neptunic works. Even the large, sharp and pointed tooth of a great white cannot penetrate the steel mesh, though a bite from a large shark would cause at least severe bruising and crushing of tissues, possible broken bones and, if the wearer were bitten on the torso, internal bleeding.

▼ If divers have to enter the water to observe or photograph sharks in their own environment, the best form of protection is undoubtedly the shark cage. Sharks cannot reach the diver if the cage's bars are sufficiently close together and the cage – and diver – can be winched out of the water in the event of damage.

scientists' attention because of its use in making lightweight bullet-proof vests. This time the suits, while they gave the divers plenty of freedom of motion, were not sufficiently resistant to shark bites.

A practical sharkproof suit has now been produced. Ron and Valerie Taylor, along with American Jeremiah Sullivan, have developed a garment composed of approximately 400 000 interlocking stainless steel rings. The suit looks exactly like the chain mail worn by medieval warriors, except the stainless steel rings are very

small so that the shark's sharp teeth cannot reach through them. The suit has been proven to be effective against the species of sharks responsible for most shark attacks. 'Neptunic' is the commercial name of the suits, which cost more than $5 000 each. Although the price may seem high, even a small shark bite can result in medical bills that are even larger. For those who must expose themselves to shark attack a Neptunic would seem to be a necessary purchase.

CHEMICAL REPELLENTS

Just after midnight on 30 July 1945, Lieutenant Commander Mochitsura Hashimoto, captain of the Japanese submarine I-58, sighted a large unescorted enemy warship steaming in a straight line instead of zigzagging to avoid submarine attack. He fired two torpedoes and twelve minutes later the heavy cruiser USS *Indianapolis*, flagship of the Fifth Fleet, disappeared from sight forever. It was steaming under radio silence and no SOS was sent. The highly classified mission it had just completed had been to deliver the first two nuclear bombs to Guam. For four long days and nights the survivors of one of the greatest tragedies in US naval history waited for rescue. Of the 1196 on board that night only 316 would come home. It will never be

Marty Snyderman

known how many were taken by sharks. Guesses range from 50 to 100, certainly far less than the 600 that Quint, the character from *Jaws,* claimed. Sharks were present for most of the four days between sinking and rescue. The survivors have a reunion every five years, and many are still bothered by the memory of those horrifying days 40 years ago. The tragedy so haunted the skipper of the *Indianapolis* that he took his own life in 1977.

While naval disasters of this magnitude did not happen often during World War II, many lesser ones did occur. Early in the war the need for some kind of shark protection for the members of the Allied Forces was clearly recognised. A crash program was instituted in the United States and a few months later a chemical shark repellent, called Shark Chaser, was produced. The scientists involved knew that shark fishermen believed (they still believe it to this day) that sharks are repelled by the presence of decaying shark flesh. So they created a repellent that combined the chemical they believed to be the important one from decaying sharks, with a black dye and a wax binder. The dye was designed to spread out around the users to effectively hide them from the sharks' view. The final package, which needed to be compact, was only two centimetres thick, ten centimetres long and seven and a half centimetres wide. The packet contained about 170 grams of the active ingredients and would dissolve at a fairly uniform rate over around three and a half hours. A similar compound was developed by the British Admiralty. It was called Admiralty Pattern 0473/1399 and was made up of the same chemicals – copper acetate and a nigrosine dye – as Shark Chaser. Hastily conducted tests seemed to show that the compound was effective in repelling sharks.

While Shark Chaser and Pattern 1399 undoubtedly provided comfort to those forced to use them, tests since World War II have shown them to be of little or no value as shark repellents and the US Navy stopped procuring Shark Chaser in 1976. No search for a replacement has ever been started. The main reason for this is that since World War II only one US military person has been injured by a shark while on active duty. On 23 September 1961, a US Navy aircraft ditched in the mid-Atlantic. The three crew members drifted, bothered by sharks, for many hours before rescue. As he was trying to climb aboard a rescue craft one of the three fell back into the sea and was attacked by a shark. Fortunately, his wounds were not serious. In the intervening period hundreds of US airmen have had to parachute into the sea. None who survived suffered a shark attack and the recovered remains of those who did not survive have shown no sign of shark bite. High performance fighter pilots carry a one-man life raft when they eject and these certainly provide adequate protection against sharks.

Marty Snyderman

▲ The design of most shark cages is a matter of compromise between optimum protection for the diver and optimum opportunity for underwater photography. Sufficient space for cameras often means that a small shark can enter the cage and could possibly injure or kill a diver thus trapped. Most sharks, however, are simply anxious to escape.

OTHER DEVICES

Even though the US Navy is not officially searching for a replacement for Shark Chaser, it does provide some funding for shark research. Most of the research is basic in character and is done at various universities and at one Navy laboratory, the Naval Ocean Systems Center (NOSC) in San Diego, California. The basic aim of the work at NOSC is to translate the available knowledge about sharks into ways of solving problems that sharks cause for the Navy. Sharks may not injure people very often but they can, and occasionally do, damage important and valuable equipment. Dozens of towed arrays – long pieces of hose filled with underwater listening devices – have been damaged by sharks. The Navy

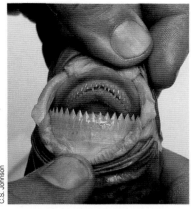

▲ Mystifying damage to the rubber coating of underwater cables in US Navy hydrophones was identified as being due to a small deepwater dogfish, the cookiecutter shark (*Isistius brasiliensis*), which attaches itself by suction to whales, tuna, marlins or megamouth sharks and cuts out a neat circular plug of flesh. A layer of fibreglass frustrated the shark's bizarre feeding method and eliminated damage to naval equipment.

tows these devices behind submarines and surface ships in order to locate enemy submarines. Companies prospecting acoustically for oil use them to collect information from echoes produced in sub-bottom structures by small explosions set off at the sea surface.

Damage to rubber covers on submarine hydrophones (underwater microphones) was a cause for concern to the US Navy until a scientist at NOSC identified the cause as the cookiecutter shark. This small species of shark (*Isistius brasiliensis*) grows to a maximum length of only around 50 centimetres. It feeds by attaching itself to the sides of large fish, dolphins, whales and other sea creatures with its suction cup lips. Then with its lower saw-blade-like set of teeth it carves out hemispherical chunks of flesh up to five centimetres in diameter. Once the cause of the damage was identified, a protective layer of fibreglass was applied and the problem was solved.

Chemical repellents continue to be developed and tested. A recent one has attracted a good deal of publicity. A few years ago Dr Eugenie Clark discovered a small fish in the Red Sea that sharks were reluctant to bite. She found that when endangered this fish, the Moses sole (*Pardachirus marmoratus*), excreted a milky white fluid that

worked extremely rapidly on the sharks she tested. Other scientists studying the sole's fluid found that it chemically resembled a group of chemicals called surfactants (the ingredients that cause the foaming action in many soaps and detergents). While surfactants have been shown to repel sharks, they are not as effective as other chemicals that have been tested. The basic problem with all chemicals tested to date is that far too great quantities are needed to produce the desired repelling effect. The Moses sole's strategy is to inject its fluid into the shark's mouth, thus producing a very high local concentration of repelling material.

One promising idea that is yet to be tested involves sharks' ability to detect extremely weak electric fields: indeed, sharks attracted to the electric field generated by trans-oceanic telephone cables have caused expensive damage by attacking the cables, perhaps in the belief the cables were prey. We now know that sharks are more sensitive to electric fields than any other known marine animal. All living things in the sea generate tiny electric fields around their bodies. As in a battery, these fields are produced by the chemical interaction of various body fluids. Nerve impulses are not detected by sharks because they occur at frequencies too high for them to sense. Instead,

SHARK SCREEN: SAFETY IN A PLASTIC BAG

While the United States Navy is not actively trying to develop shark deterrent devices, it does test some of the better ideas that come along. One device developed by scientists is called the Shark Screen. Shark Screen is simply a large dark cylindrical plastic bag that is closed at the bottom and has inflatable rings around the open top. It folds into a small package weighing half a kilogram. When it is necessary to use a Shark Screen the package is unfolded, one or more of the three inflatable rings is inflated, and the user climbs inside. The user then scoops in water to extend the bag fully.

The idea for Shark Screen originated in the knowledge that most shark bites are to the arms and legs. It was known, too, that swimmers had often been bitten on their legs when they stopped swimming and stood up to wade ashore. The logical thing to do was to cover up the arms and legs and present only one large shapeless image to the surrounding water. There are no protruding areas that might invite an exploratory bite and, with the bottom closed, blood or other body chemicals that might provoke an attack are kept inside. Tests of Shark Screens on many species of dangerous sharks have been extremely successful.

When the devices are made of dark-coloured materials sharks have been found to be reluctant to make close approaches, even when fresh fish are attached to the sides. On land Shark Screens can be used as tents, solar stills or sleeping bags. They are potentially valuable pieces of general survival gear. Although the navy has not adopted the Shark Screen for use, it is being sold by private manufacturers.

they use their electrical sensors to find prey buried in the sand and in complete darkness. This capacity for electrical detection gives sharks a great advantage over their prey. With their electrical sensory system they can also detect the earth's magnetic field, which they may use to determine directions for migrations.

The idea here would be to suspend a small electrical source, which would have characteristics resembling prey, a few metres below the person or object to be protected. The signals emitted would not be detectable more than a metre or so away. If a shark made an approach it should be attracted to the dummy prey rather than to the person or object to be protected.

As we learn more about sharks many new ideas for shark repellents will be developed and tested. We can only hope that some of them will be successful.

A great deal has been written offering advice to those who are cast away at sea and possibly endangered by sharks. In 1944 the US Navy issued a booklet titled *Shark Sense*, which contained both good and, as we now know, bad advice. More recently the US Airforce published Information Bulletin No 1, titled *Sharks*. This is much more accurate in its information.

In general the best advice to anyone floating in the water is:

1 Try to keep calm. Erratic movements may attract sharks.

2 Do not remove shoes or any other piece of clothing. Clothing helps conserve body heat, thereby reducing the onset of exposure. As well, sharks sometimes bump or rub against floating objects in order to investigate them. Their skins are often very rough and can cause painful abrasions and possibly bleeding. This may in turn provoke an attack.

3 Do not swim unless necessary. Again, swimming uses up vital energy reserves and can hasten the onset of exposure.

4 Use the Heat Escape Lessening Procedure (HELP), developed by Canadian scientist J. D. Hayward to lessen the effects of exposure. The procedure is shown in the illustration. If more than one person is present they should huddle together to conserve energy. HELP and huddling not only conserve energy; they change the outlines of those floating into shapes less likely to be bitten by sharks.

C.S. Johnson

▲ During World War II the possibility of downed airmen or shipwrecked sailors being attacked by sharks inspired a search for a chemical shark repellent. Shark Chaser, basically a package of copper acetate and nigrosine dye, was issued to all Allied military personnel but proved totally ineffective in repelling sharks; some even ate the packages!

▼ An understanding of the techniques of HELP and huddling can assist people adrift at sea. HELP — the Heat Escape Lessening Procedure — involves taking up a crouching position to expose less of the body area to the water. If two or more people are present they should huddle together to conserve heat energy.

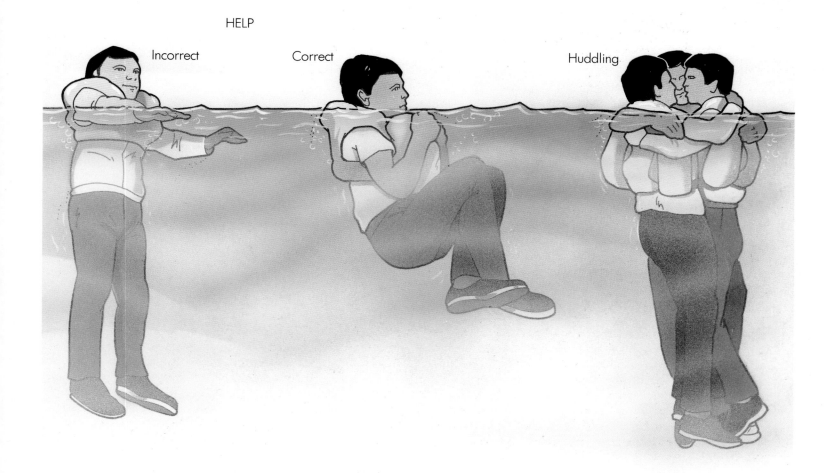

HELP

Incorrect   Correct   Huddling

PHOTOGRAPHING SHARKS

MARTY SNYDERMAN

Most species of sharks make wonderful photographic subjects. To the eyes of underwater photographers sharks are swift, powerful, sleek, exciting and potentially dangerous predators. It is difficult to imagine a more dramatic subject for a wildlife photographer than a large shark swimming mouth agape, teeth exposed, as it attacks its prey. Even when it is simply cruising, the shark's hydrodynamic design creates a potential for images that photographers dream about.

And yet, while many sport divers encounter sharks on a regular basis, only a comparative handful of underwater photographers ever acquire top quality pictures. It may seem that it is the threat of being bitten that keeps photographers from getting close to sharks; in fact, it is usually the sharks who won't approach divers, not vice versa.

What makes shark photography different and difficult? Perhaps the most fundamental difference between filming potentially dangerous predators on land and filming sharks is that underwater photographers must be very close to their subjects to achieve the desired results. The best underwater photographers use wide angle

lenses and get as close as possible to their subjects in order to shoot through as little water, and therefore as few suspended particles, as possible. How close is close? Three metres is about as far away as an underwater photographer can ever work unless he or she is shooting silhouettes. And getting closer is even better.

If you examine some photographs of sharks you might question whether the photographer was further than three metres from the subject when he or she tripped the shutter. Keep in mind that the perspective created by the use of wide angle lenses is different from that of your eyes, and even in crystal clear, shallow, tropical water you can count on the fact that if the image is of good quality and is not a silhouette, the photographer was within three metres of the shark. It might help to put the underwater photographer's problem in perspective if you realise that while 60-metre visibility is exceptional underwater, in similar conditions on land airports are closed because of restricted visibility.

And no matter how much visibility one has, water is a selective filter of the colour spectrum. At depth photographers have a difficult time trying to create visual separation between photographic subjects and backgrounds, regardless of whether the background is water or reef. In addition, many species of sharks are countershaded, being darkly coloured on the top and lightly coloured on the underside, in order to blend in with their surroundings. If you film from above a shark, looking down onto its darkly coloured back, the

animal will blend in with the dark water or reef below. The opposite is true if your perspective is looking upward. Countershading is an obvious advantage for predators and prey alike. But for underwater photographers the separation problems created by countershading and the physics of light in water combine to make it extremely challenging to obtain quality photographs. Shark photographers occasionally work from inside a protective steel cage that can be lowered and raised. However, most of us who make our living in this field do our best work when filming from the outside, so that is where we prefer to be. This holds true whether we are working with large groups of scalloped hammerheads in Mexico's Sea of Cortez, lemon sharks in the sand flats of the Bahamas, blue sharks in the middle of nowhere at two in the morning without the benefit of moonlight, and when filming great white sharks in South Australia.

It is not easy to swim face to face with a shark, simply because many sharks will not allow a diver to get close. The best way to close the gap is for photographers to use bait, often called chum. But it is important to understand that chumming extracts a fee. Normally sharks are not the proverbial frenzied feeding machines portrayed in Hollywood films. But when aroused they can become boldly aggressive, and when excited many species are among the ocean's fastest swimmers. Most sharks swim rather slowly when not feeding in order to conserve energy, but when offered food their behaviour often changes dramatically.

Potentially dangerous situations do exist when hungry sharks become excited, and it is imperative for divers to be fully aware of the exact location of the food source. Sharks almost always approach a bait source from the down current side (or downwind side if wind is causing a boat to drift in mid-ocean which creates a bait slick downwind from the boat). When swimming in the baited corridor sharks are stimulated by the presence of food, and it is easy to understand how a diver who is in the corridor close to the bait might be mistaken for the food source. But sharks are not indiscriminate feeders, and the difference in being in the odour corridor a metre in front of the bait, and being a metre on the upcurrent side is like the difference between night and day. I am convinced that even in baited situations, most shark 'attacks' are mistakes. The sharks believe they are biting a natural food source and in their excited state mistakenly bite a diver.

Filming sharks from outside a shark cage while suspended over hundreds of metres of water in the middle of nowhere is a demanding diving situation, to say the least. In mid-ocean there is no apparent bottom to help divers get their bearings. There is only blue-black water below and lighter water and sunshine near the surface. Currents and drift are difficult to detect, and it is all too easy to become involved in setting up just one more shot only to turn around after you trip the shutter and not be able to see your boat, the shark cage, or your diving buddies who have been wise enough to remain close to the cage. Being alone in the middle of the ocean surrounded by a large group of baited sharks is about as empty a feeling as one can experience.

The development of the stainless steel Neptunic anti-shark suit has been of real benefit to shark photographers. The suit is made of approximately 400 000 electronically welded stainless steel links backed up by solid Kevlar plates. While the suit cannot prevent injury from all species of sharks, it does make working with sharks that weigh less than 100 kilos and under three metres long much safer. Photographers wearing the suit can work while suspended almost motionless in the water column outside a cage rather than being

Marty Snyderman

bounced around in a cage that is jolted every time a wave passes overhead or the boat rocks with the swell. Cages do not make steady platforms, and in even moderate wind and swell being inside one is rather like being inside a washing machine.

The weight of a Neptunic suit made for a diver two metres tall of average build is approximately eight kilos. In temperate waters divers can simply exchange their weight belt for a shark suit without any significant change in buoyancy. However, the suit is difficult to swim in because of its bulk and the increased drag. Muscle cramps are common. Divers using the suit must realise that in an emergency they no longer have the option of dropping their weight belt in order to float up to the surface. Getting out of the suit in an underwater emergency would be virtually impossible. But there can be no doubt that all the extra effort is worthwhile the first time a shark chomps down on the suit and you escape without a scratch.

Most underwater photographers use Nikonos cameras with wide angle lenses to take still photographs of sharks. Nikonos 15 mm, 20 mm or 28 mm lenses are popular. Nikonos cameras are rangefinder cameras, not single lens reflex (SLR) systems. Trying to keep your focusing eye glued to the viewfinder of an SLR system without flinching while the viewfinder fills up with the face of a great white shark is a task that requires an incredible amount of discipline and

courage. When looking through the viewfinder, photographers can easily lose their perspective of sizes and distances, and experienced shark photographers know how dangerous the viewfinder illusion can be. Even large sharks swimming only a few metres away can look deceptively small and rather far away through a viewfinder. But when you look over the camera instead of through the lens, reality hits hard. Prefocused point and shoot cameras are much easier to use than SLRs, especially when filming from outside a cage. Some underwater photographers do choose to use SLR systems when filming from within the safe confines of a shark cage because of the added ability for precise focus and framing. Most professionals select Kodachrome 64 as their preferred film. Kodachrome has a pleasing look, accentuates warm colours which many photographers find pleasing, and helps build colour contrast between blue water and subjects.

Given the degree of difficulty invoved in acquiring excellent photographs of sharks, it is easy to understand why shark pictures are so highly valued by even the most experienced underwater photographers. But no matter what degree of success I enjoy or whatever failures I must endure, to me the most rewarding part of shark photography is simply the opportunity to observe sharks in their natural habitat.

CHECKLIST OF LIVING SHARKS

LEONARD J. V. COMPAGNO

ORDER HEXANCHIFORMES – SIXGILL, SEVENGILL AND FRILLED SHARKS

FAMILY CHLAMYDOSELACHIDAE – FRILLED SHARKS

Chlamydoselachus anguineus . . . . Frilled shark

FAMILY HEXANCHIDAE – SIXGILL AND SEVENGILL SHARKS

Heptranchias perlo . . . . Sharpnose sevengill shark
Hexanchus griseus . . . . Bluntnose sixgill shark
Hexanchus vitulus . . . . Bigeye sixgill shark
Notorynchus cepedianus . . . . . Broadnose or spotted sevengill shark

ORDER SQUALIFORMES – DOGFISH SHARKS

FAMILY ECHINORHINIDAE – BRAMBLE SHARKS

Echinorhinus brucus . . . . Bramble shark
Echinorhinus cookei . . . . Prickly shark

FAMILY SQUALIDAE – DOGFISH SHARKS

Aculeola nigra . . . . Hooktooth dogfish
Centrophorus acus . . . . Needle dogfish
Centrophorus granulosus . . . . Gulper shark
Centrophorus harrissoni . . . . Dumb gulper shark
Centrophorus lusitanicus . . . . Lowfin gulper shark
Centrophorus moluccensis . . . . Smallfin gulper shark
Centrophorus niaukang . . . . Taiwan gulper shark
Centrophorus squamosus . . . . Leafscale gulper shark
Centrophorus tesselatus . . . . Mosaic gulper shark
Centrophorus uyato . . . . Little gulper shark
Centroscyllium fabricii . . . . Black dogfish
Centroscyllium granulatum . . . . Granular dogfish
Centroscyllium kamoharai . . . . Bareskin dogfish
Centroscyllium nigrum . . . . Combtooth dogfish
Centroscyllium ornatum . . . . Ornate dogfish
Centroscyllium ritteri . . . . Whitefin dogfish
Centroscymnus coelolepis . . . . Portuguese dogfish
Centroscymnus crepidater . . . . Longnose velvet dogfish
Centroscymnus cryptacanthus . . . . . . Shortnose velvet dogfish
Centroscymnus macracanthus . . . . . . Largespine velvet dogfish
Centroscymnus owstoni . . . . Roughskin dogfish
Centroscymnus plunketi . . . . Plunket shark
Cirrhigaleus barbifer . . . . Mandarin dogfish
Dalatias licha . . . . Kitefin shark
Deania calcea . . . . Birdbeak dogfish
Deania hystricosum . . . . Rough longnose dogfish
Deania profundorum . . . . Arrowhead dogfish
Deania quadrispinosum . . . . Longsnout dogfish
Etmopterus baxteri . . . . New Zealand lanternshark
Etmopterus brachyurus . . . . Shorttail lanternshark
Etmopterus bullisi . . . . Lined lanternshark
Etmopterus carteri . . . . Cylindrical lanternshark
Etmopterus decacuspidatus . . . . . . Combtooth lanternshark
Etmopterus gracilispinis . . . . Broadband lanternshark
Etmopterus granulosus . . . . Southern lanternshark
Etmopterus hillianus . . . . Caribbean lanternshark
Etmopterus lucifer . . . . Blackbelly lanternshark
Etmopterus perryi . . . . Dwarf lanternshark
Etmopterus polli . . . . African lanternshark

Etmopterus princeps . . . . Great lanternshark
Etmopterus pusillus . . . . Smooth lanternshark
Etmopterus schultzi . . . . Fringefin lanternshark
Etmopterus sentosus . . . . Thorny lanternshark
Etmopterus spinax . . . . Velvet belly
Etmopterus unicolor . . . . Brown lanternshark
Etmopterus villosus . . . . Hawaiian lanternshark
Etmopterus virens . . . . Green lanternshark
Euprotomicroides zantedeschia . . . . Taillight shark
Europtomicrus bispinatus . . . . Pygmy shark
Heteroscymnoides marleyi . . . . Longnose pygmy shark
Isistius brasiliensis . . . . Cookiecutter or cigar shark
Isistius plutodus . . . . Largetooth cookiecutter shark
Mollisquama parini . . . . Softskin dogfish
Scymnodalatias sherwoodi . . . . Sherwood dogfish
Scymnodon ichiharai . . . . Japanese velvet dogfish
Scymnodon ringens . . . . Knifetooth dogfish
Scymnodon squamulosus . . . . Velvet dogfish
Somniosus microcephalus . . . . Greenland sleeper shark
Somniosus pacificus . . . . Pacific sleeper shark
Somniosus rostratus . . . . Little sleeper shark
Squaliolus laticaudus . . . . Spined pygmy shark
Squalus acanthias . . . . Piked dogfish
Squalus asper . . . . Roughskin spurdog
Squalus blainvillei . . . . Longnose spurdog
Squalus cubensis . . . . Cuban dogfish
Squalus japonicus . . . . Japanese spurdog
Squalus megalops . . . . Shortnose spurdog
Squalus melanurus . . . . Blacktail spurdog
Squalus mitsukurii . . . . Shortspine spurdog
Squalus rancureli . . . . Cyrano spurdog

FAMILY OXYNOTIDAE – ROUGHSHARKS

Oxynotus bruniensis . . . . Prickly dogfish
Oxynotus caribbaeus . . . . Caribbean roughshark
Oxynotus centrina . . . . Angular roughshark
Oxynotus japonicus . . . . Japanese roughshark
Oxynotus paradoxus . . . . Sailfin roughshark

ORDER PRISTIOPHORIFORMES – SAWSHARKS

FAMILY PRISTIOPHORIDAE – SAWSHARKS

Pliotrema warreni . . . . Sixgill sawshark
Pristiophorus cirratus . . . . Longnose sawshark
Pristiophorus japonicus . . . . Japanese sawshark
Pristiophorus nudipinnis . . . . Shortnose sawshark
Pristiophorus schroederi . . . . Bahamas sawshark

ORDER SQUATINIFORMES – ANGELSHARKS

FAMILY SQUATINIDAE – ANGELSHARKS

Squatina aculeata . . . . Sawback angelshark
Squatina africana . . . . African angelshark
Squatina argentina . . . . Argentine angelshark
Squatina australis . . . . Australian angelshark
Squatina californica . . . . Pacific angelshark
Squatina dumeril . . . . Sand devil
Squatina formosa . . . . Taiwan angelshark

Squatina japonica . . . . Japanese angelshark
Squatina nebulosa . . . . Clouded angelshark
Squatina oculata . . . . Smoothback angelshark
Squatina squatina . . . . Angelshark
Squatina tergocellata . . . . Ornate angelshark
Squatina tergocellatoides . . . . Ocellated angelshark

ORDER HETERODONTIFORMES –
BULLHEAD SHARKS
FAMILY HETERODONTIDAE – BULLHEAD SHARKS

Heterodontus francisci . . . . Horn shark
Heterodontus galeatus . . . . Crested bullhead shark
Heterodontus japonicus . . . . Japanese bullhead shark
Heterodontus mexicanus . . . . Mexican hornshark
Heterodontus portusjacksoni . . . . Port Jackson shark
Heterodontus quoyi . . . . Galapagos bullhead shark
Heterodontus ramalheira . . . . Whitespotted bullhead shark
Heterodontus zebra . . . . Zebra bullhead shark

ORDER ORECTOLOBIFORMES –
CARPETSHARKS
FAMILY PARASCYLLIIDAE – COLLARED CARPETSHARKS

Cirrhoscyllium expolitum . . . . Barbelthroat carpetshark
Cirrhoscyllium formosanum . . . . Taiwan saddled carpetshark
Cirrhoscyllium japonicum . . . . Saddled carpetshark
Parascyllium collare . . . . Collared carpetshark
Parascyllium ferrugineum . . . . Rusty carpetshark
Parascyllium multimaculatum . . . . Tasmanian carpetshark
Parascyllium variolatum . . . . Necklace carpetshark

FAMILY BRACHAELURIDAE – BLIND SHARKS

Brachaelurus waddi . . . . Blind shark
Heteroscyllium colcloughi . . . . Bluegrey carpetshark

FAMILY ORECTOLOBIDAE – WOBBEGONGS

Eucrossorhinus dasypogon . . . . Tasselled wobbegong
Orectolobus japonicus . . . . Japanese wobbegong
Orectolobus maculatus . . . . Spotted wobbegong
Orectolobus ornatus . . . . Ornate wobbegong
Orectolobus wardi . . . . Northern wobbegong
Sutorectus tentaculatus . . . . Cobbler wobbegong

FAMILY HEMISCYLLIIDAE – LONGTAILED CARPETSHARKS

Chiloscyllium arabicum . . . . Arabian carpetshark

Chiloscyllium burmensis . . . . Burmese bambooshark
Chiloscyllium caerulopunctatum . . . . . . Bluespotted bambooshark
Chiloscyllium griseum . . . . Grey bambooshark
Chiloscyllium hasselti . . . . Indonesian bambooshark
Chiloscyllium indicum . . . . Slender bambooshark
Chiloscyllium plagiosum . . . . Whitespotted bambooshark
Chiloscyllium punctatum . . . . Brownbanded bambooshark
Hemiscyllium freycineti . . . . Indonesian speckled carpetshark
Hemiscyllium hallstromi . . . . Papuan epaulette shark
Hemiscyllium ocellatum . . . . Epaulette shark
Hemiscyllium strahani . . . . Hooded carpetshark
Hemiscyllium trispeculare . . . . Speckled carpetshark

FAMILY GINGLYMOSTOMATIDAE – NURSE SHARKS

Ginglymostoma brevicaudatum . . . . Shorttail nurse shark
Ginglymostoma cirratum . . . . Nurse shark
Nebrius ferrugineus . . . . Tawny nurse or giant sleepy shark

FAMILY STEGOSTOMATIDAE – ZEBRA SHARKS

Stegostoma fasciatum . . . . Zebra shark

FAMILY RHINCODONTIDAE – WHALE SHARKS

Rhincodon typus . . . . Whale shark

ORDER LAMNIFORMES –
MACKEREL SHARKS
FAMILY ODONTASPIDIDAE – SAND TIGER SHARKS

Eugomphodus taurus . Sand tiger, spotted raggedtooth, or grey nurse shark
Eugomphodus tricuspidatus . . . . Indian sand tiger
Odontaspis ferox . . . . . Smalltooth sand tiger or bumpytail raggedtooth
Odontaspis noronhai . . . . Bigeye sand tiger

FAMILY PSEUDOCARCHARIIDAE –
CROCODILE SHARKS

Pseudocarcharias kamoharai . . . . Crocodile shark

FAMILY MITSUKURINIDAE – GOBLIN SHARKS

Mitsukurina owstoni . . . . Goblin shark

FAMILY MEGACHASMIDAE – MEGAMOUTH SHARKS

Megachasma pelagios . . . . Megamouth shark

FAMILY ALOPIIDAE – THRESHER SHARKS

Alopias pelagicus . . . . Pelagic thresher
Alopias superciliosus . . . . Bigeye thresher
Alopias vulpinus . . . . Thresher shark

1. The Fox Shark. 2. The Picked Dog Fish.

FAMILY CETORHINIDAE – BASKING SHARKS

Cetorhinus maximus . . . . Basking shark

FAMILY LAMNIDAE – MACKEREL SHARKS

Carcharodon carcharias . . . . Great white shark
Isurus oxyrinchus . . . . Shortfin mako
Isurus paucus . . . . Longfin mako
Lamna ditropis . . . . Salmon shark
Lamna nasus . . . . Porbeagle shark

ORDER CARCHARHINIFORMES – GROUND SHARKS

FAMILY SCYLIORHINIDAE – CATSHARKS

Apristurus atlanticus . . . . Atlantic ghost catshark
Apristurus brunneus . . . . Brown catshark
Apristurus canutus . . . . Hoary catshark
Apristurus federovi . . . . Federov's catshark
Apristurus herklotsi . . . . Longfin catshark
Apristurus indicus . . . . Smallbelly catshark
Apristurus investigatoris . . . . Broadnose catshark
Apristurus japonicus . . . . Japanese catshark
Apristurus kampae . . . . Longnose catshark
Apristurus laurussoni . . . . Iceland catshark
Apristurus longicephalus . . . . Longhead catshark
Apristurus macrorhynchus . . . . Flathead catshark
Apristurus maderensis . . . . Madeira catshark
Apristurus manis . . . . Ghost catshark
Apristurus microps . . . . Smalleye catshark
Apristurus nasutus . . . . Largenose catshark
Apristurus parvipinnis . . . . Smallfin catshark
Apristurus pinguis . . . . Fat catshark
Apristurus platyrhynchus . . . . Spatulasnout catshark
Apristurus profundorum . . . . Deepwater catshark
Apristurus riveri . . . . Broadgill catshark
Apristurus saldanha . . . . Saldanha catshark
Apristurus sibogae . . . . Pale catshark
Apristurus sinensis . . . . South China catshark
Apristurus spongiceps . . . . Spongehead catshark
Apristurus stenseni . . . . Panama ghost catshark
Apristurus verweyi . . . . Borneo catshark
Asymbolus analis . . . . Australian spotted catshark
Asymbolus vincenti . . . . Gulf catshark
Atelomycterus macleayi . . . . Australian marbled catshark
Atelomycterus marmoratus . . . . Coral catshark
Aulohalaelurus labiosus . . . . Blackspotted catshark
Cephaloscyllium fasciatum . . . . Reticulated swellshark
Cephaloscyllium isabellum . . . . Draughtsboard shark
Cephaloscyllium laticeps . . . . Australian swellshark
Cephaloscyllium nascione . . . . Whitefinned swellshark
Cephaloscyllium silasi . . . . Indian swellshark
Cephaloscyllium sufflans . . . . Balloon shark
Cephaloscyllium ventriosum . . . . Swellshark
Cephalurus cephalus . . . . Lollipop catshark
Galeus arae . . . . Roughtail catshark
Galeus boardmani . . . . Australian sawtail catshark
Galeus eastmani . . . . Gecko catshark
Galeus melastomus . . . . Blackmouth catshark
Galeus murinus . . . . Mouse catshark
Galeus nipponensis . . . . Broadfin sawtail catshark
Galeus piperatus . . . . Peppered catshark
Galeus polli . . . . African sawtail catshark
Galeus sauteri . . . . Blacktip sawtail catshark
Galeus schultzi . . . . Dwarf sawtail catshark

Halaelurus alcocki . . . . Arabian catshark
Halaelurus boesemani . . . . Speckled catshark
Halaelurus buergeri . . . . Blackspotted catshark
Halaelurus canescens . . . . Dusky catshark
Halaelurus dawsoni . . . . New Zealand catshark
Halaelurus hispidus . . . . Bristly catshark
Halaelurus immaculatus . . . . Spotless catshark
Halaelurus lineatus . . . . Lined catshark
Halaelurus lutarius . . . . Mud catshark
Halaelurus natalensis . . . . Tiger catshark
Halaelurus quagga . . . . Quagga catshark
Haploblepharus edwardsii . . . . Puffadder shyshark
Haploblepharus fuscus . . . . Brown shyshark
Haploblepharus pictus . . . . Dark shyshark
Holohalaelurus punctatus . . . . African spotted catshark
Holohalaelurus regani . . . . Izak catshark
Parmaturus campechiensis . . . . Campeche catshark
Parmaturus macmillani . . . . New Zealand filetail
Parmaturus melanobranchius . . . . Blackgill catshark
Parmaturus pilosus . . . . Salamander shark
Parmaturus xaniurus . . . . Filetail catshark
Pentanchus profundicolus . . . . Onefin catshark
Poroderma africanum . . . . Striped catshark or pyjama shark
Poroderma marleyi . . . . Barbeled catshark
Poroderma pantherinum . . . . Leopard catshark
Schroederichthys bivius . . . . Narrowmouth catshark
Schroederichthys chilensis . . . . Redspotted catshark
Schroederichthys maculatus . . . . Narrowtail catshark
Schroederichthys tenuis . . . . Slender catshark
Scyliorhinus besnardi . . . . Polkadot catshark
Scyliorhinus boa . . . . Boa catshark
Scyliorhinus canicula . . . . Smallspotted catshark
Scyliorhinus capensis . . . . Yellowspotted catshark
Scyliorhinus cervigoni . . . . West African catshark
Scyliorhinus garmani . . . . Brownspotted catshark
Scyliorhinus haeckelii . . . . Freckled catshark
Scyliorhinus hesperius . . . . Whitesaddled catshark
Scyliorhinus meadi . . . . Blotched catshark
Scyliorhinus retifer . . . . Chain catshark
Scyliorhinus stellaris . . . . Nursehound
Scyliorhinus torazame . . . . Cloudy catshark
Scyliorhinus torrei . . . . Dwarf catshark

FAMILY PROSCYLLIIDAE – FINBACK CATSHARKS

Ctenacis fehlmanni . . . . Harlequin catshark
Eridacnis barbouri . . . . Cuban ribbontail catshark
Eridacnis radcliffei . . . . Pygmy ribbontail catshark
Eridacnis sinuans . . . . African ribbontail catshark
Gollum attenuatus . . . . Slender smoothhound
Proscyllium habereri . . . . Graceful catshark

FAMILY PSEUDOTRIAKIDAE – FALSE CATSHARKS

Pseudotriakis microdon . . . . False catshark

FAMILY LEPTOCHARIIDAE – BARBELED HOUNDSHARKS

Leptocharias smithii . . . . Barbeled houndshark

FAMILY TRIAKIDAE – HOUNDSHARKS

Furgaleus macki . . . . Whiskery shark
Galeorhinus galeus . . . . Tope shark
Gogolia filewoodi . . . . Sailback houndshark
Hemitriakis japanica . . . . Japanese topeshark
Hemitriakis leucoperiptera . . . . Whitefin topeshark
Hypogaleus hyugaensis . . . . Blacktip topeshark
Iago garricki . . . . Longnose houndshark
Iago omanensis . . . . Bigeye houndshark
Mustelus antarcticus . . . . Gummy shark

Mustelus asterias . . . . Starry smoothhound
Mustelus californicus . . . . Grey smoothhound
Mustelus canis . . . . Dusky smoothhound
Mustelus dorsalis . . . . Sharpnose smoothhound
Mustelus fasciatus . . . . Striped smoothhound
Mustelus griseus . . . . Spotless smoothhound
Mustelus henlei . . . . Brown smoothhound
Mustelus higmani . . . . Smalleye smoothhound
Mustelus lenticulatus . . . . Spotted estuary smoothhound or rig
Mustelus lunulatus . . . . Sicklefin smoothhound
Mustelus manazo . . . . Starspotted smoothhound
Mustelus mento . . . . Speckled smoothhound
Mustelus mosis . . . . . . Arabian, hardnose, or Moses smoothhound
Mustelus mustelus . . . . Smoothhound
Mustelus norrisi . . . . Narrowfin or Florida smoothhound
Mustelus palumbes . . . . Whitespot smoothhound
Mustelus punctulatus . . . . Blackspot smoothhound
Mustelus schmitti . . . . Narrownose smoothhound
Mustelus whitneyi . . . . Humpback smoothhound
Scylliogaleus quecketti . . . . Flapnose houndshark
Triakis acutipinna . . . . Sharpfin houndshark
Triakis maculata . . . . Spotted houndshark
Triakis megalopterus . . . Sharptooth houndshark or spotted gully shark
Triakis scyllium . . . . Banded houndshark
Triakis semifasciata . . . . Leopard shark

FAMILY HEMIGALEIDAE – WEASEL SHARKS

Chaenogaleus macrostoma . . . . Hooktooth shark
Hemigaleus microstoma . . . . Sicklefin weasel shark
Hemipristis elongatus . . . . Snaggletooth shark
Paragaleus leucolomatus . . . . Whitetip weasel shark
Paragaleus pectoralis . . . . Atlantic weasel shark
Paragaleus tengi . . . . Straighttooth weasel shark

FAMILY CARCHARHINDIDAE – REQUIEM SHARKS

Carcharhinus acronotus . . . . Blacknose shark
Carcharhinus albimarginatus . . . . Silvertip shark
Carcharhinus altimus . . . . Bignose shark
Carcharhinus amblyrhynchoides . . . . Graceful shark
Carcharhinus amblyrhynchos . . . . Grey reef shark
Carcharhinus amboinensis . . . . Pigeye or Java shark
Carcharhinus borneensis . . . . Borneo shark
Carcharhinus brachyurus . . . . . . Copper shark or bronze whaler
Carcharhinus brevipinna . . . . Spinner shark
Carcharhinus cautus . . . . Nervous shark
Carcharhinus dussumieri . . . . Whitecheek shark
Carcharhinus falciformis . . . . Silky shark

Carcharhinus fitzroyensis . . . . Creek whaler
Carcharhinus galapagenisis . . . . Galapagos shark
Carcharhinus hemiodon . . . . Pondicherry shark
Carcharhinus isodon . . . . Finetooth shark
Carcharhinus leucas . . . . Bull or Zambezi shark
Carcharhinus limbatus . . . . Blacktip shark
Carcharhinus longimanus . . . . Oceanic whitetip shark
Carcharhinus macloti . . . . Hardnose shark
Carcharhinus melanopterus . . . . Blacktip reef shark
Carcharhinus obscurus . . . . Dusky shark
Carcharhinus perezi . . . . Caribbean reef shark
Carcharhinus plumbeus . . . . Sandbar shark
Carcharhinus porosus . . . . Smalltail shark
Carcharhinus sealei . . . . Blackspot shark
Carcharhinus signatus . . . . Night shark
Carcharhinus sorrah . . . . Spottail shark
Carcharhinus wheeleri . . . . Blacktail reef shark
Galeocerdo cuvier . . . . Tiger shark
Glyphis gangeticus . . . . Ganges shark
Glyphis glyphis . . . . Speartooth shark
Isogomphodon oxyrhynchus . . . . Daggernose shark
Lamiopsis temmincki . . . . Broadfin shark
Loxodon macrorhinus . . . . Sliteye shark
Nasolamia velox . . . . Whitenose shark
Negaprion acutidens . . . . Sharptooth lemon shark
Negaprion brevirostris . . . . Lemon shark
Prionace glauca . . . . Blue shark
Rhizoprionodon acutus . . . . Milk shark
Rhizoprionodon lalandei . . . . Brazilian sharpnose shark
Rhizoprionodon longurio . . . . Pacific sharpnose shark
Rhizoprionodon oligolinx . . . . Grey sharpnose shark
Rhizoprionodon porosus . . . . Caribbean sharpnose shark
Rhizoprionodon taylori . . . . Australian sharpnose shark
Rhizoprionodon terraenovae . . . . Atlantic sharpnose shark
Scoliodon laticaudus . . . . Spadenose shark
Triaenodon obesus . . . . Whitetip reef shark

FAMILY SPHYRNIDAE – HAMMERHEAD SHARKS

Eusphyra blochii . . . . Winghead shark
Sphyrna corona . . . . Mallethead shark
Sphyrna couardi . . . . Whitefin hammerhead
Sphyrna lewini . . . . Scalloped hammerhead
Sphyrna media . . . . Scoophead shark
Sphyrna mokarran . . . . Great hammerhead
Sphyrna tiburo . . . . Bonnethead shark
Sphyrna tudes . . . . Smalleye hammerhead
Sphyrna zygaena . . . . Smooth hammerhead

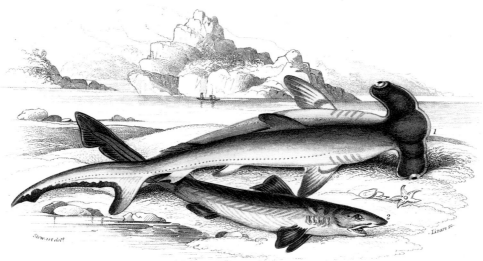

BBC Hulton Picture Library   1. The Hammer Headed Shark. 2 Common Tope.

BIBLIOGRAPHY

Much of the information in this book derives from original research undertaken by the contributors. However, the following publications may be of value to those readers who would like to explore more fully the fascinating world of sharks.

SHARK BIOLOGY
Bone, Q. and Roberts, B.L. 1969. The density of elasmobranchs. *Journal of the Marine Biological Association of the United Kingdom* 49, 913–37.
Carey, F.G. and others. 1985. Temperature, heat production and heat exchange in lamnid sharks. *In:* Biology of the white shark. *Memoirs of the Southern California Academy of Sciences* 9, 92–108.
Gilbert, P.W. 1981. Patterns of shark reproduction. *Oceanus* 24, 30–9.
Gruber, S.H. 1981. Lemon sharks: supply–side economists of the sea. *Oceanus* 24, 56–64.
Moss, S.A. 1984. *Sharks: an Introduction for the Amateur Naturalist.* Prentice–Hall, Englewood Cliffs, New Jersey.
Thomson, K.S. and Simanek, D.E. 1977. Body form and locomotion in sharks. *American Zoologist* 17, 343–54.

THE SHARK'S SENSES
American Society of Zoologists. 1977. Recent advances in the biology of sharks. *American Zoologist* 17, 2.
Baldridge, H.D. 1974. *Shark Attack.* Berkeley Medallion Books, New York.
Ellis, R. 1976. *The Book of Sharks.* Grosset & Dunlap, New York.
Hodgson, E.S and Mathewson, R.F. (eds). 1978. *Sensory Biology of Sharks, Skates and Rays.* US Government Printing Office, Washington DC.
Moss, S.A. 1984. *Sharks: an Introduction for the Amateur Naturalist.* Prentice–Hall, Englewood Cliffs, New Jersey.
Zahuranec, B.J. (ed.) 1983. *Shark Repellents from the Sea.* AAAS Selected Symposia, Westview Press, Boulder, Colorado.

SHARK BEHAVIOUR
Budker, P. 1971. *The Life of Sharks.* Weidenfeld and Nicholson, London.
Clark, E. 1963. Maintenance of sharks in captivity with a report on their instrumental conditioning. *In:* P.W. Gilbert (ed). *Sharks and Survival.* D.C. Heath and Co, Boston, 115–49.
Clark, E. 1981. Sharks: magnificent and misunderstood. *National Geographic* 160, 138–87.
Corwin, J.T. 1981. Audition in elasmobranchs. *In:* W.N.Tavolga, A.N. Popper and R.R. Fay (eds). *Hearing and Sound Communication in Fishes.* Springer–Verlag, New York, 81–102.
Gilbert, P.W. 1962. The behavior of sharks. *Scientific American* 207, 60–8.
Graeber, R.C. 1974. Food intake patterns in captive juvenile lemon sharks, *Negaprion brevirostris. Copeia* 1974, 554–6.
Gruber, S.H. and Keyes, R.M. 1981. Keeping sharks for research. *In:* A.D. Hawkins (ed). *Aquarium Systems.* Academic Press, London, 373–402.
Hass, H. and Eibl–Eibesfeldt, I. 1977. *Der Hai.* C. Bertelsmann Verlag, Munich.
Hodgson, E.S. and Mathewson, R.F. (eds). 1978. *Sensory Biology of Sharks, Skates and Rays.* US Government Printing Office, Washington DC.
Holden, M.J. 1977. Elasmobranchs. *In:* J.A. Gulland (ed). *Fish Population Dynamics.* Wiley, New York, 187–215.
Johnson, R.H. 1978. *Sharks of Polynesia.* Les Editions du Pacifique, Papeete.
Kalmijn, A.J. 1984. Theory of electromagnetic orientation: a further analysis. *In:* L. Bolis, R.D. Keynes and S.H.P. Maddrell (eds). *Comparative Physiology of Sensory Systems.* Cambridge University Press, Cambridge, 525–60.
Klimley, A.P. 1985. Schooling in *Sphyrna lewini,* a species with low risk of predation: a non-egalitarian state. *Journal of Comparative Ethology* 70, 297–319.
Longval, M.J., Warner R. and Gruber, S.H. 1982. Food intake of the lemon shark, *Negaprion brevirostris,* under controlled conditions. *Florida Scientist* 45, 25–33.
McKibben, J.N. and Nelson, D.R. 1986. Patterns of movement and grouping of grey reef sharks, *Carcharhinus amblyrhynchos,* at Enewetak Atoll, Marshall Islands. *Bulletin of Marine Science* 38, 89–110.
Myrberg, A.A. Jr and Gruber, S.H. 1974. The behavior of the bonnethead shark, *Sphyrna tiburo. Copeia* 1974, 358–74.
Myrberg, A.A. Jr, Gordon, C. and Klimley, A.P. 1978. Rapid withdrawal from a sound source by open ocean sharks. *Journal of the Acoustical Society of America* 64, 1289–97.
Sibley, G., Seigel, J.A. and Swift, C.C. (eds). 1985. Biology of the white shark. *Memoirs of the Southern California Academy of Sciences* 9, 1–150.
Springer, S. 1967. Social organization of shark populations. *In:* P.W. Gilbert, R.F. Mathewson and D.P. Rall (eds). *Shark, Skates and Rays.* John Hopkins Press, Baltimore, 149–74.
Wallett, T. 1978. *Shark Attack.* Purnell, London.
Zahuranec, B.J. (ed.) 1975. *Shark Research: Present Status and Future Direction.* Office of Naval Research. Reprint, ACR-208.

SHARK ECOLOGY
Bigelow, H.B. and Schroeder, W.C. 1948. *Fishes of the Western North Atlantic.* Part I. *Lancelets, Cyclostomes, and Sharks.* Memoirs of the Sears Foundation, New Haven, Connecticut.
Budker, P. 1971. *The Life of Sharks.* Columbia University Press, New York.
Hobson, E.S. 1963. Feeding behavior of three species of sharks. *Pacific Science* 17, 2, 171–94.
Nelson. J. and Johnson, R.H. 1980. Behavior of the reef sharks of Rangiroa, French Polynesia. *National Geographic Society, Res. Repts* 12, 479–99.
Randall, J.E. 1977. Contribution to the biology of the whitetip reef shark (*Triaenodon obesus*). *Pacific Science* 31, 2, 143–64.
Randall, J.E. and Helfman, G.E. 1973. Attacks on humans by the blacktip reef shark. (*Carcharhinus melanopterus*). *Pacific Science* 27, 3, 226–38.

Tricas, T.C. 1979. Relationships of the blue shark *Prionace glauca* and its prey species near Santa Catalina Island, California. *United States Fisheries Bulletin* 77, 1, 175–82.
Tricas, T.C., Taylor, L.R. and Naftel, G. 1981. Diel behavior of the tiger shark, *Galeocerdo cuvier,* at French Frigate Shoals, Hawaii. *Copeia* 1981, 4, 904–8.
Tricas, T.C. and McCosker, J.E. 1984. Predatory behaviour of the white shark, *Carcharodon carcharias,* and notes on its biology. *Proceedings of the California Academy of Sciences* 43, 14. 221–38.

SHARK ATTACK IN NEW ZEALAND
Ayling, A.M. and Cox, G.J. 1982. *Collins Guide to the Sea Fishes of New Zealand.* Collins.
Doogue, R.B. and Moreland, J.M. 1961. *New Zealand Sea Anglers Guide.* 2nd edn. Reed, Auckland.
Moreland, J.M. and Heath, E. 1983. *Marine Fishes 1.* Reed, Auckland.
Paul, L.J. and Heath, E. 1985. *Marine Fishes 2.* Reed Methuen, Auckland.
Paul, L.J. 1986. *New Zealand Fishes.* Reed Methuen, Auckland.

SHARK ATTACK IN THE PACIFIC
Bagnis, R. 1968. A propos de 10 cas de blessures par requins chez des pêcheurs sousmarins en Polynésie Francaise. *Médecine Tropicale* 28, 3, 368–73.
Balazs, G. and Kam, A. 1981. A review of shark attacks in the Hawaiian Islands. *Elepaio* 41, 10, 97–106.
Baldridge, H.D. 1973. *Shark Attack Against Man.* Mote Marine Laboratory, Sarasota, Florida.
Brown, C. 1980. Terror of shark and sea, 35 years after. *Washington Post* 6 August, E1–E3.
Cook, C. 1985. Shark 'wipes out' surfers at Pakala. *Garden Isle* (Kaui), 27 May.
Fellows, D.P. and Murchison, A.E. 1967. A non-injurious attack by a small shark. *Pacific Science* 21, 1, 150–1.
Fouques, M. and others. 1972. Traumatismes et blessures par les poissons en Polynésie Française. *La Nouvelle Presse Médicale* 1, 47, 3175–9.
Johnson, R. and Nelson, D.R. 1972. Agonistic display in the gray reef shark, *Carcharhinus menisorrah* and its relationship to attacks on man. *Copeia* 1, 76–84.
Jones, R.S. 1971. Two nonfatal shark attacks in the Truk district, eastern Caroline Islands. *Micronesia* 7, 230–3.
Lagraulet, J. and others. 1972. Les morsures par requins en Polynésie Française (à propos de 14 cas). *Bulletin de la Société de Pathologie Exotique* 4, 592–605.
Lipman, V. 1983. When shark meets man. *Honolulu Magazine* April, 58–94.
Randall, J.E. 1977. Contribution to the biology of the whitetip reef shark (*Triaenodon obesus*). *Pacific Science* 31, 2, 143–64.
Randall J and Helfman, G.S. 1973. Attacks on humans by the blacktip reef shark (*Carcharhinus melanopterus*). *Pacific Science* 27, 3, 226–38.
Read, K.R.H. 1971. Nonfatal shark attack, Palau Islands. *Micronesia* 7, 233–4.
Schulz, L.P. and Malin, M.H. 1963. A list of shark attacks for the world. *In:* P.W. Gilbert (ed). *Sharks and Survival,* D.C. Heath & Co, Boston.
Schweitzer, D. 1982. Shark attack defense. *Wind Surf Magazine,* November, 71.

THE LEGENDARY SHARK
Baldridge, H.D. 1974. *Shark Attack.* Berkeley Medallion Books, New York.
Baldridge, H.D. 1974. Shark attack: a program of data reduction and analysis. *Contributions From the Mote Marine Laboratory* 1, 2.
Benchley. P. 1974. *Jaws.* Doubleday, New York.
Coppleson, V.M. 1958. *Shark Attack.* Angus & Robertson, Sydney.
Davies, D.H. 1964. *About Sharks and Shark Attacks.* Routledge and Kegan Paul, London.
Ellis, R. 1976. *The Book of Sharks.* Grosset & Dunlap, New York.
Ellis, R. 1983. Chiller from the depths. *Geo,* 5, 3, 90–7.
Hemingway, E. 1952. *The Old Man and the Sea.* Scribners, New York.
McCormick, H.W., Allen, T. and Young, W. 1963. *Shadows in the Sea: the Sharks, Skates and Rays.* Chilton, Philadelphia.
Mattheissen, P. 1971. *Blue Meridian: the Search for the Great White Shark.* Random House, New York.
Stead, D.G. 1963. *Sharks and Rays of Australian Seas.* Angus & Robertson, Sydney.
Wise, H.D. 1937. *Tigers of the Sea.* Derrydale Press, New York.
Young, W.E. and Mazet, H. 1934. *Shark! Shark!* Gotham House, New York.

USING SHARKS
Olsen, A.M. 1984. Synopsis of biological data on the school shark, *Galeorhinus australis* (Macleay 1881). FAO Fish. Synop. 139.
Olsen, A.M. 1954. The biology, migration and growth rate of the school shark, *Galeorhinus australis* (Macleay) (Carcharhinidae) in south-eastern Australian waters. *Australian Journal of Marine Freshwater Research* 5, 353–410.
Ripley, W.E. 1946. The soupfin shark and the fishery. *Calif. Div. Fish. Game Fish Bull* 64, 7–37.
Tenison-Woods, J.E. 1882. *Fish and Fisheries of New South Wales.* New South Wales Government Printer, Sydney.

REPELLING SHARKS
Baldridge, H.D. 1974. *Shark Attack.* Berkeley Medallion Books, New York.
Clark, E. 1969. *The Lady and the Sharks.* Harper & Row, New York.
Cook, S.F. 1985. *Cook's Book: a Guide to the Handling and Eating of Sharks.* G.A. Bonham Books.
Ellis, R. 1976. *The Book of Sharks.* Grosset & Dunlap, New York.
Gilbert, P.W., Mathewson, R.F. and Rall, D.P. (eds). 1967. *Sharks, Skates and Rays.*
Gilbert, P.W. (ed). 1963. *Sharks and Survival.* D.C Heath & Co, Boston.
McCormick, H.W., Allen, T. and Young, W. 1963. *Shadows in the Sea: the Sharks, Skates and Rays.* Chilton, Philadelphia.
Moss, S.A. 1984. *Sharks: an Introduction for the Amateur Naturalist.* Prentice–Hall, Englewood Cliffs, New Jersey.

NOTES ON CONTRIBUTORS

LEONARD J.V. COMPAGNO

Leonard Compagno was born in San Francisco, California, in 1943 and is a citizen of the United States. He became interested in the taxonomy, morphology, evolution, distribution and biology of cartilaginous fishes (sharks, rays and chimaeras) at about age ten and has written two books and over fifty papers, chapters for books and other articles on these fishes, including the *Catalogue of World Sharks*. His studies have taken him around the world, on work for the Food and Agriculture Organisation of the United Nations and the US Office of Naval Research. While a graduate student, he was the technical consultant for the first *Jaws* movie, which he now regrets because of the damage to sharks promulgated by *Jaws* and subsequent flights of Hollywood fancy. He is a founding director of the American Elasmobranch Society and has been a research associate of the California Academy of Sciences, Tiburon Center for Environmental Studies and American Museum of Natural History. Apart from cartilaginous fishes, Dr Compagno is particularly interested in vertebrate biology and paleontology, microtechnique, photography (particularly avian photography), microcomputers, aviation and space exploration, science fiction and philosophy, and dabbles in other subjects too numerous to mention.

CARSON CREAGH

Carson Creagh was born in Sydney in 1951 and has been involved with natural history since childhood. His interest in marine biology (especially the anatomy, behaviour and taxonomy of sharks and cetaceans) led to studies at Macquarie University, where he obtained a BSc in 1974 with majors in zoology and geography. For the past six years he has worked as a magazine journalist and production editor, and has written three books on natural history subjects for schools: *The Ones That Got Away, Animal Tracks* and *Life Between the Tides*. He is a founder member of Trees On Farms, a Sydney-based volunteer organisation devoted to assisting landholders with tree regeneration, and works as a consultant on a number of large-scale environmental management projects. His wife Joanne is a childbirth educator and they have four children.

GUIDO DINGERKUS

Formerly curator of the New York Aquarium and then field associate of the American Museum of Natural History in New York City, Dr Dingerkus is presently director of Natural History Consultants. He has extensively studied and collected fishes and especially sharks around the world, including North and Central America, the Caribbean, Europe, Africa, Japan, Taiwan, Australia and New Zealand. While curator of the New York Aquarium he oversaw the setting up of the aquarium's new shark exhibit and routinely dived in the tank where he hand-fed the sharks. An avid scuba diver, he has participated in several dozen scientific research cruises to study fishes and sharks around the world and has been chief scientist of several. He has published numerous scientific papers on sharks and fishes, as well as several books. Recently he was elected as president of the American Elasmobranch Society.

HUGH EDWARDS

Hugh Edwards is a West Australian diver and marine photographer and the author of nineteen books, mostly about the sea. He began diving with an ex-army gasmask as a boy of twelve after World War II and had his first scuba gear in 1952. In 1958 he was a member of a Cambridge University expedition diving on Greek wrecks off Sicily and exploring the sunken Graeco-Roman city of Apollonia off North Africa. In 1963 he was involved in the discovery of the Dutch treasure ship *Batavia* wrecked in 1629, and was leader of the first expedition to explore the wreck. His book *Islands of Angry Ghosts* won the Sir Thomas White Memorial Prize for the best book by an Australian in 1966. In 1968 he discovered the wreck of the 1727 Dutch ship *Zeewyk* in the Abrolhos Islands and wrote *Wreck on the Half Moon Reef*. But perhaps his most exciting diving period came between 1976 and 1978, filming *The Great White Shark* alongside dead whales off the now-defunct Albany Whaling Station.

RICHARD ELLIS

Richard Ellis is considered the foremost painter of marine natural history subjects in America. He has illustrated all the world's cetaceans and pinnipeds, and 106 of his original paintings are in the permanent collection of Whaleworld, the whaling museum in Albany, Western Australia. His paintings hang in museums and private collections throughout the world and he has recently completed a mural of sperm whales for the New Bedford Whaling Museum in Massachusetts. He is the author of *The Book of Whales* (Knopf, 1980), *Dolphins and Porpoises* (Knopf, 1982) and *The Book of Sharks* (Harcourt Brace Jovanovich, 1983). He has shipped out aboard a Japanese whaler, dived with right whales in Patagonia, with humpbacks in Hawaii, and recently with great white sharks in South Australia. He is a member of the Explorers Club and has been a member of the US delegation to the International Whaling Commission since 1980.

EDWARD S. HODGSON

Professor Edward Hodgson, chairman of the Biology Department at Tufts University (Boston), previously taught at Columbia University (New York). His research on the senses and behaviour of sharks has included field studies in all the world's tropical oceans and at laboratories in the Bahamas, Hawaii, Australia, Micronesia, Japan, the Philippines and Egypt. He was awarded a Fulbright Fellowship for research in sensory physiology at the Australian National University and the Commonwealth Scientific and Industrial Research Organisation, which included studies at the Heron Island Research Station on the Great Barrier Reef in the 1960s – which began his continuing interest in all coral reef ecosystems and animals. He has returned frequently to Australia for work on the Great Barrier Reef. From his home base in Boston, he has directed research on the sense of smell and the behaviour of sharks for the US Office of Naval Research. He is a research associate of the American Museum of Natural History in New York as well as a frequent lecturer on animal behaviour and natural history. Both his wife, Valorie, and his son, Gregor, are professional marine biologists. Whenever possible, all the Hodgsons take delight in organising their field studies into cooperative family expeditions.

ROLAND HUGHES

Roland Hughes has twelve years' experience as an author, editor and science communicator. After majoring in zoology and marine sciences, and obtaining a science degree from the University of Sydney, he entered the field of journalism. He was formerly editor of the Australian Museum's quarterly nature magazine, *Australian Natural History*, and today can regularly be heard on national radio. Apart from writing for newspapers and magazines he also heads his own communications company, Roland Hughes & Associates, which specialises in public relations, writing and media liaison. He is the general editor of *Australia's Underwater Wilderness* (1985) and author of *What to Do in Sydney* (1987).

C. SCOTT JOHNSON

Scott Johnson received his BSc degree in physics from the University of Missouri at Rolla, Missouri, in 1954 and his PhD in physics from Washington University at St Louis, Missouri, in 1959. Following four years as research associate at the University of Chicago's Enrico Fermi Institute for Nuclear Studies he joined the US Naval Ocean Systems Center, a government research and development laboratory in San Diego, California. Since then he has done basic research on dolphin hearing and echolocation, shark behaviour, shark counter measures and shark electrosensing. After spending several years in various management positions he has returned to scientific research on dolphins and sharks. He has authored or coauthored scientific papers on the subjects of cosmic rays, high energy nuclear physics, cetacean hearing, shark behaviour, shark countermeasures and biosonar. He has also received ten patents on diving gear devices, anti-shark devices and sonar systems.

JOHN G. MAISEY

Born in London in 1949, John Maisey became interested in fossils at the age of eight. After studying geology and zoology at university, he went on to teach at Exeter University and St Alban's College, England. In 1979 he joined the American Museum of Natural History, New York, which houses one of the world's largest collections of fossil fishes. He has been investigating fossil sharks and related fishes since 1970, and has published numerous papers on their anatomy and phylogenetic relationships. He was a consultant to the National Museum of Natural History, Washington DC, in reconstructing the jaws of the extinct giant white shark, which went on public display in 1985. Dr Maisey lives about fifty kilometres north of Manhattan with his wife Vivien, small son Alexander and two large dogs. He has developed a great interest in naval history, and enjoys building wooden models of seventeenth and eighteenth century warships.

ARTHUR A. MYRBERG JR

Arthur Myrberg was born in Chicago Heights, Illinois, in 1933. He grew up in northern Illinois and attended Ripon College, Ripon, Wisconsin. After graduating in 1954 with a BA degree in biology, he spent two and a half years in the army. After completing that service, he went to the University of Illinois, Urbana, and received an MSc degree in zoology in 1958. From there, he entered the University of California, Los Angeles, receiving a PhD in zoology in 1961. He then travelled to the Max-Planck-Institute for Behavioural Physiology in Seewiesen, West Germany, as a National Institutes of Health post-doctoral fellow, spending three years working with the Nobel laureate Konrad Lorenz. He accepted a position as a member of faculty at the School of Marine and Atmospheric Science of the University of Miami in 1964 and has been there ever since. His scientific interests centre on the ethology and sensory biology of teleost fishes and sharks. His publications exceed fifty, the majority of which deal with the effects of underwater sound upon social behaviour.

A.M. OLSEN

After studying science at the University of Tasmania, A.M. Olsen held a number of research and administrative positions with government authorities and the CSIRO until his retirement in 1979. Between 1967 and 1972 he was permanent head and director of fisheries and fauna conservation at the Department of Fisheries, South Australia. He became director of fisheries research in 1973 and from 1977 to 1979 was chief fisheries officer with the Department of Agriculture and Fisheries in that state. Throughout his career, Mr Olsen conducted specialist research into the biology of school sharks, scallops and rock lobsters, with particular reference to the commercial utilisation of these species.

LARRY J. PAUL

Larry Paul has had a longstanding association with the sea, marine biology and fisheries. As a boy he lived by the sea, beachcombed and went fishing; his family firm owned commercial fishing vessels and processed fish. Since graduating from Victoria University, Wellington, in 1962 he has worked as a fisheries scientist. His main research programs and interests have been snapper biology, flounder fisheries, marine fish distribution patterns, identification and biology of New Zealand elasmobranchs, climatic influences on coastal sea temperatures, estimation of sustainable yields for coastal fisheries and investigations into deepwater fish resources, all of which have involved considerable fieldwork at sea on various research vessels. An honorary research associate of the National Museum of New Zealand, Larry Paul has published a number of scientific papers and articles and two books on New Zealand marine fish and fisheries.

MARTY SNYDERMAN

Marty Snyderman is an assignment photographer, cinematographer, author and speaker specialising in the marine environment. During his career, Marty has worked in wilderness settings with many species of sharks, whales and other large and potentially dangerous animals in oceans all over the world. His cinematography has been utilised by the National Geographic Society, Nova, Mutual of Omaha's Wild Kingdom, Public Broadcasting System documentaries, Living Ocean Society films and many other organisations. The author of a book titled *The Complete Guide to California Marine Life*, Marty's writing and/or still photography have been used by the National Wildlife Federation, the National Geographic Society, *Oceans Magazine*, *Skin Diver*, *Ocean Realm*, Nikon, *Newsweek*, Sea World and other institutions expressing interest in marine life. Marty lives in San Diego, California.

JOHN D. STEVENS

John Stevens was born in the southwest of England and obtained a BSc (Hons) from London University in 1970. He subsequently worked on the biology and ecology of blue sharks (*Prionace glauca*) off southwest England for his doctorate while based at the Marine Biological Laboratory, Plymouth. He gained a PhD from London University in 1976 and then travelled extensively, particularly in the United States, while doing consultancy work on sharks and visiting numerous fisheries agencies and marine laboratories. He spent a year on Aldabra, a remote, uninhabited coral atoll south of the Seychelles, studying the biology of tropical reef sharks. Dr Stevens joined the CSIRO in Cronulla, New South Wales, in 1979 and was transferred in 1984 when the laboratories were moved to Hobart, Tasmania. He now works at the CSIRO on the biology and population dynamics of commercially important shark species off northern Australia.

LEIGHTON R. TAYLOR JR

Leighton Taylor has been conducting research on temperate and tropical sharks in the laboratory and in the field for the past twenty years. In addition to scientific studies his work has involved the collection of live sharks for maintenance and display in public aquariums. As director of the Waikiki Aquarium in Honolulu, he pioneered the collection and display of the now widely exhibited blacktip reef shark. Taylor has discovered a number of new shark species, ranging from the tiny 30-centimetre long Mexican catshark to the novel giant megamouth. In addition to his shark research, Taylor is also an active open-ocean swimmer and occasionally thinks, quite subjectively, about the possibility of shark attack.

VALERIE TAYLOR

Valerie Taylor is an internationally acclaimed marine photographer whose work has appeared in a wide range of publications, films and television documentaries. She began skindiving in 1956 under the tutelage of her husband Ron and since then has worked with Ron on a number of photographic assignments. Their first underwater film, *Shark Hunters*, appeared on American television in 1963. In 1969-70 they featured as actors in the film *Blue Water, White Death* and in the following year filmed a 39-episode television series on the Great Barrier Reef. In 1974 they filmed the live shark sequences for *Jaws*; other filming assignments include the *Wild Wild World of Animals* series, *Orca* and *The Blue Lagoon*. Valerie's contribution to a wider understanding of marine life was recognised in 1981 when she was awarded the NOGI award by the Underwater Society of America and again in 1986 when she was appointed Ridder of the Order of the Golden Ark by Prince Bernhard of the Netherlands. During her career Valerie has only twice been bitten by sharks, which she considers to be more than adequate testimonial to the fact that sharks are not the vicious maneaters of popular myth.

TIMOTHY C. TRICAS

Timothy Tricas has studied the behaviour and ecology of sharks in temperate and tropical oceans for the past fifteen years. Much of his research has focused on the relationships between shark predators and their prey, and the movement patterns of sharks in the field by ultrasonic telemetry tracking. He has also examined the mating behaviour of sharks and rays in the wild. He has studied the attack patterns, feeding ethology and food habits of great white sharks in Australia and California. He is an expert on the behavioural ecology of butterflyfishes and is currently involved in neuro-ethological studies of fishes.

ACKNOWLEDGMENTS

The publishers would like to thank the following people for their assistance in the preparation of this book:

H. David Baldridge for advice about mapping cases of shark attack around the world; Perry W. Gilbert for providing information and photographs about repelling sharks; Rudy van der Est of the Oceanographic Research Institute, Durban, for photographs and information; Beulah Davis of the Natal Sharks Board for details of anti-shark measures in South Africa; Anne Burke for background research; Cecille Haycock, John Owen and Mary-Dawn Earley for advice and encouragement; Judy Hamilton for searching out information; Debra Wager for assistance with photographic sources; Claire Leimbach for information about the Pacific Islands; Tony Gordon and Guy Mirabella for design conceptualisation; Mark McGrouther for assistance at the Australian Museum in Sydney; John Paxton, J.A.F. Garrick and Bobb Schaeffer for suggestions about contributors; Jane Fraser, Jennie Phillips, Tracey Peakman, Penny Pilmer and Kate Smyth for administrative assistance.
The extract from Peter Benchley's *Jaws* is reproduced by permission of Doubleday & Company Inc. and International Creative Management; the extract from Ernest Hemingway's *The Old Man and the Sea* is reproduced by permission of Jonathan Cape. Diagrams are reproduced by permission of Prentice-Hall Inc. (from Sanford Moss, *Sharks*, 1984) and C. Struik (from Tim Wallett, *Shark Attack* in South Africa, 1983). The extract from *Art of the Pacific* (Brake, McNeish and Simmonds) is reproduced by permission of Oxford University Press.

BLUE SHARK.
BBC Hulton Picture Library

Lizars sc

INDEX

The Spinous Shark.
BBC Hulton Picture Library